LION HANDBOOK OF SCIENCE

AND CHRISTIANITY

LION HANDBOOK OF SCIENCE

AND CHRISTIANITY

EDITED BY
R. J. BERRY

LION

Copyright © 2012 R. J. Berry
This edition copyright © 2012 Lion Hudson

The author asserts the moral right
to be identified as the author of this work

A Lion Book
an imprint of
Lion Hudson plc
Wilkinson House, Jordan Hill Road,
Oxford OX2 8DR, England
www.lionhudson.com
ISBN 978 0 7459 5346 5

Distributed by:
UK: Marston Book Services, PO Box 269, Abingdon, Oxon, OX14 4YN
USA: Trafalgar Square Publishing, 814 N. Franklin Street, Chicago,
IL 60610
USA Christian Market: Kregel Publications, PO Box 2607, Grand
Rapids, Michigan 49501

First edition 2012
10 9 8 7 6 5 4 3 2 1 0

326591

Acknowledgments
Scripture quotations are from The New Revised Standard Version of the
Bible copyright © 1989 by the Division of Christian Education of the
National Council of Churches in the USA. Used by permission. All rights
reserved.

A catalogue record for this book is available
from the British Library

Typeset in 10/13 New Baskerville ITC by BT and 10/13 Futura BT
Printed and bound in Singapore

ADVISORY BOARD

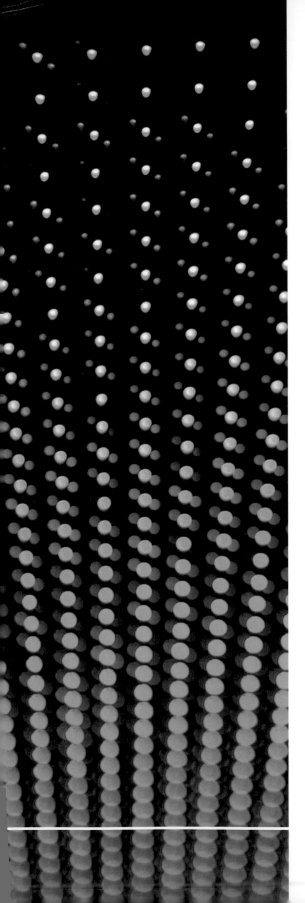

CONTRIBUTORS

Denis R. Alexander, Faraday Institute for Science & Religion, Cambridge University [**Life Sciences**; *Origin of Life; Intelligent Design*]

William T. Arnold, Asbury Theological Seminary [*Ancient Cosmology*]

R. J. (Sam) Berry, University College London [**Life Sciences**; *"Days" in Genesis; On the Creation of Woman*]

Russell C. Bjork, Gordon College [*Artificial Intelligence and the Soul*]

Andrew Briggs, Oxford University [*Belief Systems*]

John Hedley Brooke, Oxford University [*Huxley* versus *Wilberforce*]

Donald Bruce, Edinethics Ltd, Edinburgh [*Ethics and Risk; Nuclear Power; Human Enhancement*]

John A. Bryant, Exeter University [**Science, Ethics, and Christianity**; *Genetic Manipulation; Pre-implantation Genetic Diagnosis; DNA Sequencing and the Human Genome Project; The "Moral Status" of the Early Human Embryo*]

Roland Chia, Trinity Theological College, Singapore [*God and Time*]

Peter G. H. Clarke, Lausanne University [**Humanity and Humanness**; *Schizophrenia; Genes for Religiosity*]

John Clifton-Brown, Aberystwyth University [*Biofuels*]

E. David Cook, Oxford University and Fuller Seminary [**Philosophy and Theology;** *"Proofs" for the Existence of God; Providence and Miracles*]

Joel B. Green, Fuller Seminary [**Science, Faith, and the Bible;** *Neoplatonism*]

Peter Harrison, Oxford University [*Conflict Thesis; The "Two Books"*]

Elaine Jensen, Aberystwyth University [*Biofuels*]

Ernan McMullin, Notre Dame University [*The Galileo Affair*]

Ronald L. Numbers, University of Wisconsin–Madison [*Creationism*]

Dónal P. O'Mathúna, Dublin City University [*Nanotechnology and the Environment; Nanotechnology and Health*]

Alan G. Padgett, Luther Seminary [*The "Spiritual Body"*]

Michael Poole, King's College London [**Nature of Science;** *Positivism and Logical Positivism*]

Michael Ruse, Florida State University [*Teleology*]

Richard Sosis, University of Connecticut [*Evolution of Religion*]

Robert S. White, Cambridge University [**Physical and Earth Sciences;** *Dating Methods; Historical Understanding of the Age of the Earth; Theological Perspectives on the Age of the Earth*]

David L. Wilcox, Eastern University [*Modern Human Origins*]

David B. Wilkinson, Durham University [**Physical and Earth Sciences;** *God's Action in the Universe; The Search for Extraterrestrial Intelligence; Stephen Hawking and Quantum Gravity; Anthropic Balances, Design, and Many Universes*]

Christopher Wilmott, Leicester University [**science, ethics, and Christianity**]

Key
Major contributions to chapters in **bold italics**
Contributions to feature articles in *italics*

HOW TO USE THIS BOOK

The book is meant to help readers understand the issues raised where Christianity meets science. It is not designed to be read from beginning to end – although there can be no objection for anyone wanting to do so. But be advised: in order to make each section self-contained, there is intentional repetition and some issues are dealt with in more than one place. Readers unfamiliar with certain terminology will find such terms highlighted in **bold** along the way, as an indication that an explanation can be found in the Glossary.

CONTENTS

In-depth feature articles are indicated by this symbol.

1

The Nature
of Things

In the fourth century BC, Aristotle (384–322 BC) wrote about the nature of things. For him, everything should be studied and understood: he wrote about geology, physics, chemistry, biology, and philosophy; he believed these all depended on and blended into each other. He called this "physics", but it included most of what we today call natural science, including sensory experience and memory. From here Aristotle went on to what he called "metaphysics", which today is used to refer to how we think about the world, reality, space, time, and human nature. For us, the way we approach the world already assumes some aspects of philosophy (or metaphysics); in contrast, Aristotle made a rigid distinction between physics and metaphysics.

The Greeks were not unique in their speculations. Chinese, Assyrians, Egyptians, the Arab nations, and Western thinkers all had – and have – views of what the world is, how we know things, and what we ought and ought not to do with all that. And all these views contribute to what we today would call a philosophy of science and religion – which in turn affects the way we approach science. We study **ontology** – what there is; **epistemology** – how we know what there is; and ethics – what we do with what there is. Sometimes these philosophies are called worldviews. They are the assumptions we bring to the practice of science and technology and include the way we live in the world and how we treat each other and the world around us.

Oxford University Museum of Natural History, built (1858) to provide "knowledge of the great material design of which the Supreme Master-Worker has made us a constituent part". Venue for the British Association for the Advancment of Science debate in 1860 between Thomas Henry Huxley and Samuel Wilberforce, Bishop of Oxford.

Our ancestors gradually came to believe that the world was not chaotic but ordered and that we could not only understand but also control and direct things. This meant we could be seen not to be at the mercy of nature – natural events or whatever else may happen. We are able to make sense of the world around us because it makes sense and we have the capacity to make sense of that. The Edinburgh theologian T. F. Torrance described this as the inherent intelligibility of the nature of things and the inherent intelligence in the nature of people.

WHAT WE DON'T KNOW

Inevitably, this understanding leads to discussion about from where we and the world originated; whether there is some purpose in and to the world; and what we can do to direct the processes and objects around us. The ancient Greeks believed that all reality consisted of four major elements: earth, air, fire, and water. Their scientific and philosophical outlook was built round a belief that you could describe everything in these four terms. Initially, there was little distinction between astronomy – the study of the stars – and astrology – the belief that behind the stars was a world of gods whose natures controlled the elements of the world, what happened in nature, and how people behaved. Gradually that belief in a divine realm gave way to a naturalistic description of reality or the notion that divine revelation helped humanity understand itself and the world.

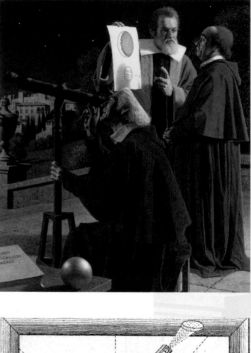

Galileo Galilei (1564–1642) explaining details of astronomy to skeptical churchmen

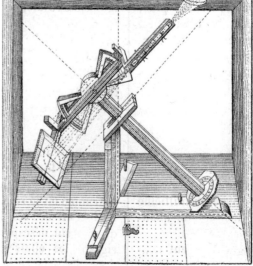

Le télescope de Galilée, exposé à South-Kensington. à Londres.

Bottom: Galileo did not invent telescopes, but he significantly improved their design and made many new observations in the night sky.

Philosophers dispute whether purpose and order are human constructs where we impose our sense of order on things or whether order and purpose are something intrinsic to things themselves. Are they simply the way things are or are they the way that God created the world and humanity so that purpose can be known and discovered? Is order objective, subjective, or some mixture? Our grasp and expression of order varies as we discover more about the world around us. Ptolemy (AD C. 85–C. 165) believed that the earth was the centre of the universe, and nobody doubted it. Galileo (1564–1642) observed that certain planetary alignments only made sense if the sun was at the centre, and our worldview adapted in light of the new evidence (pp. 62–63). This ability to make sense, discover, and codify our observations and form laws so we can act appropriately is part of our humanity. There is order to be known, and we have the capacity to grasp that order. Our subjective interpretations are corrected by objective facts and evidence. Part of the confusion is that "subjective" can mean "just a matter of opinion" rather than its original sense of "belonging to a human subject". In this sense, a fact is only known if it is recognized (or appreciated) by a human subject. There may be facts about the world which we do not yet know or have forgotten, but until a human knows those facts they don't really count as facts and it makes no sense other than speculation to talk about what we don't know.

Historically, Aristotle, Thomas Aquinas (1225–74), and apologists such as William Paley (1743–1805) looked to features of order in the world as proof of the existence of a prime mover or God. Paley argued that the design we see in the world shows that there must have been a designer who imbued reality with those features of design. Such teleological arguments for the existence of God were hotly criticized by David Hume (1711–76), Immanuel Kant (1724–1804), and the logical positivists. They argued that at best order proved only some previous cause and at worst cheated by leaping from this immanent world to a transcendent realm with which we have no direct, empirical link. There is a key distinction between explaining the cause and purpose of a particular thing and trying to explain the cause and purpose of everything as a whole. We have nowhere to stand to experience universes or galaxies as a whole because we stand inside a universe; even our observations, including that of other universes, may affect what we record as experiencing.

The Scottish empiricist philosopher David Hume maintained that so much of the world is disordered and chaotic, lacking purpose and order (**dysteleology**), that we cannot argue for a designer. Religious believers respond that we live in an imperfect world because human sin, bad choices, and the fall have affected not only human relationships but the world itself. Thus the perfect creation has become influenced by evil and does

"PROOFS" FOR THE EXISTENCE OF GOD

Scientists and philosophers have argued from a general perception about the world to try to prove the existence of God. Anselm (1033–1109) argued ontologically: that if a being greater than which no greater being can be conceived, he must be God. Anselm began from the concept or idea of God and reasoned from that that he exists. In contrast, cosmological arguments use the notion of cause and explanation to argue from things we experience in the world to God himself.

Thomas Aquinas developed five key aspects of this. For him, the facts of motion, causation, being, value, and purpose in the world all demanded some idea of a First Mover, Cause, Being, Source of Value and Purpose. The only alternative would be an infinite regress of movers or causes, and then there would be no reason for there to be motion, cause, being, value, or purpose – unless there was a first cause, mover, being, source of value, or designer.

Other elements of human experience like the fact of morality, religious experience, and a common consensus that there is a God have also been used as the bases for proofs of God. The persistence of the idea that our human experiences need a solid grounding in reason and first cause suggests that there is a way that the heavens declare not only the reality of God but also his glory.

not function as was meant. For both atheist and theist, there is a fine line between arguing that there is chaos which would make science impossible and arguing that what seems chaotic is evil and a result of human choice rather than failure to understand the purpose. This kind of thinking led to the "God of the gaps" approach to philosophy, where what we don't understand is explained by God (see pp. 38–39). In this way, evil can become a kind of non-explanation.

The human desire to know and to act underlies all scientific endeavours. A scientific approach requires that we are honest in our recording. This is seen in "peer group review" where any experiment or theory is rigorously tested, and affirmed or denied. What science tells us must be shown to be true. We can then reliably act on those theories. Morality is at the centre of science. Morality, philosophy, science, and technology – the practical application of science – go together.

David Hume (1711–76), Scottish empirical philosopher, "the first post-sceptical philosopher of the early modern age", once described as "God's greatest gift to the infidel".

Modern science developed after the Renaissance and the Reformation led to a blossoming of discovery in exploration, knowledge, and literature. Francis Bacon (1561–1626) is generally credited as the founder of the modern scientific method of observation, hypothesis, testing, and formulating laws. He firmly believed in God's "twin books" of words and works, of Bible and nature. These "books" were in harmony with each other and offered two distinct pathways to know something of God and his dealings with the world and humanity (pp. 57–58). Bacon's methodology of science was inductive, inferring general rules from hypothesis and observed particular cases. He believed this led inexorably to understanding. Induction has now been largely replaced in science by **deduction** – arguing from the general to the particular.

Public perception, strongly influenced by the successes of science and its applications in areas like media, communication, travel, and medicine, tends to assume that religion and morality are matters of personal opinion. In contrast, science is seen as objective and factual. This implies that scientific knowledge is reasonable whereas religion and morality are no more than prejudices and essentially irrational. This is a false dichotomy. Rational understanding and subjective choices and preferences are involved in all we do, including both scientific research and religious practice. Many scientists are both practising scientists and religious believers and see no conflict with their faith in understanding physics, chemistry, mathematics, and cosmology. However tension between science and religion often boils over into aggressive anti-religion and, particularly in biology, fuels the "new atheism" of Richard Dawkins (1941–), Christopher Hitchens (1949–), and the like. It is important to realize that their evangelistic fervour for atheism does not automatically lead to coherence and intellectual rigour.

One of my assumptions had been that faith was the opposite of reason and hence that there could be no evidence to undergird it – it was merely a blind leap in the absence of evidence. It surprised me when I found the definition of faith in Hebrews 11:1: "Faith is the substance of things hoped for, the evidence of things not seen." It was astounding for me to realise that word "evidence" was in the very definition of faith in the Bible. What I began to realise was that faith and reason are, in fact, linked together, but faith

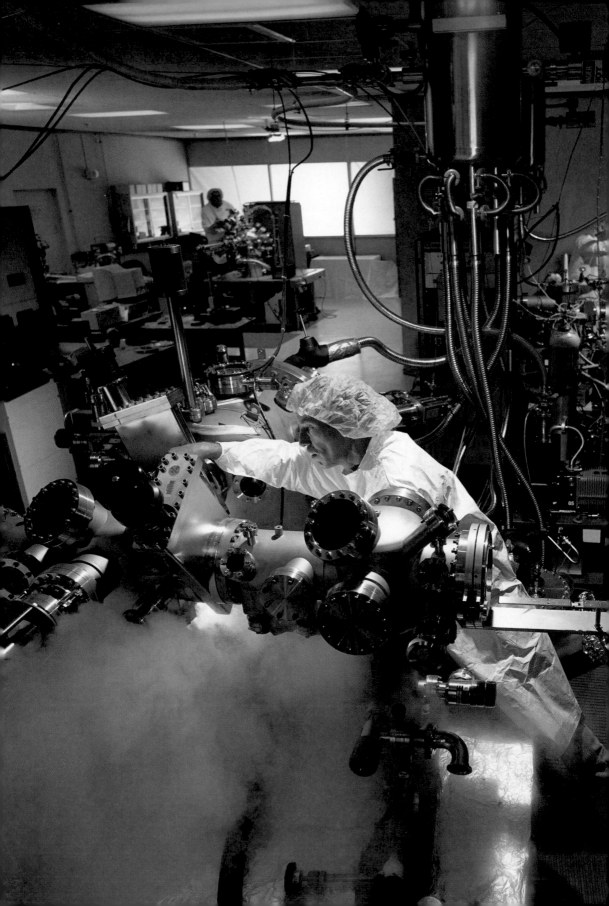

has the additional element of revelation. At the same time, I began to appreciate that there were pointers to God's existence in the study of nature, some of which I had spent time on without really thinking about it.
Francis Collins, Director of the National Institutes of Health, USA

All this makes the public understanding of science and scientific education highly important. Our social and moral values affect the funding of scientific research and education in the sciences. In an age of limited resources, scientists have to compete with each other and with different projects. Society and funding agencies decide what research should be pursued, guided by what scientists claim will be produced. There are yawning gaps between claims of magical cures and the sad reality of research. Too often reports of scientific results are accompanied by hyperbole and exaggeration of what and how soon cures are achievable.

Both philosophy and religion have been important motivations and bases for scientific advance. It is no exaggeration to say that without Christianity modern science would not have developed in the way it has. Obviously there have been and remain tensions between religious beliefs and some aspects of scientific thought. The very fact of there being so many scientists who are unreservedly Christian in their beliefs and find no contradiction between their faith and their science shows that there is no necessary conflict between religion and science.

[A] source of conviction in the existence of God, connected with the [human] reason… follows from the extreme difficulty or rather impossibility of conceiving this immense and wonderful universe, including man with his capacity of looking far backwards and far into futurity, as the result of blind chance or necessity…. But then arises the doubt – can the mind of man, which has, as I fully believe, been developed from a mind as low as that possessed by the lowest animals, be trusted when it draws such grand conclusions?
Charles Darwin, *Autobiography* (1887)

Origins, creation, providence, **immanence**, transcendence, miracles, space, time, design, and evil create hard questions for scientists, philosophers, and religious people alike. The way to conduct, direct, and cope with science and its fruits and consequences is to be transparent about our fundamental view of the nature of reality, life, humanity, and the values we hold and practise. Science involves faith, and religion involves rationality; faith and reason are not in essential conflict, nor are science and religion.

Human knowledge requires both inductive and deductive reasoning. Our judgments, living and working, whether in the practice of science or in its outworking through technology in work, sales, or the service industry, are a mixture of the objective and factual and the subjective, personal, and communal. All of us operate with assumptions and presuppositions. Our values, religious, philosophical and scientific thinking and practice are integral to who and what we are and to our lives in human community. Mutual understanding and sympathy are vital as we seek to understand each other and the practices of science and religion. Clear communication rather than verbal invective is the way to appreciate the truths in science and religion.

THINKING ABOUT THINKING

"I am here" is as good as any a starting point for enquiry about thinking, including about science and religion. In an attempt to discard belief in all things which are not absolutely certain, the seventeenth-century French philosopher, René Descartes (1596–1650) came up with his famous and apparently incontrovertible assumption *cogito ergo sum*: "I think, therefore I am." He was seeking for some bedrock for what has come to be called "Cartesian certainty". But he was forced to admit "there is nothing at all which gives me assurance of their truth beyond this, that I see very clearly that in order to think it is necessary to exist."

Man is but a reed, the weakest in nature; but he is a thinking reed.
Blaise Pascal, *Pensées* (1670)

The assumption of human rationality – that our thinking processes make

Blaise Pascal (1623–62), French mathematician and philosopher. After his death, a scrap of paper was found sewn into his cloak, "God of Abraham, God of Isaac, God of Jacob, not of the philosphers or the learned. Certitude. Joy. Peace. God of Jesus Christ. My God and your God...."

Rene Descartes (1596–1650),
French rationalist philosopher

sense, is absolutely fundamental. Without this, we cannot even meaningfully *discuss* human rationality – whether our thinking processes *do* make sense. Without human rationality, writing and speaking are no more than squiggles and sounds.

If my mental processes are determined wholly by the motion of atoms in my brain, I have no reason to suppose my beliefs are true. They may be sound chemically, but that does not make them sound logically.... In order to escape from this necessity of sawing away the branch on which I am sitting, so to speak, I am compelled to believe that mind is not wholly conditioned by matter. But as regards my own very finite and imperfect mind, I can see its limitations are largely at least due to my body. Without my body, it may perish altogether, but it seems to me quite as probable that it will lose its limitations and be merged into an infinite mind or something analogous to a mind which I have reason to suspect exists behind nature. How this might be accomplished I have no idea.
J. B. S. Haldane, *Possible Worlds* (1927)

Metacognition – thinking about thinking – is important for *any* study, not just science. There are a number of basic beliefs (or presuppositions) other than *cogito ergo sum* that have to be taken for granted before the scientific enterprise itself can even begin. They include:

- The *orderliness* of the natural world. There appear to be regular patterns of behaviour in nature, such as the dynamics of moving bodies. Without these regularities there could be no concise summaries of their motion, embodied in scientific laws.

- *The uniformity of nature*. This phrase, which is closely allied to the matter of orderliness, encapsulates the idea that, although there is change and development in nature, the underlying matter and laws appear to be the same throughout time and space.

- *Intelligibility*. All the foregoing is still of no avail unless the natural world is capable of being understood.

The most incomprehensible thing about the universe is that it is comprehensible.
Attributed to Albert Einstein

- *Beauty.* To human *rationality* and the *orderliness, uniformity,* and *intelligibility of nature,* scientists and mathematicians often add beauty/elegance, which provides food for thought. G. H. Hardy, propounder of the Hardy–Weinberg Law of Population Genetics, expressed this idea by saying "Beauty is the first test; there is no permanent place in the world for ugly mathematics." This thought is buried even deeper in history when, over three centuries ago, Galileo marked out mathematics as the language of science.

Philosophy is written in this grand book, the universe, which stands continually open to our gaze. But the book cannot be understood unless one first learns to comprehend the language and read the letters in which it is composed. It is written in the language of mathematics…
Galileo Galilei, *Il Saggiatore* **(1623)**

Not only can mathematics be seen as beautiful but it is amazing as well. In a famous paper on "The Unreasonable Effectiveness of Mathematics in the Natural Sciences", Eugene Wigner concluded "The miracle of the appropriateness of the language of mathematics for the formulation of the laws of physics is a wonderful gift which we neither understand nor deserve". Like Charles Darwin (1809–82) and Haldane, he found that "it is hard to believe that our reasoning power was brought, by Darwin's process of natural selection, to the perfection which it seems to possess."

[A surprising feature of the laws of nature is] that the regularity… is independent of so many conditions which could have an effect on it…. If there were no phenomena which are independent of all but a manageably small set of conditions, physics would be impossible.
Eugene Wigner, "The Unreasonable Effectiveness of Mathematics in the Natural Sciences", *Communication in Pure and Applied Mathematics* **(1960)**

Eugene Wigner (1902–95), Nobel Prize-winning Hungarian American mathematician

So, the world excites our curiosity and both science and mathematics provide us with tools to satisfy our puzzlement, but it also generates wonder. The physicist Erwin Schrödinger, famous for his "wave equation" was amazed by the hereditary mechanism. He asked:

> *How can the events in space and time which take place within the spatial boundary of a living organism be accounted for by physics and chemistry?... The obvious inability of present-day [1944] physics and chemistry to account for such events is no reason at all for doubting that they can be accounted for by those sciences. That is a marvel – than which only one is greater... I mean the fact that we, whose total being is entirely based on a marvellous interplay of this very kind, yet possess the power of acquiring considerable knowledge about it.*
> Erwin Schrödinger, *What Is Life?* (1944)

SCIENCE AND ITS STRENGTHS

> *Science is a great and glorious enterprise – the most successful... that human beings have ever engaged in...*
> Peter Medawar, *The Limits of Science* (1984)

The fascination of solving mysteries is one factor that attracts people into studying science at school and pursuing science as a career. A key to the success of science is its openness to publicly available evidence.

EVIDENCE IN SCIENCE
Science appeals to evidence drawn from the physical world to establish general principles that can be expressed in scientific laws. From these laws certain future events may be predicted, based upon precedent. Francis Bacon believed that science proceeded by the simple process of its practitioners going out to look at the natural world, collecting their data, and generalizing their findings in laws. This process of arguing from specific instances to generalizations is known as induction. But, as the philosopher Karl Popper (1902–94) realized, you cannot verify a generalization in this way because there is always the possibility of an undetected counter-example which would falsify the generalization. Philosophers often illustrate this by pointing out that however many white swans are observed, one cannot justifiably *induce* the generalization "all swans are white". It only requires one black swan to be seen – and they are around – to falsify

the generalization. This limitation is known as *the problem of* **induction**. Popper saw the task of the scientist as trying to knock down a provisional hypothesis – to *falsify* it. If it survives such attempts, the hypothesis is to be retained as belonging to the scientific corpus, at least for the time being. But even the criterion of falsification has its problems. For example, how can one be absolutely sure that the hypothesis has been truly falsified and it is not just the result of a bad measurement or erroneous reasoning?

Another problem associated with going out to look at the natural world and collecting data is highlighted by the question, "what data do you collect from the near-infinite amount there is?" It is now accepted that scientists go out with some kind of an idea about what might be expected. Their search is "theory laden". For instance, scientists investigating the dynamics of falling bodies consider distance, time, mass, velocity, and acceleration as relevant; but without a murmur they ignore the colour or the shape of the falling body, how old it is, or who it belongs to. These data are not considered relevant. Interestingly, making allowance for air resistance, it turns out that mass is *not* a factor needing consideration. Bodies of different masses, falling in a vacuum, drop at the same rate.

> *[There is] a widely accepted distinction between two allegedly different types of science; the* nomothetic *[Greek nomos – law] which seeks to establish abstract general laws for indefinitely repeatable events and processes [in the natural and some social sciences], and the* ideographic, *which aim to understand the unique and non-recurrent [e.g. aspects of the Earth sciences which explore the non-repeatable development of Earth's history]*
> **Ernest Nagel,** *The Structure of Science* **(1961)**

Scientists seek for explanations and understanding by appealing to direct, indirect, and cumulative physical evidence, although after positivism (see pp. 33–35) overlooked the interpretative element involved, more care came to be exercised in recognizing the theory laden nature of evidence. Good science education emphasizes this. Evidence is also a key element in religious explanations and understanding, although that is not our concern at this point. Conclusions are not "proved" according to some "traditional philosophical ideal of Cartesian absolute certainty", but more along the lines of the word "prove" in the archaic use of the term – testing, trying out, in order to arrive at what is termed "empirical fit". There is a provisionality about all this; scientific conclusions are corrigible in the light of new data and new interpretations of the old. Theories are always *underdetermined* by the available data. Where explanations are arrived at, the principle is that they result from an "inference to the best explanation". Aphorisms like "all seeing is *seeing as*" and "there is more to seeing than meets the eyeball" are constant reminders that all "facts" are interpreted.

THE SOCIOLOGY OF SCIENCE

The above comments recognize that science is a human activity. Attitudes to science (often including technology) are a complicated mixture of approval and distrust involving domestic benefits, pollution, medicine, climate change, transport, wars, costs of "unnecessary" research, and so on – the list is almost endless. Often complex ethical issues are involved. One of the limitations of science is that it can only tell us what *is* the case, not what *ought* to be the case in any moral sense. However, a strength is that science can often give us an indication of the likely consequences of an action, helping us to make informed decisions based on successful predictions. It can do this by virtue of warranted assumptions about the *uniformity of nature* and human rationality. Science can also lead to extreme attitudes, either through its virtual deification

Karl Popper (1902–94), Austrian-born philosopher of science, known for his insistence that the key criterion of a scientific theory is its verifiability.

THE MERTON THESIS

In 1938 a long paper by a famous American sociologist, Robert K. Merton on "Science, technology and society in seventeenth-century England" appeared in the science journal, *Osiris* (Volume 4, pp. 360–632). In it Merton treated science and technology as social phenomena, not merely or even mainly the relentless search for truth or utility that was their traditional image. Merton has been widely praised, particularly by those who, like Marx and others, insist that science is essentially a social phenomenon, mainly reflecting society's cultural values. Such people are *externalists*, insisting on the importance of external factors in scientific practice. Others, especially those who actually do scientific research, find this implausible and stress the importance of hard evidence. Classically these are the *internalists*. Such people may simply shrug off external factors, and for them the Merton Thesis is something to be reviled and denied.

Merton's paper has been revisited many times since it first appeared. There is general agreement that his argument has an element of truth. Few scientists could survive without camaraderie with their fellows, a stable financial situation, a culture in which their science was appreciated, and a stable scientific community in which they worked. All of these things are external to the theories they construct and sometimes even the experiments they do. Equally, however, it is absurd to suppose that measurements of physical or biological data have nothing to do with a reality "out there". There must be some kind of internal logic to science.

Merton presented his ideas in the framework of faith and science, and that makes them particularly relevant here. He attempted to show in the early days of modern science there was a strong connection between science and (of all things) Puritanism. He was not the first to suggest this, but he did bring a new level of sophisticated and detailed historical reasoning to his argument.

Merton's thesis has stimulated much debate. The main conclusions are:

- Much of modern science has its roots in England in the early seventeenth century. This was, after all, the time and place of Isaac Newton's majestic work on gravity and the laws of nature. One can be even more precise: a great deal of early modern science was located in London and at the infant Royal Society (founded in 1660).

The foundation of the Royal Society of London as recorded in its minute book of 28 November 1660. The Society is the oldest National Academy of Science in the world, established for the purpose of "improving natural knowledge".

This is not to deny the importance of Oxford, Cambridge, and centres much further afield at this time, but the main generalization is sound.

- A great deal of that work was done by men who held to strong Protestant values — and did not mind admitting it. The Protestant Reformation had brought with it a return to the Bible, and much in that book was seen as conformable to the new scientific enterprise.

- Thanks to the work of Reijer Hooykaas and others it has now become clear that Puritanism was extremely important in the early days of science. This was a very English phenomenon, but something like it can be encountered in the Low Countries as well. It is hard for some people to accept this image of the Puritans, who have been depicted as killjoys, austere, and quite uninterested as such topics as worldly science. But as many have shown, this is a caricature of Puritanism, and many pioneers, such as the chemist Robert Boyle, accepted Puritan values without being maligned as narrow-minded or bigoted.

- Nevertheless, science did prosper in countries where Puritanism was unknown or anathema. Roman Catholics, for instance, did notable scientific work in France and Italy, so a causal link with Puritanism is unfounded.

- Beyond the seventeenth century a Puritan culture no longer existed, but science marched ahead. By the twentieth century an explicit link between science and biblical religion had largely been forgotten.

- Despite this fact, many scientists today hold to a strong Christian faith, and the common parody of a "conflict model" has little to commend it. Furthermore, science still owns concepts like the regularity of the universe, the existence of scientific laws, the importance of honesty and integrity which, though certainly present elsewhere, are compatible with, or even dependent on, a biblical theology of nature.

(usually by non-scientists but sometimes by scientists themselves, as was the case with the logical positivists – see below), or by the denigration of science/technology for failing to "deliver the goods" or answer the sort of question not in its gift. But it is no use kicking the cat because it fails to bark at intruders. Other attitudes have manifested themselves in cults of irrationality in science which, if pursued, could only lead to the demise of science itself. This was the charge laid against the Austrian philosopher, Paul Feyerabend in the 1970s with his claims that "Science is an essentially anarchistic enterprise… The only principle that does not inhibit progress is: *anything goes.*"

SCIENCE
• • • •

1. The study of *nature* (Greek *phusis* from which we get our word physics). It *methodologically* excludes *metaphysics* and *religion*, while not denying them. The term *methodological naturalism* is misleading as "naturalism" is more than a methodological principle.

2. Reduces systems to their components to understand them better (analytic) – methodological **reductionism**, but also recognizes the emergence of higher order properties resulting from increasing the complexity of organization (synthetic).

3. Causality – methodologically, science only deals with *proximate* causes, not first/final causes.

4. Scientific laws are concise descriptions of the normal behaviour of the natural world. The uniformity of nature is a methodological assumption.

5. Science is one form of knowledge, differing from forms such as historical, personal, mathematical.

6. Assumes rationality in the interpretation of empirical data.

7. Deals with the processes of *evolution*, *natural selection*, and *chance* but avoids metaphysical extrapolations.

8. Offers explanations of physical structures and processes, while recognizing the logical possibility of other compatible types of explanations (such as religious).

All of which raises the question of what may be classed as "genuine" science. As we have seen, verifiability is not an adequate criterion for a scientific theory, and Popperian *falsification*, too, has its problems. How might astronomy and astrology be classified, for example? What about the traditional distinction between *science* and *scientism*? A generalization about scientism could be that many things that science takes simply as *methodological principles*, such as the "bracketing out" of *metaphysical* concepts like God, are "hardened up" by scient*ism* into matters of faith – which can lead to the claim that science does away with God.

SCIENTISM

● ● ● ● ●

1. Denies that anything other than the natural world exists – naturalism (rejects metaphysics and religion).

2. Matter/energy is all there is – ontological reductionism (ontology – the study of being, of what is) is dubbed "nothing-buttery" – "we are 'nothing but' atoms and molecules"! There is more to be said about people than their physical components.

3. Denies that there are first/final causes (teleology), Some biologists are rethinking teleology.

4. Denies the world could ever exhibit behaviour other than law-like. Miraculous behaviour would be impossible, as it would "break" scientific laws.

5. Science is the supreme form of knowledge.

6. Exalts reason and the empirical, denying revelation.

7. Reifies concepts such as nature, chance, evolution, and natural selection and vests them with God-like attributes.

8. Regards scientific explanations as superior to other types of explanation and as replacing religious explanations [about agency and purpose].

The need for *demarcation criteria* to distinguish science from scientism and non-science points in the direction of the carefully thought-out attempts of philosophers to say what science *is*. In practice, we look to a hypothesis or proposed law to explain why things happen. It enables us to predict what is going to happen. If there is an exception, we do not simply throw away the hypothesis but revise it to allow for occasional exceptions. We would look for good reasons why an exception happened; if there were too many exceptions then we would reject the proposed hypothesis and law. We can use similar criteria with miracles. The God who created order and gave purpose to natural processes, may interrupt that order for a particular purpose. The miracles of Jesus are described in the New Testament as signs that God is at work. Miracles point to the special nature of the person or the moment of revelation. Whether it is Moses seeing a burning bush that is not consumed or Jesus stilling a Galilean storm, we can ask, "What is the purpose of this exceptional event?" Some, like the theologian John Hick, believe that miracles are merely a matter of how we interpret or see a natural event. Such people regard timing as that which makes us "see" a happening as miraculous. This reduces everything to the miraculous and empties all real significance from any "miracle" event. We cannot talk of the miraculous if these happen all the time or whenever we pray or expect them. That would in fact be no longer exceptional but rather a new kind of order and subject to new natural or supernatural laws.

Scientists look for order and forms laws, but they also look for exceptions, aware that if these exist, there may be a need to refine the law; there must be some good reason for the exception. Science tells us something of how an event happened, while religion offers an account of the purpose and why what has happened has done so.

> *We must agree with Hume that, if there is absolutely "uniform experience" against miracles (in other words, if they have never happened), why then, they never have. Unfortunately, we know the experience against them to be uniform only if we know that all the reports of them are false. And we know the reports to be false only if we know already that miracles have never occurred. In fact, we are arguing in a circle.*
> C. S. Lewis, *Miracles* (1947)

As religion and science began to grow apart in the eighteenth century, philosophy entered a phase critical of religious belief. Thomas Jefferson (1743–1826), US president and the principal author of the United States Declaration of Independence, revered Jesus for his benevolence and ethical teaching but rejected miracles and mysteries (such as the Trinity) as incompatible with nature and reason. He produced his own edition of the

PROVIDENCE AND MIRACLES

Philosophy, religion, and science have often clashed about whether the world and life just happened or whether there is some divine purpose at work in and behind things, events, and processes. There is a sense of amazement that there is a world at all, that it operates as a consistent whole, that it is remarkably fitted and integrated to support life, and that the human body functions in such a balanced way. Modern medicine seeks to restore broken functioning. It puts right what has gone wrong. We have got to a stage where nanotechnology, genetics, and modern plastic surgery can enhance human performance and even alter human nature. In an age of transplantation and **xenotransplantation** (using organs from animals to save human lives), we can change and adapt our appearance, bodies, and performance in the interests of sex, sport, disability, weakness, ageing, or preferences.

Human choices seem to drive such discoveries, developments, and applications. Is this the way things and we are, simply a contest for survival of the fittest? Or are we upheld and supported by a divine creator, who sustains the world and all life and gives

humanity the capacity to understand, control, and direct the elements of life?

For many scientists, belief in God and a sense of his handiwork in the world helps them to understand and deal with the world and life as it is. The complex interrelatedness of everything and the way things fit and function together indicate that it is not a matter of chance but an expression of a loving God who is involved in everything. It is not just that in "Him we live, move and have our

---

Moses and the Burning Bush, painted by William Blake. Miracles are rare events, but to deny their impossibility is as much an act of faith as the acknowledgment of their occurrence.

"Jesus rebuked the wind and sea, and there was a dead calm. The men were astonished and exclaimed, 'What sort of man is this? Even the wind and sea obey him'" (Matthew 8:26–27). *The Storm on the Sea of Galilee*, painted by Rembrandt.

• •

being", but that "all things consist in him and are sustained by his good will" (Acts 17:24–31; Colossians 1:16–20).

A sense of the order of the world raises the question as to what sense we make of disturbances of that order. David Hume defined a miracle as "an interruption of the laws of nature by the volition of a deity". This implies that there is such a thing as a natural order to things and processes; it is what makes science possible. If there were no regularity, we could not understand what was and was about to happen. Hume and, later, Antony Flew argued that if there is an interruption of a natural law this means there is no natural law. If there is no natural law, there cannot be exceptions to that law, so miracles cannot happen. This is to misunderstand how science, laws, and exceptions operate.

Gospels, leaving out all the miracles, including the resurrection, the greatest miracle of all. The modern model for analytic philosophy stems from Hume, who distinguished between matters of fact and subjective opinions. Morality and religion belonged in the world of subjective opinion. Logical positivists, like Bertrand Russell and A. J. Ayer stressed that statements were meaningful only if they could be verified by sense experience. This ruled out religious, moral, and aesthetic language. Scientific objectivity and empirical evidence became the only standard and religious thinkers largely withdrew from debate. It seemed that positivism had won, but it contained the seeds of its own destruction (see p. 33–35). Philosophical thought in science, religion, and metaphysics now stresses that all thinking depends on a wider range of key assumptions and that religion can be rational and meaningful. Indeed, the theologian T. F. Torrance argued that theology has its own science in the study of God and the standards of truth and meaningfulness need to be appropriate to the nature of the object.

Are there questions that science cannot answer, or even address? Nobel Laureate, Peter Medawar, has examined the limitations of science in depth (*The Limits to Science*, 1984). He concluded that:

[It is not] possible to deduce from the axioms and postulates of Euclid a theorem to do with how to cook an omelet or bake a cake.... To reproach it [science] for its inability to answer all the questions we should like to put to it is no more sensible than to reproach a railway locomotive for not flying... The existence of a limit to science is made clear by its inability to answer childlike elementary questions having to do with first and last things – questions such as "How did everything begin?" "What are we all here for?" "What is the point of living?"... It is not to science but to metaphysics, imaginative literature or religion that we must turn for answers to questions having to do with first and last things. Doctrinaire positivism – now something of a period piece – dismissed all such questions as nonquestions or pseudoquestions such as only simpletons ask and only charlatans of one kind or another profess to be able to answer....

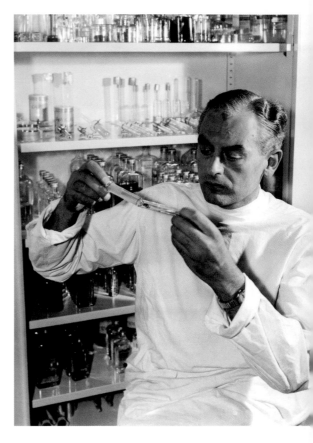

The "positivism" that Medawar refers to was a classic example of worldviews affecting perceptions of the *nature of science*. Positivism and its younger brother Logical Positivism well illustrate the limitations of science.

An enduring legacy of logical positivism is muddling up the types of questions that science can and cannot address. It spawns the kind of demand such as "prove to me scientifically that God exists". This is an odd request because the subject matter of science is the natural world, while religion includes questions like "is there anything *other* than the natural world to which the world of nature owes its existence?" Surprisingly, it seems to need pointing out that it is no use going to science (the study of the natural world) to answer the question "is there anything *other* than the natural world" (that is, God) to which the world of nature owes its existence.

Peter Medawar (1915–87), Nobel Prize winner for his pioneering discoveries in immunology. He was a non-believer, but one who clearly accepted that there are limits to science.

POSITIVISM AND LOGICAL POSITIVISM

The positivist belief, popular in the early twentieth century, was that the world is all there is; it held that physical unobservables have no existential status. The challenge to religious belief was obvious. It was called *positivism* because it postulated that our senses gave us direct knowledge of the physical world, enabling us to be positive about what science tells us. But it became apparent that we cannot avoid interpreting what we "see"; all our observations are "theory laden".

A group of philosophers in Vienna in the 1920s and 30s saw philosophy as "the handmaiden of science". They regarded science as the subject of the "first order" because it was "talking about the world", which they believed was everything. Philosophy was a "second order subject", applying logic to analyse what scientists were saying. For them, philosophers were merely "talking about 'talking about the world'". Their campaign, for such it was, was directed against metaphysics and the belief that there might be other entities than those which sensory perception revealed. They came to be called the "Vienna Circle", seeking to combine positivist principles with logic and thence to develop a wholesale theory of the meaning of language; they were also known as Logical Positivists or Logical Empiricists. Their main doctrine was the "Principle of Verification", which asserted: "The meaning of a proposition is its method of verification." This meant that a proposition like "white light can be split up into colours by passing it through a prism" means something because it can be verified empirically (experimentally)

Alfred Ayer (1910–89), humanist and enthusiast for logical positivism, who later came to realize its core tenet of "verifiability" was meaningless.

by actually shining white light through a prism and observing the dispersion into colours. "God is love", on the other hand, said the Logical Positivists, has no way of being scientifically verified, so this proposition, according to them, was meaningless.

The English champion of logical positivism was A. J. Ayer. His manifesto on the subject was first published in 1936 under the title *Language, Truth and Logic* when he was aged only 24. However, the original "Principle of Verification" encountered difficulties, and Ayer was forced to reformulate it in the second edition of his book (1946), by saying that "a statement is held to be literally meaningful if and only if it is either analytic or empirically verifiable."

The effect of this was that logical positivists had to regard two kinds of propositions as meaningful: analytic propositions like "a bachelor is an unmarried man", which are tautologies and true by definition; and synthetic propositions like "forget-me-nots are blue", which synthesize the concepts of "forget-me-nots" and "blueness". Such propositions can be tested empirically. In this example, a qualifier "most" is necessary when observation reveals that there are pink "forget-me-nots". If the claim expressed by the Principle of Verification could be sustained, we would have to concede Ayer's point that "there is no logical ground for antagonism between religion and natural science... For since the religious utterances of the theist are not genuine propositions at all, they cannot stand in any logical relation to the propositions of science." With a sweep of their arms the positivists dismissed religion and metaphysics, and in many cases, ethical claims of right and wrong. It was a polite way of doing this, not by saying

The philosopher Thomas Kuhn (1922–96) addressed the psychological, social, and historical development of scientific theories. He argued that the scientific enterprise goes through various stages from a *pre-scientific phase* to *the emergence of a paradigm*, which then becomes *normative science*. Paradigms are "universally recognized scientific achievements that for a time provide model problems and solutions to a community of practitioners". Working within a paradigm very occasionally gives rise to unexpected results which do not fit in with what has been hitherto classed as normal science. This, in Kuhn's view, leads to a

• •

it, itself, really belong to one of the only two allowable classes of meaningful propositions? It became clear that it contained the seeds of its own downfall. Clearly it was not analytic – it was not a tautology – but on careful examination neither could its truth be verified empirically – so it was not synthetic: it seemed therefore that it must itself be classed as meaningless on the positivists' own definition. Disaster! Various efforts to reformulate the Principle of Verification were made, consistent with the foundation principles of logical positivism, but to no avail. In a televised discussion A. J. Ayer was forced to admit to Bryan Magee that "nearly all of it was false" and "in detail very little survived".

Logical positivism in its heyday seemed to offer a severe threat to religion, but it is now no more than a relatively distant chapter in recent philosophy.

such things were untrue, but that their propositions, which included religious ones, were meaningless.

The movement spread rapidly after the Second World War, but awkward questions began to be asked about the status of the very proposition on which the logical positivism edifice had been erected: the Verification Principle. Did

period of *crisis and extraordinary science*, which in turn becomes *revolutionary science* and leads to a new paradigm. The process is iterative. An example of this has been the overthrow of the reigning paradigm of Newtonian physics and replacement by an Einsteinian, relativistic one when dealing with very high velocities near that of light.

The philosophies of science inspired by Karl Popper and Thomas Kuhn argued that attempting to falsify rather than verify was more in keeping with scientific method than the positivists' assumptions. They saw a structure for scientific revolutions whereby new ways

"Let me explain" said John to the curious stranger watching what he was doing. "This little heap of chemicals contains saltpetre, sulphur, carbon, and iron filings in certain proportions. When I raise the temperature by lighting a match, the oxygen in the saltpetre oxidizes the sulphur and carbon quite quickly and it gets hot enough to melt the filings and make a shower of sparks." The stranger frowned a little as though he did not know much chemistry, so John explained, "It's my mother's birthday today and, when it's dark, I'm going to set light to this as a surprise for her." A different surprise was in store, however, when the stranger produced a warrant card and asked for an explanation of why John was breaking the law by constructing home-made fireworks.

For most things there is no single explanation, *the* explanation. In this case there was (i) a scientific explanation; (ii) an explanation in terms of the agent (one who acts) who made the mixture; (iii) an explanation of purpose – to celebrate a birthday; and (iv) a forensic explanation (or lack of it!) which could be quoted if John had to appear before a juvenile court!

These four different types of explanation are not in competition. They are logically compatible with each other. If this point about the plurality of compatible explanation is fully grasped, many of the perceived tensions between science and Christianity would disappear. Notable among these are the notions that you have to choose between the Big Bang and creation or between evolution and creation. Neither of these pairs are alternatives; to pose them as such is wrong and rests on a misunderstanding of the theological concept of creation. The creation of the world by God is a timeless act of bringing-into-being-and-sustaining-in-being everything there is. It is completely independent of any particular physical origins (Big Bang or otherwise) or timescales. Augustine (354–430) argued that if God created everything then he must have created time as well. Modern physics teaches that not only does time come into being with the Big Bang, but space does as well. Living as we do in space–time, we find it almost impossible to conceive of this, but it illustrates an important point, that much of modern science is counterintuitive.

"Creation" and "physical origins" need to be recognized as logically distinct concepts. They can never be alternatives. Creation is the act of a divine agent –

God – in both making and maintaining the universe – what theologians came to call *creatio ex nihilo* and *creatio continua* respectively. Explanations of the physical beginnings of the world and of the origin of species by natural selection are irrelevant as to whether or not it is a created world. To claim otherwise is to commit what the philosopher Gilbert Ryle called a category mistake. To maintain that one has to choose between creation and natural selection would be rather like claiming one has to choose between whether James Dyson was responsible for bringing into being a particular type of vacuum cleaner or whether it was the result of automation on a production line. Once the distinction between creation and physical origins is clear, the questions that then need to be addressed relate to the two creation accounts in Genesis 1:1–2:4a and Genesis 2:4b–3:24.

In philosophy, there is what is known as the Fallacy of the Excluded Middle. This is committed if it is claimed there are only two positions between which one has to choose, when others are logically possible. Richard Dawkins frequently paints the picture of evolution and creation as alternatives, and much atheist belief is built on this insecure foundation.

In his book *The Blind Watchmaker*, Dawkins claimed that "although atheism might have been logically tenable before Darwin, Darwin made it possible to be an intellectually fulfilled atheist". But this is philosophically a category mistake in Gilbert Ryle's terminology. Atheism – the denial of God – is not entailed by understanding the mechanisms of biological adaptation. It is coherent to accept both creation and evolution as well as both creation and the Big Bang without doing violence to the biblical text.

Richard Dawkins (1941–), Oxford University evolutionist and evangelist for atheism

of perceiving the world affect our understanding and practice of science. Science is – like all of life and knowledge – a blend of our subjective and objective understandings; our worldviews undergird and shape our science.

In the box differentiating "science" from "scientism" (pp. 26–27), the last entry in each list highlights a key *raison d'être* for doing science: to find explanations of how our world is made up and how it works, a topic to which we now turn.

It is just as much a philosophical and theological mistake to think that gaps in scientific explanations can be plugged by "God" as to think the converse, that complete scientific explanations could "replace" God. The act of an agent, human or divine, is unaffected by an explanation of the means employed by that agent. It is meaningless to argue that John didn't "create" his firework because we now understand the scientific explanation for how igniting a mixture of certain chemicals results in a shower of sparks.

"GOD OF THE GAPS"

Different types of explanations are not interchangeable with each other. They are answering different questions. Obviously any lack of a fully comprehensive explanation of the chemistry of fireworks could not justifiably lead to filling in what was missing by saying "that's John's bit"! And yet, because to many ears it has sounded plausible to ascribe to God that which cannot currently be explained scientifically, it has led to an explanatory type error – the hoary old chestnut dubbed "God of the gaps".

There are reverent minds who ceaselessly scan the fields of Nature and the books of Science in search of gaps – gaps which they will fill up with God. As if God lived in the gaps? What view of Nature or of Truth is theirs whose interest in Science is not in what it can explain but in what it cannot, whose quest is ignorance not knowledge, whose daily dread is that the cloud may lift, and who, as darkness melts from this field or from that, begin to tremble for the place of His abode? What needs altering in such finely jealous souls is at once their view of Nature and of

Henry Drummond (1851–97), Scottish evangelist and friend of Dwight Moody

Discovering explanations of physical events is an ongoing task of science and one of its huge strengths. At the macroscopic and the sub-microscopic ends of the scale of size, things can get quite mysterious. **Cosmogony** (the study of the physical origins of the universe) and **cosmology** (the astronomical study of the structure and space–time relationships within the universe) raise all sorts of intriguing conundrums. The furthest stars visible to us were formed earliest, so we are not seeing things as they "are" but rather we are looking into the past. They may no longer even exist. At the opposite end of size, the question arises whether "quarks" and "God particles" are actual "things" or just mental

God. Nature is God's writing, and can only tell the truth; God is light, and in Him is no darkness at all.
Henry Drummond, *The Ascent of Man* (1894)

This logical point was made in the nineteenth century by Henry Drummond, a Scottish preacher, but the neat phrase "God of the gaps" is more usually associated with the theoretical physicist, Charles Coulson. In a classic statement Coulson wrote:

I believe that the limits of science are only those which are presented by the following words: if a question about nature can be posed in scientific terms, then ultimately it will be susceptible of a scientific answer. Science does not lead us through its own country to the boundary of the scientifically unknown, explaining to us that this is where we have to deal with God. When we come to the scientifically unknown, our correct policy is not to rejoice because we have found God: it is to become better scientists.
Charles Coulson, *Science and Religion* (1954)

constructs to enable us to interpret sense data. For reasons like these, taking a *realist* view of science needs some caution and critical scrutiny, so a *critical realist* position is usually adopted by practising scientists, to take into account such points, summarized earlier by saying that much modern science is *counterintuitive*.

EVIDENCE IN CHRISTIANITY

In evaluating the truth of Christianity, evidence is just as vital as in science, but the kinds of evidence are more varied. As in science they make an appeal similar to *"the legal standards of proof established by preponderance of evidence and proof beyond reasonable doubt"*. And just as in the law courts, such evidence is of a cumulative nature. Many small pieces of valid evidence, none of which on their own might be convincing, may nevertheless add up to a rational, cumulative, and persuasive case for belief and consequent action. But each piece must contribute to the whole.

> *Nor, incidentally, will it do to recognize that of a whole series of arguments each individually is defective, but then to urge that nevertheless in sum they comprise an impressive case… We have here to insist upon a sometimes tricky distinction: between on the one hand, the valid principle of the accumulation of evidence, where every item has at least some weight in its own right; and on the other hand, the "Ten-leaky-buckets-Tactic", applied to arguments none of which hold water at all.*
> Antony Flew, *God and Philosophy* (1974)

The Central Criminal Court in London. Like justice, science depends on the accurate reporting of facts and robust questioning of possible explanations.

[There are elements in the Bible] (the story of the flood, the exodus, the life of Christ, etc.) which look as if they relate in some way to facts which we might discover (or have already discovered) by scientific enquiry. What purpose then should these scientific facts serve? Are we meant to regard them as verifying the inspiration of Scripture or of augmenting revelation – or do they have some other, quite different function in God's economy?

Obviously a surface meaning of many passages could be tested, for example, against archaeological discoveries, and the meaning of others can be enriched by scientific and historical knowledge. But I want to suggest that the primary function of scientific enquiry in such fields is neither to verify nor to add to the inspired picture, but to help us in eliminating improper ways of reading it.

Donald MacKay, *The Open Mind* (1988)

Care is needed to avoid reading science into the Bible. It is also necessary to recognize which forms of literary *genre* are being used in specific passages. The Bible includes allegory, elevated prose, euphemism, history, joke, letter, metaphor, parable, paradox, personification, poetry, prayer, prophecy, riddle, and song. Failure to take account of *genre* can end up as "Wonderful things in the Bible I see; some put there by you, some put there by me" – *eisegesis* instead of *exegesis*.

> *There have been apparent contradictions within science itself as formidable and difficult to resolve as any that have arisen between science and religion. Conflict between rival views is common in science.*
> **Malcolm Dixon**, *Science and Irreligion* (1964)

The Parting of the Red Sea, as depicted by Richard Mcbee

Superficiality and a lack of sufficient care when studying the text can create unnecessary difficulties and tensions between science and the Bible. Like shadow boxing, in which an imaginary opponent is created and then has to be knocked about, so unnecessary difficulties can be created which help contribute to the quite widespread view of science and religion as being at loggerheads – the so-called *conflict thesis* (see pp. 60–61). Those who fail to recognize the plurality of possible *compatible explanations* of objects and events, for instance, may overestimate science's considerable explanatory power and dismiss other types of explanation. Science itself is often able to achieve tidy resolution of puzzles – though certainly not always.

CHRISTIAN PERSPECTIVES ON SCIENCE

Those with a religious faith or not can work together on common problems in science. It is customary to omit references to God in contemporary science. But Christian beliefs have played a significant part in the development of modern science.

Wigner's conclusion was "that the enormous usefulness of mathematics in the natural sciences is something bordering on the mysterious and that there is no rational explanation for it". While it is true that mathematics, which is a product of the human mind, maps very elegantly onto a physical world which existed long before we arrived, for Christians there *is* a rational explanation – that they are "thinking God's thoughts after him", a phrase attributed to the sixteenth/seventeenth-century astronomer Johannes Kepler to describe his astronomical work. Christians over the centuries have found their beliefs give them additional incentives to pursue science because:

- The presuppositions of science, already referred to, are consistent with belief in the non-capricious nature of God.

- God's command to be good stewards of the creation appears to encourage science as a way of helping achieve that goal. The created order, surely, can be managed better if one knows how it is constructed and the way it works.

- It seemed that God could be glorified through scientific studies of the world, since this could both help alleviate suffering and reveal God's wisdom and power.

- Christians believe that creation is a free act of God. In philosophical language, it is *contingent* (in other words, it could have been otherwise) rather than *necessary* (had to be that way). Hence experiments need to be done to find out about it, rather than simply looking to reason for answers, or consulting the writings of authorities such as Aristotle.

- The pantheism of the ancient Greeks, which identified God with the world, discouraged experiment. By contrast, Christian belief removed that obstacle by making a clear distinction between Creator and the creation.

Why did modern science, the mathematization of hypotheses about Nature, with all its advanced technology, take its meteoric rise only in the West at the time of Galileo?...

... the available ideas of a Supreme Being, though certainly present from the earliest times, became depersonalized so soon, and so severely lacked the idea of creativity, that they prevented the development of the conception of laws ordained from the beginning by a celestial law-giver for non-human nature. Hence the conclusion did not follow that other lesser rational beings could decipher or reformulate the laws of a great rational Super-Being if they used the methods of observation, experiment, hypothesis and mathematical reasoning.

Joseph Needham, world authority on Chinese science, in *The Grand Titration: Science and Society in East and the West* **(1969)**

If Needham was right about science in China, it is not surprising that the Arabic world, with its belief in a creator, also made great contributions to science. The reasons why modern science arose only in the West remains a paradox, much debated by historians.

GOD: IMMANENCE AND TRANSCENDENCE

Science deals with the relationships between what there is and how we make sense of, affect and interact with reality. What is immanent is understood in terms of our world in all its relationships and with our human experiences and knowledge. In early times, humanity believed that there were gods and spirits everywhere and these had to be treated with respect and even worshipped. There was also an awareness of some kind of reality beyond and transcendent to our human experience. Monotheistic religions claimed that this immanent reality is created by and dependent upon a transcendent deity who started off and maintains everything. God became the explanation of what humans could not themselves explain. As human knowledge developed and extended, the explanatory power of God declined to the extent of becoming obsolete.

One consequence of this was a rise of deism. Deists believed that God initiated creation, but then left the machine to run itself. Science could explain everything else, given enough time and effort (p. 124). Modern religious and scientific thinking offer a more nuanced view of the relationship between the Creator, Sustainer God and the world. It is one affirmed by the incarnation and resurrection of Christ, where God himself became part of the immanent world. He will ultimately transform and redeem that world so that humanity and the world will function and flourish, as they were meant to do.

> *Deism, even when it struggled to be orthodox, constantly spoke of God as we might speak of an absentee landlord, who cares nothing for his property so long as he gets his rent. Yet nothing more opposed to the language of the Bible and the Fathers can hardly be imagined… For Christians the facts of nature are the acts of God. Religion relates these facts to God as their Author, science relates them to one another as integral parts of a visible order. Religion does not tell us of their interrelations, science cannot speak of their relation to God. Yet the religious view of the world is infinitely deepened and enriched when we not only recognize it as the work of God but are able to trace the relation of part to part…. The break up of the mediaeval system of thought and life resulted in an atomism, which if it had been more perfectly consistent with itself, would have been fatal alike to knowledge and society… Its theory of knowledge was a crude empiricism; its theology unrelieved deism. God was "throned in magnificent inactivity in a remote corner of the universe" and "a machinery of secondary causes" had practically taken His place…. Slowly but surely that theory of the world has been undermined…. Science had pushed the deist's God farther and farther away, and at the moment when it seemed as if He would be pushed out altogether, Darwinism appeared and under the disguise of a foe, did the work of a friend. It conferred upon philosophy and religion an inestimable benefit by showing that we must choose between two alternatives: either God is everywhere present in nature or He is nowhere.*
> **Aubrey Moore, "The Christian Doctrine of God" in Charles Gore (ed.),**
> *Lux Mundi* (1889)

Humanity affects the world and has responsibility for the uses to which we put our knowledge. Atomic science can be used to create power for human benefit or weapons of mass destruction. Our worldviews of the nature of reality, humanity, and knowledge affect what we do and whether these are self-explanatory in some kind of mechanistic, reductionist way or only make ultimate sense in light of divine revelation.

Philosophy enables us to ask and attempt to answer fundamental questions about ontology, epistemology, and morality. Immanence gives answers in terms of reality and humanity themselves; transcendence gives answers by stressing the interaction and relationship of the world and humanity with the Divine Creator and Sustainer.

CREATION AND THE BEGINNING OF THE UNIVERSE

When Augustine was asked to define time he complained that when no one asked he understood it, but when someone asked he couldn't explain it. Space and time are similarly problematic. Are they absolute and real things in themselves or simply relative to our perceptions and relationships between things and events? Space has been regarded as an all-pervading reality and as a container medium within which objects relate. Newton regarded space and time as absolute, while for Einstein they were part of relativity.

Our view of space developed with the practical exercise of surveying of land in Egypt and with theoretical reflections on geometry, physics, and mathematics. Scientists have devised different concepts and measurements of space and time – in the speeds of sound and light, and in metric or imperial systems; they debate whether space can be understood as straight or curved and time as rational or intuitive. Subjectively we talk about time "flying" or "dragging", but that is more about our experience and attention than something in and of itself. We know how to talk about space and time without any

clear definition of what they are. Language and experience are crucial as we cannot easily imagine objects as not in time nor space.

Our use of different tenses places objects and events in the past, present, or future. Cosmology, physics, and quantum mechanics all depend on our descriptions of space and time. This matches our ordinary human experiences of position, perception, duration, and change. Existentialists such as Henri Bergson and J. P. Sartre have sought to describe the link between our conscious experiences and our language. The present has no duration. The past and present do not exist without our human memories and expectations. Our perceptions are of things changing, and this raises questions of the nature and definitions of space and time. Kant argued that all our human experience is mediated in space and time, and these are necessary to have any experience at all. Perhaps this is a reason why we tend to be fascinated by the notion of space travel and of time machines, as in the science fiction writings of Jules Verne, H. G. Wells, Isaac Asimov, and a host of others.

The Genesis account insists that the world is not self-explanatory. God has the priority in explanation and is the Creator of everything. He is before all things and there is nothing that exists without him. He sustains the world; it operates and functions in dependence on him. The universe has purpose and meaning and we can make sense of those purposes. Religion and science offer complementary accounts of how the world began and operates today and how humanity began and is as it is. Science depends on order, purpose, and our capacity to understand and codify that order in scientific laws and hypotheses. Problems arise when we pretend that religion can explain everything scientifically or that science can explain all about religion.

The biblical, philosophical, and religious accounts of how and why human beings were created are all necessary to explain the complex totality of humanity with the physical, psychological, and spiritual aspects of each human being. People are combinations of what traditionally has been called body and soul. Our human experience reveals that we are different from animals in both our inner life, imagination, thought, and emotion as well as in our relationships in community and family. It is untrue that human beings are "nothing but" material objects. We are not just complicated machines, but also whole people aware of the world, other forms of life, ourselves, and each other. Religion and human history stresses that life extends beyond the here and now and that there is more to the meaning and nature of our life than this world. Religion rejects any dualist notion that we are simply material and spiritual somehow stuck together. We are intrinsically integrated persons.

Life after death, our understanding of an "inner" world of feelings, thoughts, the will, and the acceptance of the revelation of God, especially in the life, death, and resurrection of Jesus Christ all show that science and religion should go hand in hand.

The biblical account from Genesis to Revelation, but especially in Colossians (see 1:13–20), stresses that Christ is the Lord of creation, God's revelation and visual aid to humanity to understand God and what it means to be fully human.

Francis Collins (1950–), Director of the US National Institutes of Health and US leader of the Human Genome Project. For him, "Great are the works of the Lord, studied by all who delight in them" (Psalm 111:2).

WORLDVIEWS

Theology and philosophy ask questions beyond those posed by science: "If God created space and time, where was God?" "Was there any sense of time before creation?" Hard questions also arise with our understanding of freedom and determinism, infinity and eternity. Are these merely extrapolations of our current understanding of space and time or is there some objective reality to these? Our worldviews and physical observations and measurements are expressed in terms of time and space, and we have to agree conventions by which to communicate the nature of things, events, change, development, or consistency.

Along with Kepler's (attributed) response to studying our vast universe as "thinking God's thoughts after him", Francis Collins, Director of the US National Institutes of Health, reacted to the sub-microscopic components of the same universe four centuries later by saying:

> *For me the experiencing of sequencing the human genome, and uncovering this most remarkable of all texts, was both a stunning scientific achievement and an occasion of worship.*

For Kepler and Collins, "The heavens declare the glory of God; the skies proclaim the work of his hands" (Psalm 19:1). Richard Dawkins has, despite his claims, a much more restricted worldview. He rejoices in the "wonder" of the world, referring to "a sumptuous planet, sparkling with colour, bountiful with life". But for Dawkins, "there is no Creator, no plan and no purpose other than being machines for propagating DNA… [which] is every living object's sole reason for living".

Perhaps this difference is because Dawkins is comparing a modern perception of the universe with a medieval one, rather than between a Christian and an atheist one. Whatever the reason, it shows how worldviews, theistic, atheistic, or otherwise, can colour views about

The "astronomical" clock in Strasbourg Cathderal, seen by many as modelling the mechanical regularities of the universe.

the discoveries of science – and even about the nature of science itself.

An excellent example of this is the Steady State Theory of the universe – that the universe is undergoing continuous creation and has no beginning – formulated in 1948 by Fred Hoyle, Hermann Bondi, and Thomas Gold. In 1965, this was contraindicated by Arno Penzias and Robert Wilson discovering residual radiation in space – a kind of "echo" of the so-called "Big Bang". For Penzias and Wilson it was comparable to finding some ashes in a wood that were slightly warm and concluding "there was a fire here some while ago". But for Bondi, Gold, and Hoyle the idea of a beginning sounded too suggestive of a "Beginner"; Hoyle, an atheist, disparagingly coined the term the "Big Bang".

Some worldviews are not entirely religious or antireligious. Two hybrids including elements of religion with a base of metaphors are:

- In the heyday of ancient Greek science (600 BC to AD 200) the world was often conceived of as an *organism.* The religious element was that it was also seen as semi-divine. To the Greeks, the performing of experiments on a semi-divine nature seemed to be what they called *hubris,* an outrage. This *organismic* view of nature obviously hindered the growth of experimental science. A modern organismic worldview is the Gaia hypothesis.

- Robert Boyle (1627–91), a founder member the Royal Society (of London) widely known for his Gas Law, saw the world with it regularities and continuance as like the great clock at the church of Notre Dame in Strasbourg, whose works were visible. This mechanical metaphor, a *mechanistic* worldview, resonated with Boyle's Christian belief as implying a clockmaker. The deists, who were influential throughout the eighteenth century, built on this idea. They believed God had created the world and then moved off-stage; they pointed out that a clock, once made, does not need the continual attention of the clockmaker. This illustrates one of the pitfalls of metaphors: trying to press every detail into service. If every detail fitted it would no longer be a *comparison*, but an *identity.*

BELIEF SYSTEMS

• **Atheism**. Disbelief in, or denial of, the existence of a God. "A little superficial knowledge of philosophy may incline the mind of man to atheism." Francis Bacon (1561–1626).

• **Deism**. Belief in the existence of a God, with rejection of revelation: "natural religion". "Deism being the very same with old Philosophical Paganism." Richard Bentley (1662–1742).

• **Agnostic**. One who holds that the existence of anything beyond material phenomena cannot be known. Thomas Henry Huxley (1825–95).

• **Theism**. Belief in a deity or deities, as opposed to atheism. Belief in one God as creator and supreme ruler of the universe, without denial of revelation; in this use distinct from deism.

Since atheism denies the existence of God, an atheist believes neither that God created the world nor that he subsequently sustains it; there is little more to be said. Deism asserts that God created the world, but that he subsequently left it to itself and has no further interaction with it. A consequence is that there is no revelation from God to man. Knowledge of God comes instead through so-called natural theology, whereby man is able to deduce through the exercise of his reason what God is like. The sciences play a special role in this, since they provide the empirical evidence to which reason is applied.

Thomas Huxley coined the word "agnostic" in 1869 at a party held to mark the formation of the short-lived Metaphysical Society, allegedly taking it from Paul's mention of the altar to "the Unknown God" in Acts 17:23. Uniquely of the four belief paradigms, the term for this one was created by its chief advocate. Huxley quickly lost control of the meaning. There is a story that Benjamin Jowett, the Master of Balliol, replied to an undergraduate who proclaimed himself an agnostic, "Young man, in this university we speak Latin not Greek, so when speaking of yourself in that way, use the word ignoramus." It was quickly recognized that agnosticism could be a veneer. In nine cases out of ten Agnosticism is but old atheism writ large.

RELATIONSHIPS BETWEEN SCIENCE AND CHRISTIANITY

Science and Christianity may be viewed as "***interactionist***" or "*non-interactionist*".

Interactionist views may be seen either as supporting science against religion or, conversely, as upholding religious beliefs by the findings of science. Non-interactionist views may also be used in opposing ways. One group may use them supposedly to render all religious claims immune from possible discredit by scientific discoveries by claiming a total separation between them, while another group may use them to claim, like the logical positivists, that religious propositions are meaningless because they are not open to empirical tests.

NON-INTERACTIONIST ("WATERTIGHT-COMPARTMENT") POSITIONS

Arguments for a complete separation between theology and natural science fall into two major classes: instrumentalist arguments, and two-realms arguments.

Instrumentalist arguments hinge on denying, either of scientific statements or of religious ones, that they in fact make assertions about what is the case, and ascribing to them some other function instead. In two-realms arguments it is allowed that both scientific and religious statements are assertions, but they are said to be about such entirely different things that they can neither support nor conflict with each other.
William Austin, *The Relevance of Natural Science to Theology* (1976)

INSTRUMENTALIST ARGUMENTS

A classical example of **instrumentalism** in science is the two prefaces to Copernicus's book *On the Revolution of the Heavenly Spheres.* In Copernicus's time a major issue was whether astronomical theories described how the heavens actually were (*physical* theories) or were just convenient calculating devices (*mathematical* theories). The Roman Catholic authorities did not, in principle, object

---

Nicolaus Copernicus (1473–1543), Polish astronomer and author of *De Revolutionibus Orbium Coelestium* (1543) which argued that the movements of the planets could be better explained by assuming they revolved around the Sun rather than the Earth.

to a fresh calculating device, but they did object to a new *physical* theory if it conflicted with their favoured *world picture* of a central Earth. Copernicus anticipated problems and wrote a preface to his book, dedicated to Pope Paul III, making it clear that he *was* advancing a realist position, a physical theory:

> *I may well presume, most Holy Father, that certain people, as soon as they hear that in this book* On the Revolutions of the Spheres of the Universe *I ascribe movement to the earthly globe, will cry out that holding such views, I should at once be hissed off the stage… How I came to dare to conceive such motion of the Earth, contrary to the received opinion of the Mathematicians and indeed contrary to the impression of the senses, is what your Holiness will rather expect.*

But Copernicus was dying and the book was seen through the press by one Andreas Osiander on behalf of Copernicus's friend, the Bishop of Kulm. Osiander, also anticipating trouble, inserted an anonymous preface without Copernicus knowing. Headed "Concerning the Hypothesis of the Work", he tried to protect Copernicus and claimed it was simply a mathematical theory – an *instrumentalist* position:

> *The author of this work has done nothing blameworthy, for it is the duty of an astronomer to… conceive and devise, since he cannot in any way attain to the true causes, such hypotheses as, being assumed, enable the motions to be calculated correctly from the principles of geometry… they are not put forward to convince anyone that they are true, but merely to provide a correct basis for calculation.*

Copernicus was deeply disturbed when he received a printed copy of *De Revolutionibus Orbium Coelestium* on his deathbed and read the additional preface.

Instrumentalism in religion shifts the focus on to what religion does for people, rather than asking the question "is it true?" Its unsatisfactory nature arises because believers place a high importance on the truth or falsity of what they believe. This latter criticism of instrumentalism is also valid for science and, as indicated earlier, most practising scientists hold to some form of a *realist* position. Neither in science, nor in religion are cognitive claims regarded simply as "useful fictions". The issue which instrumentalism ducks is that of truth.

TWO-REALMS ARGUMENTS

These avoid the explanatory type-error of the "God of the gaps" by using a range of metaphorical terms to convey the idea of science and religion occupying different and separate *domains, dimensions, fields, levels, realms, spaces, spheres,* or *areas* and as being *complementary.* But such terms introduce a different problem. How can one define these metaphorical terms in ways that avoid what philosophers call *persuasive* definitions, ones that necessarily force either non-interactionist or interactionist conclusions? The attempt at clarifying possible relationships between science and religion through this kind of imprecise classification turns out to be unsatisfactory.

Charles Coulson in his influential book, *Science and Christian Belief,* argued that science and religion are "complementary", extending the idea of complementarity in physics, which seeks to explain the well-known paradox that light and electrons can behave – or be described – as either particles or waves. Others have followed him (see p. 55), although Ian Barbour, who has developed his own typology of science and religion, objects that the "use of the Complementarity Principle outside physics is *analogical not inferential.* There must be independent grounds for justifying in the new context the value of two alternative sets of constructs." For Barbour, the Complementarity Principle "refers to *different ways of analyzing a single entity* (such as an electron)" and although it might be possible to extend the principle to "mind-and-brain" relationships, it would be illegitimate to apply it to science and religion since "science and religion are not simply two views of one world – unless one subscribes to pantheism…"

MacKay has argued for a more sophisticated use of complementarity, expressed as a logical relationship and not dependent on the original use of the concept in physics by Neils Bohr, even though MacKay considered the wave–particle duality exemplified it.

In biological research, references to features of wholeness and purposeful reactions or organisms are used together with the increasingly detailed information on structure and regulatory processes… It must be realized that the attitudes termed mechanistic and finalistic are not contradictory points of view, but rather exhibit a complementary relationship which is connected with our position as observers of nature.
Niels Bohr, *Atomic Physics and Human Knowledge* (1958)

INTERACTIONIST POSITIONS

These come in a variety of forms. At one end of the spectrum, religious writings may be judged at "face value" by current views of the content and processes of either science or of religious concepts. Between these extremes lies a range of positions in which the

A TV image is the product of electronic ingenuity – but it also depends on the original pictures being transmitted, and the producer who can switch the image at will.

literary genre of language employed in religion plays a key role. The extreme positions often draw upon and therefore encourage the idea of a war between science and religion. This may result in the acceptance of science and rejection of religion, or vice versa. At this point, the ways in which language is used in science and in religion become important.

The God in whom the Bible invites belief is no "Cosmic Mechanic". Rather is he the Cosmic Artist, the creative Upholder, without whose constant activity there would be not even chaos, but just nothing. What we call physical laws are expressions of created events that we study as the physical world. Physically they express the nature of the entities "held in being" in the pattern. Theologically they express the stability of the great Artist's creative will. Explanations in terms of scientific laws and in terms of divine activity are thus not rival answers to the same question; yet they are not talking about different things. They are complementary accounts of different aspects of the same happening, which in its full nature cannot be explained by either alone. To invoke "natural processes" is not to escape from divine activity, but only to make hypotheses about its regularity… . A painting can be described both in terms of the distribution of chemicals on a two-dimensional surface and also as the physical expression of a design in the mind of an artist. In other words, the same material object can have two or more "causes", which do not contradict or overlap, but are undeniably complementary.
Donald MacKay, *Science and Christian Faith Today* **(1960)**

LEARNING THE LINGO

One aspect of how a specific literary genre is employed by both science and religion is the use of analogical language, without which our literacy in both science and religion would be severely limited. Advocates of the more moderate positions described above recognize the need to grapple with complex ideas, both in science and in religion, by drawing on various literary devices in order to be articulate about certain classes of subjects. These may be any, or all of the following:

• invisible;

• novel;

• conceptually difficult;

• difficult to handle by any other means.

Model of an atom, with electrons orbiting around a central nucleus

Time and time again we employ comparisons between familiar things and the apparently intractable entities which confront us. This is done in the hope and expectation that what we are familiar with may share characteristics with what is unfamiliar, thus helping us to gain a purchase on what is inhibiting literacy in the subject of our investigation. In other words, we resort to analogical thinking. We say light is *like* a wave motion, God is *like* a father (similes); or we drop the "like" and say light *is* a wave motion, God *is* a father (metaphors). We have, of course, already encountered metaphors in worldview comparisons with *organisms* and *mechanisms*, and, indeed with a list of eight of them in the "two-realms" arguments.

Sometimes a metaphor turns out to embody useful insights – such as good fatherhood in religion and waves in science. Such metaphors can be highly fruitful in developing understanding, lending themselves to being systematically developed as helpful comparisons. For example, in science we commonly compare electricity with water flowing through pipes: batteries/pumps, switches/taps, voltmeters/pressure gauges, ammeters/flow meters, wires/pipes, and so on. In theology, a comparable example would be "light", which can encourage growth, make the way ahead clear, generate a sense of well-being, dispel our fears of darkness, warn us of dangers, and expose what needs to be cleared away.

We need to beware of how we employ such metaphors. For example, is an atom best conceived of as a positively charged "pudding" in which are embedded negatively charged electrons? Or does a miniature solar system, having a central, positively charged nucleus circulated by negatively charged electrons, make a better comparison? Another model is that of water waves, which gives some understanding of how light and other electromagnetic phenomena such as radio, infrared, gamma, and cosmic radiations behave. In the scientific arena, we have refined the way we use such conceptual models to illuminate complex ideas. So too in religion our conceptual apparatus needs to be developed to enable us to speak intelligibly about such notions as an invisible God, the Holy Spirit, and a future afterlife. Here, the problem of invisibility (addressed in the incarnation) means we have to make comparisons with things we are familiar with – good fathers, loving mothers, wind, shepherds, kings, and so forth. A key feature of a good model is its extensibility and consequent fruitfulness, aiding understanding, stimulating fresh thought, giving rise to novel avenues of enquiry, and generating new research programmes. The understanding of God's two "books", nature and the Bible (more metaphors!), requires care in "reading" them intelligently. A lack of care may have misleading consequences.

THE "TWO BOOKS"

The metaphor of the "two books" conveys the idea that God is the author of nature and the Bible, and that something of his power, wisdom, and goodness can be discerned from both of these "books".

While the general notion that God can be known from his creation is a biblical motif, set forth most explicitly in the Psalms and somewhat more ambivalently in Romans 1, the specific idea of nature as a book written by God dates from the patristic period. John Chrysostom (c. 347–407), Archbishop of Constantinople, wrote that the heavens are a volume in which the unlearned can read of the power of God. The greatest of the Latin fathers, Augustine of Hippo (354–430), used the phrase "book of nature" to castigate the Manicheans who doubted that the material world was the creation of a good God.

During the Middle Ages the idea of "the book of the creatures" became commonplace. God was said to have invested the whole created order with symbolic meanings that directly reflected a range of profound theological truths. Christian teachings were associated with particular creatures – mythical and real – because of their appearance, characteristics, and behaviours. The pelican thus symbolized Christ's atonement, because of a widespread belief that the parent bird's blood could revivify its expired offspring. Similarly, the phoenix was a sign of the resurrection, while the lion and unicorn represented Christ. Other creatures symbolized the wiles of the devil, or particular virtues to be emulated. Hugh of St Victor (c. 1078–1141) captured the essence of this symbolic worldview in his declaration that "the whole sensible world is like a book written by the finger of God" in which each of the creatures is a figure "not invented by human decision, but instituted by the divine will to manifest the invisible things of God's wisdom". One distinctive feature of the "book of nature" metaphor during this period was the way in which the widespread use of allegorical interpretation provided an intimate connection between the interpretation of the Bible and the interpretation of nature. The Bible and nature could both be interpreted allegorically and when interpreted in this way bore witness to the same set of truths.

With the emergence of modern science in the seventeenth century the "two books" metaphor persisted and, if

• •

anything, became even more prevalent. However, it now took on a rather different complexion. Galileo announced in a famous passage that the book of nature was written in mathematical language, and that only those skilled in mathematics could read it. This signalled a significant divergence from the older approach, in which nature and the Bible were "read" together as part of a unified interpretative practice. Now, moreover, the reading of the book of nature was increasingly the province of scientific experts. The theological content of the book of nature was radically contracted, too, since readers of nature could now only infer truths about God from their experience of the world. As Francis Bacon expressed it, the book of nature exhibits the power of the Creator, but not his image. The book of nature, on this new understanding, tells of God the mathematician or God the ingenious designer, but not of a triune God who became incarnate in Christ. The prevalence of the "two books" metaphor in the seventeenth and eighteenth centuries nonetheless illustrates the close and positive relationship that then existed between the natural sciences and Christianity. Many natural historians saw themselves as engaged in an enterprise that would yield significant dividends for natural theology. In this way, the idea of the book of nature underscored the theological importance of natural science and sanctified the endeavours of its practitioners.

From the nineteenth century onwards, for a variety of reasons, the metaphor fell into decline. Natural theology began to attract criticisms from philosophers and, increasingly, theologians, too. Related to this, the design argument, as traditionally understood, seemed less credible as the theory of evolution by natural selection gained almost universal acceptance. The professionalization and fragmentation of the sciences also challenged the idea of a single, unified "book of nature". At the same time, biblical criticism sorely tested the notion of a unitary "book of scripture" that was unequivocal in its meaning. That said, the expression has enjoyed a long and interesting life – one that offers key insights in the historical relations between science and religion. And the metaphor encapsulates what must surely still be the conviction of the religious believer: that verifiable facts about the natural world cannot ultimately be in conflict with religious truths.

SCIENCE AND RELIGION IN THE MODERN PERIOD

In Bacon's time the church dominated every branch of learning, but tensions arose when scientific advances seemed to contradict church dogma. This was typified by the debate between Galileo and the church over whether the earth or the sun was the centre of the universe. In fact, it was Galileo's telescope that conclusively refuted the contemporary interpretation of Psalm 96:10, that the "world is fixed immovably". Religion and philosophy started to diverge in the Enlightenment. Many scientists in the early seventeenth century were believing Christians, motivated in their scientific work by their faith that God had made the world and proper worship, service, and obedience was "to think God's thoughts after him". However, with the rise of Enlightenment thinking, the focus moved away from God to human nature and indeed to nature itself. Humanism became the contemporary worldview and increasingly humanity became the basis of all explanation. Humankind was regarded as the measure of all things. Often God was seen as the initial Creator, who had started the whole process, but then left the world to run itself (deism). This meant we could understand how things worked and what they were without referring to God or divine intervention. By the late nineteenth century, Darwin in science and Marx in social understanding, joined a few years later by Freud in psychological thinking, had created tensions between anthropomorphic views of human beings and the world itself, and religious and biblical accounts of the origin of the world and humanity. These were heightened by a critical view of the Bible and its interpretation, and a failure of the church to respond adequately and comprehensively to these philosophical and scientific challenges. As science progressed into every area of life and the world, religion retreated from occupying the centre of explanation with God at the heart of all knowledge and understanding to a "God of the gaps" view: God was only invoked when human explanations could go no further. With scientific explanation expanding more and more, the perceived need for belief in God became less and divine accounts more irrelevant.

An illustration from the cosmographical atlas *Harmonia Macrocosmica* (1660) by Andreas Cellarius, showing the Sun, rather than the Earth, at the centre of the universe, as envisaged by Nicolaus Copernicus.

THE CONFLICT THESIS

The idea of a conflict between science and Christian belief is a relatively recent phenomenon. Perhaps the first use of "conflict" to represent the idea of warfare between science and religion was John Draper's book, *History of the Conflict between Science and Religion* (1874).

THE CONFLICT THESIS

Advocates of the Conflict Thesis hold that there has been a perennial conflict between science and religion, and that such conflict is inevitable. The thesis found its definitive formulation in the writings of the nineteenth-century controversialists John Draper (1811–82) and Andrew Dickson White (1832–1918) and despite powerful criticism by historians, is still commonly encountered in contemporary debates about science and religion. The conflict thesis has a number of related elements. First is the belief that history offers incontestable evidence of the inevitability of science–religion conflict. Second is the idea that "science" and "religion" are discrete human enterprises with distinct boundaries that change little over time. Third is the conviction that science and religion seek to offer explanations for the same phenomena and that, accordingly, conflict between them is inescapable.

The chief historical episodes that lend plausibility to the conflict thesis are the trial of Galileo in 1632 and the reception of Darwin's ideas about evolution in the latter half of the nineteenth century. Close examination of these episodes, however, reveals a more complicated picture. In the case of Galileo, it is clear that the Catholic Church was affirming the scientific consensus of the time, and thus its position could not be characterized as anti-science per se. Moreover, the Galileo affair was by no means typical of religious attitudes towards science, since the Catholic Church was the major supporter of astronomical research during this period. Moving to the nineteenth century, it is undoubtedly true that Darwin's ideas elicited religious opposition. But these same ideas attracted strong support in some religious circles and were initially criticized by reputable scientific authorities. The examples of Galileo and Darwin do not offer unambiguous support for the conflict thesis.

It is also important to bear in mind a larger historical perspective in which religious ideas and institutions played a significant and positive role in motivating

Further comments on the frequently quoted episodes to support a conflict thesis are given in the following sections (pp. 62–67), which summarize key points from the Galileo affair, and the well-known, but poorly understood, encounter between Professor Thomas Henry Huxley and Bishop Samuel Wilberforce at the Oxford Museum on 30 June 1860.

and legitimating scientific enquiry. It has been plausibly argued that religion was a necessary (if insufficient) condition for the emergence of modern science in the West. Accordingly, the current consensus among historians is that the history of science–religion relations is too complex to fit into any simple pattern of unremitting conflict.

Adding further to the complexity of this picture is the fact that the boundaries between science and religion have been somewhat fluid over time. While the study of nature in the West has long been concerned with naturalistic explanation, in the past these patterns of explanation were often assumed to have deep theological significance. Religion, in other words, was at times inextricably bound up with "science". It is a mistake, therefore, to assume that in all periods of history science and religion were distinct enterprises in the way that they are today.

Following on from this, proponents of the conflict thesis typically assume that science and religion compete for the same intellectual territory. Religion is thought of as offering explanatory hypotheses that are in direct competition with scientific theories. The doctrine of creation, to take a key example, is seen as being on a par with scientific accounts of origins. There necessarily follows from this conception the inevitability of the struggle between science and religion. A further assumption of this view is that with human progress, scientific explanations will ultimately triumph over religious ones. Of course, while scientific theories may have implications for religious doctrines and vice versa, the idea that religious conceptions are merely crude scientific hypotheses fails to do justice to the nature of religious belief.

In sum, since its inception in the nineteenth century the conflict thesis has continued to attract adherents and inform popular views about the relations between science and religion. Despite this, it is conceptually simplistic and at odds with the historical evidence.

THE GALILEO AFFAIR

What was the Galileo affair all about? Was it because the disputed worldview displaced man's abode from the centre of the universe? Because it conflicted with the Aristotelian worldview? Because theology took priority over the science of the day? In fact, it was none of those.

When Galileo turned his new-fangled telescope to the skies in 1609, what he saw amazed him. Above all, the sunlit phases of Venus showed that it could not possibly be orbiting the earth, as the earth-centred systems of Aristotle and Ptolemy had maintained. What was left? Galileo was familiar with the *De Revolutionibus* of Copernicus (1543), which set the sun at the centre with the planets, including the earth, circling it. This seemed the obvious answer. But difficulties loomed: setting the earth in motion contravened common sense as well as the accepted Aristotelian physics of the day. And Galileo was soon reminded that the literal interpretation of those biblical passages that mention the sun's motion or the earth's immobility excluded the Copernican alternative. Catholic biblical scholars had, in fact, maintained this for some time before.

In a worried letter to his friend, Benedetto Castelli, Galileo argued that the theological criticism of Copernicanism was mistaken. First, the writers of the Bible accommodated their language to the capacity of ordinary people. (This principle had a respectable precedent in medieval theology.) Second, the Bible ordinarily lends itself to multiple interpretations; hence, if a particular interpretation conflicts with "necessary demonstration" about nature, a different interpretation should be sought. Third, the authority of the Bible extends only to matters of faith, not to matters accessible to human reasoning like astronomy.

A copy of the letter was forwarded to Rome in 1615 by one of Galileo's critics. To complicate matters further, a respected theologian, Paolo Foscarini, also published a short work defending the Copernican view from theological attacks. Cardinal Robert Bellarmine, the leading Roman theologian, wrote to Foscarini and, implicitly, Galileo warning them that the Council of Trent had prohibited interpreting the Bible in a sense contrary to that of the fathers, as they were doing. Even the mention that Abraham had two sons, he said, is a matter of faith as God's word. After consultation with a committee of theological advisors, the Congregation of the Index, in 1616, declared that the Copernican theses were "false and contrary to Holy Scripture" and Galileo was privately admonished by Bellarmine to abandon them. If he resisted, he was to be given a more specific injunction. Bellarmine reported back to the Holy Office that Galileo had acquiesced.

What was at issue here, as the theologians saw it, was the integrity of the Bible. The Protestant Reformation a century before had led to a new emphasis, among Protestant

and Catholic theologians alike, on the literal sense of the Bible. Over the course of his career, Bellarmine, in particular, had proved a staunch defender of literal interpretation. Furthermore, the theologians regarded themselves as being on the side of the science of their day, not opposed to it: their colleagues in natural philosophy had not yet come to terms with the new worldview. Mathematical astronomy for them was still no more than a device for calculating planetary movements.

In 1624, the new Pope, Urban VIII, an admirer of Galileo, permitted the astronomer to publish a work on Copernican astronomy provided that it did not claim to demonstrate that worldview. The *Dialogue on Two Chief World Systems* appeared in 1632. Urban was enraged by it: Galileo, he said, had betrayed his confidence. Was it because he believed that Galileo had, in effect, supported the Copernican claim? Or that he had put Urban's strongly held objection to such demonstration in the mouth of the consistently refuted Simplicio of the *Dialogue*? Or because Urban was beset by critics who needed to be placated by his treating Galileo harshly? We shall never know for sure. What we do know is that Urban decided that the offence should be treated harshly on suspicion of heresy, requiring a formal trial.

Galileo was brusquely ordered to Rome, though permitted to be lodged at the Villa Medici. The merits of the case he had made for the Copernican system in the *Dialogue* never appear to have come up for discussion. The charge was finally (after considerable manoeuvring) to be the simplest and least controversial one: that Galileo had defended a work that had earlier been declared to be contrary to the Bible. After protracted interrogation he was found guilty, required to abjure the condemned view, and sentenced to permanent house arrest. In his letter to Castelli, echoing Augustine, Galileo had written that prudence alone should dictate that theologians not commit irrevocably to an interpretation of the Bible in regard to nature where the contrary could conceivably be proven later by the "senses or demonstration". How right he would prove to be!

Galileo was tried by the Inquisition for defending an interpretation of the Bible that was not accepted by the Church.

HUXLEY V. WILBERFORCE: "GREAT DEBATE" OR HISTORICAL MYTH?

The idea of perpetual conflict between science and religion gains popular support from colourful historical anecdotes. Who has not heard of the "great debate" between Charles Darwin's "bulldog", Thomas Henry Huxley, and the Bishop of Oxford, "Soapy Sam" Wilberforce? The occasion was the 1860 Oxford meeting of the British Association for the Advancement of Science, held only months after Darwin had published his *Origin of Species*. The imprudent bishop taunted Huxley by asking whether he would prefer to think of himself having an ape for an ancestor on his grandfather's or grandmother's side. He soon had his comeuppance. Huxley replied to the effect that he would rather have an ape for an ancestor, than a man who used his great gifts to obscure the truth. Hurrah for Huxley, who in most accounts is the decisive victor for science over religion. It is a great story; but, put like that, it is a myth – and in two different senses.

Retrospectively, it became a foundation myth for professional scientists, symbolizing the emancipation of serious science from clerical interference. But it is also a myth in the commoner sense because Huxley did not score a victory. Nor did his son Leonard, who edited the *Life and Letters* of his father, claim that he had. A contemporary account in the *Athenaeum* magazine probably came closest to the truth: the two men had "each found foemen worthy of their steel, and made their charges and countercharges very much to their own satisfaction and the delight of their respective friends".

Thomas Henry Huxley (1825–95), inventor of the word "agnostic" and tireless propagandist for the freeing of science from religion.

As with many myths, the anecdote captures elements of truth. Darwin's theory undoubtedly was shocking to traditional religious sensibilities. Wilberforce underlined his opposition in the *Quarterly Review*, giving himself no room for manoeuvre:

> *Man's derived supremacy over the earth; man's power of articulate speech; man's gift of reason; man's free-will and responsibility; man's fall and man's redemption; the incarnation of the Eternal Son; the indwelling of the Eternal Spirit, – all are equally and utterly irreconcilable with the degrading notion of the brute origin of him who was created in the image of God, and redeemed by the Eternal Son assuming to himself his nature.*

It is also true that Huxley valued Darwin's theory as a resource for promoting the cultural authority of a rising generation of scientists for whom the sciences would enjoy independence. Inventor of the word "agnosticism", he contrasted his position with the arrogance of those claiming privileged knowledge of the deity.

Placed in a wider context, however, it soon becomes clear that the debate was not the "great debate" it has become. Wilberforce was not the scientific ignoramus of the mythology.

Samuel Wilberforce (1805–73), son of the slave emancipator William Wilberforce and Bishop of Oxford (1845 until his death). He was far from being a scientific ignoramus; he had a first-class honours degree in mathematics.

His published review identified what, at the time, were the weakest points in Darwin's rhetoric, Darwin admitting that "he quizzes me quite splendidly". Nor was Wilberforce entirely representative of Christian responses. One of Darwin's first converts was the Anglican clergyman Charles Kingsley who saw in the model of creation through natural laws a nobler understanding of the Creator's work. The day following the Wilberforce/Huxley exchange a sermon was preached in Oxford by Frederick Temple, a future Archbishop of Canterbury, who positively welcomed the expansion of scientific knowledge, turning his back on a "God of the gaps".

As for the debate itself, far from a victory for Huxley, at least one convert to Darwin's theory, the naturalist Henry Baker Tristram, was de-converted as he reacted adversely to the Darwinian offensive. Significant repercussions are hard to find once the initial publicity waned. It was almost 30 years before the event was reconstituted and sanctified in the *Life and Letters of Darwin*, of *Joseph Hooker*, and of *Huxley*. Among the few references that appear during those 30 years most were made by churchmen distancing themselves from Wilberforce's peremptory judgment. As for Huxley, he continued his non-conformist assault on the Anglican establishment and pulled no punches when attacking the cosmology he found in Genesis. It was not, however, Huxley's view that Darwin's theory was incompatible with theism. He even allowed for a "wider" teleology inscribed in the preconditions of an evolving universe. Darwin's theory, as with all science, was neither Christian nor anti-Christian, but a-Christian. It had no more to do with theism than had the writings of Euclid. Crucially, Huxley did not see inevitable conflict between science and religion when each was properly qualified and understood. He wrote: "The antagonism between science and religion, about which we hear so much, appears to me to be purely factitious – fabricated, on the one hand, by short-sighted religious people who confound a certain branch of science, theology, with religion; and, on the other, by equally short-sighted scientific people who forget that science takes for its province only that which is susceptible of clear intellectual comprehension."

Theology and philosophy ask questions beyond those enquired about by science: "If God created space and time, where was God?" "Was there any sense of time before creation?" Hard questions also arise with our understanding of freedom and determinism, infinity and eternity. Are these merely extrapolations of our current understanding of space and time or is there some objective reality to these? Our worldviews and physical observations and measurements are expressed in terms of time and space and we have to agree conventions by which to communicate the nature of things, events, change, development, or consistency.

VALUES IN SCIENCE AND THE WORLD

A sunset can be described as the consequences of particles of matter refracted in the air by light; a kiss as the mutual approach of two pairs of lips, followed by the reciprocal transmission of carbon dioxide and microbes, and the juxtaposition of two orbicular muscles in a state of contraction. Neither account does justice to the significance and appreciation of the aesthetic beauty of a glorious sunset or the meaning of an embrace. There are values attached far beyond purely material, physical, chemical, or other scientific descriptions. For families, children are not just objects of physical existence or more mouths to feed but part of a community which sets great emotional, psychological, and spiritual store by relationships. Likewise, the very practice and theory of science is loaded with values.

Truth is fundamental to the presenting, testing, and application of the fruits of scientific research. Truth, accuracy, and the desire to pursue truth and knowledge for the importance of the search itself as well as for the benefit and good of humanity is fundamental to science. Scientific communities check and assess each other's work to establish its validity and guarantee what results, building on that research.

We make moral judgments about the character and behaviour of each other and praise or blame individuals, teams, governments, funding organizations, and the institutions we work for. Our value systems depend on our views of humanity, the world, knowledge, religion, and philosophy. These values are applied not only to how we obtain scientific knowledge, but also what we do with it.

Science has created incredible media and communication opportunities, but also the possibility of pornography and anti-social abuse. Values affect what we do in science and why we do it. It is part of our motivation, but where do our values come from?

THE BASES OF VALUES

Values are either intrinsic to the world and humanity, created by human beings; or they are revealed by God. The Natural Law tradition claims that right and wrong are part of the natural world itself and human nature. But many things we regard as evil, such as natural disasters, floods, and famine, are part of this world. Human beings are not all good, but a mixture of good and evil in thought and action. This does not mean there are no general, natural laws which indicate the purposes and goals of human flourishing and human harm.

Science does not exist in a vacuum. Value systems shape our approach to and practice of science as well as the applications we make with knowledge gained from science. What we study, how and why we study the various sciences, and what we do with the fruits of science and technology are all part of our value systems and worldviews. They need to be expressed, defended, and lived.

Philosophers like Hume, argue that morality is of our own human making; it is entirely subjective. They maintain that it is we who decide what is right or wrong, good or bad, and assign moral value to things and animals; that values are subjective human preferences and choices, whether made by an *emotivist* (who believes that values are expressions and the encouragement of emotion), a *relativist* (who believes that there are no absolute values but morality depends on and is shaped by the context we live in), an *existentialist* (who believes that morality is a matter of the will and choice), or a *prescriptivist* (who believes that values are universal prescriptions we create and make). We make morality.

This contrasts to religious claims that God reveals morality both in the world itself, human nature, and through holy books and holy people. For Christians, these focus on Jesus Christ. He shows how humans ought to live and relate to the world and each other. His role in creation, sustaining, and the climactic transformation of the world and his life, death, resurrection, and promised return in glory reveal and embody values for all humanity.

These different accounts surface in debates in the environmental sciences. James Lovelock has suggested that Gaia and the world itself has value and needs to be respected; some of his followers believe that Gaia should be worshipped. Others argue that since humanity has done so much environmental damage it needs to take responsibility to conserve, preserve, and restore the world, both for the sake of the earth itself and for future generations of its inhabitants. There is also a direct appeal to avoid the harm that environmental degradation and depletion is doing to human life. Christians, Jews, and Muslims stress that God created the world and humanity and that our responsibility is to be good stewards of all that God has given including the world itself, animal life, and each other. God demands from us respect of the world, not worship.

SO WHAT FOR PHILOSOPHY, SCIENCE, AND RELIGION?

Many universities have created an academic post for the public understanding of science. This acknowledges that the general public do not easily understand scientists, science, or what scientists do. The success of science has created an optimistic belief that science can solve everything and perform new miracles daily. The US commentator Walter Lippmann spoke for many in suggesting that scientists have become the new priests of today and science the new religion. Technical expertise and years of scientific education distance scientists from ordinary non-scientists.

Understanding science is made harder when we realize that the perception of science may not match the reality of how science is conducted and the presuppositions and even prejudices scientists bring to their work. Medical practitioners are only too well aware how little they understand disease and the limitations of what can be achieved. Patients and families are constantly optimistic that science will cure their illnesses and become angry when that does not happen.

> *All scientific work of an experimental or exploratory character starts with some expectation about the outcome of the enquiry. This expectation one starts with, this hypothesis one formulates, provides the initiative and incentive for the enquiry and governs its actual form. It is in the light of this expectation that some observations are held relevant, and others not; that some methods are chosen, others discarded; that some experiments are done rather than others. It is only in the light of this prior expectation that the activities that the scientist reports in his scientific papers really have any meaning at all.*
> **Peter Medawar, "Is the Scientific Paper a Fraud?" (1963)**

Scientists are people too and are subject to all the pressures and problems human beings face. Science and scientists operate within frameworks of meaning, skill, and community testing; they have worldviews which undergird and direct their practice. Understanding these worldviews and their interpretations of the nature of reality, the world, human beings, and the value systems scientists operate with is crucial because science is part of our social and political structures and society funds, permits, encourages, or denies and rejects some of what scientists can and are doing. Debates over the genetic modification of food and animals show how divided society can be and what restrictions can be placed on the practice of science.

Science, Faith, and the Bible

2

During the past 400 years, the relationship between natural science and the Bible has become increasingly complicated. This complexity has grown considerably in the last 100–150 years. Christian interest in natural science has long been grounded in the Bible, since the Bible presents the cosmos as God's good creation and commends the natural world as a means to understanding something about God, God's character, and the contours of faithful response to God. Indeed, when science emerged as a discrete discipline in seventeenth-century Europe, the new science was seen as nothing other than the simple investigation of God's creation (see pp.24–25).

Although the materialistic focus of new science *could* marginalize the need for God, it need not do so – and, if it did, this was thought to be neither a necessary consequence of scientific investigation nor an appropriate use of science. Thomas Browne's *Religio Medici*, first published in 1642, insisted that the physician was not doomed to unbelief, because the physician's work leads to God; the Bible and the natural world form a dual pathway to God. Similarly, Richard Cumberland argued in his *De Legibus Naturae* (1672) that physics need not lead to unorthodoxy in ethical theory or to atheism; if unbelief were the consequence of scientific investigation, not science but impiety was to blame. Perhaps most famous is Robert Boyle's *A Free Enquiry into the Vulgarly Received Notion of Nature* (1686), which insisted that the new, mechanistic science of his day was actually religion's invincible ally.

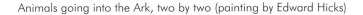

Animals going into the Ark, two by two (painting by Edward Hicks)

Despite all this, for many people today science and the Bible have nothing to contribute to each other. They point to such classic struggles as the experiences of Galileo, Copernicus, and Darwin, never mind more recent tension surrounding portraits of the human person emerging from study of the brain. For such people, the best-case scenario might be that science speaks to one set of concerns while the Bible speaks to another and completely separate set of issues. For example, science might answer questions about "what" or "how", whereas the Bible tells us "so what" or "why". According to this way of thinking, science and Bible are not really in dialogue or conflict, because they address reality in different ways (p. 57). More commonly, though, science and the Bible are assumed either to stand in tension or simply to contradict each other. According to this perspective, one must choose to accept the authority of the Bible or of science.

This warfare model – science against the Bible or the Bible against science – is popular, but neither helpful nor accurate (p. 61). For Christians at least, the interaction between science and the Bible is inescapable. This judgment is grounded in the unavoidable invasion of science in our reading of the Bible, never mind the witness of theology and the Bible itself.

READING THE BIBLE, READING THE WORLD

Most of us studied science as a separate discipline in school. Indeed, we might have studied language, then turned to arithmetic, then to history, and then to geography – all in the same day. We think of these as explorations of different things, and school textbooks tend to keep them separate. There are even specialists within these disciplines – a scientist might work in molecular biology but know little about astronomy, for example, just as someone might work in "Southeast Asian Studies" but lack specialized knowledge of Oceania. This approach to education and study, largely taken for granted in the modern world, was not at all characteristic in the ancient world. Philosophy, religion, and science were generally practised by the same people; and regarded as part of an undivided narrative. For example, the ancient physician Galen (129– c. 197), whose writings dominated medicine for almost 1,400 years, entitled one of his books, *That the Best Physician Is also a Philosopher*. The modern problem of how to relate science and religion is just that, a modern problem. Typologies for describing the interaction of religion and science are therefore not well suited to intellectual activity in the centuries before the rise of the new science in the 1600s, or even to some scientific work in the 1600s and 1700s. It makes no sense to examine the relationship of science and religion – Conflict? Independence? Dialogue? Integration? – when science and religion are inseparable. The one informs the other in such an organic way that it is virtually impossible to identify where one stops and the other starts.

With the early sixteenth century, though, we encounter a basic change in "**hermeneutics**", a term which refers to how we understand the world around us, including the Bible. There was a marked and significant shift towards "literal interpretation", opening up the possibility of new ways of understanding not only the Bible but also the natural order. Two assumptions are especially important if we are to understand the nature of this shift. The first has to do with dethroning the Bible as authority for faith and life, the second with the move toward "literal interpretation".

"LIKE ANY OTHER BOOK"

In the premodern world, people who studied the Bible or heard it expounded generally supposed that the Bible was to be believed and obeyed; its essential truth and its capacity to communicate the divine voice, was unquestioned. When biblical scholarship emerged as a distinct discipline during the past three or four centuries, this assumption or commitment would be undermined – and, for some, overturned.

The Bible was not alone in this regard; other venerable traditions and authorities were dethroned too. Well into the seventeenth century, for example, the works of Aristotle and Galen were read word for word in university teaching and followed scrupulously. The standard procedure for carrying on scientific research was described by the anatomist and physician Andreas Vesalius (1514–64):

The Gutenberg Bible, printed c.1455 by Joseph Gutenberg in Mainz, the first major book to be produced using movable type.

Galen of Pergamon (129–199/217), Roman physician who wrote widely and influentially on medicine.

How much has been attributed to Galen, easily leader of the professors of dissection, by those physicians and anatomists who have followed him, and often against reason! In confirmation there is that blessed and wonderful plexus reticularis [that is, a network of vessels thought to exist at the base of the brain] which that man everywhere inculcates in his books. There is nothing which physicians speak more often. They have never seen it (for it is almost non-existent in the human body), yet they describe it from Galen's teaching. Indeed, I myself cannot wonder enough at my own stupidity and too great trust in the writings of Galen and other anatomists; yes, I who so much laboured in my love for Galen that I never undertook to dissect a human head in public without that of a lamb or ox at hand, so as to supply what I could in no way find in that of man, and to impress it on the spectators, lest I be charged with failure to find that plexus so universally familiar by name. For the soporal [that is, internal carotid] arteries quite fail to produce such a "plexus reticularis" as that which Galen recounts!
Andreas Vesalius, *On the Fabric of the Human Body* (1543)

Thus Vesalius castigates those who depend on books and traditions rather than firsthand observation. Thomas Willis (1621–75), the Father of Neurology, described his research agenda in similar terms:

I determined with my self seriously to enter presently upon a new course, and to rely on this one thing, not to pin my faith on the received Opinions of others, nor on the suspicions and guesses of my own mind, but for the future to believe Nature and ocular demonstrations: Therefore thenceforward I betook my self wholly to the study of Anatomy: and as I did chiefly inquire into the offices and uses of the Brain and its nervous Appendix, I addicted my self to the opening of Heads… and so a firm and stable Basis might be laid, on which not only a more certain Physiologie than I had gained in the Schools, but what I had long thought upon, the Pathologie of the Brain and nervous stock, might be built.
Thomas Willis, *The Anatomy of the Brain* (1664)

These comments mirror the more direct criticism levelled by Vesalius against the long-standing convention of following unquestionably in the footsteps of the ancients. Indeed, the path to knowledge set out by Vesalius and Willis was followed in numerous writings in the seventeenth century, and resides in the motto of England's Royal Society: *Nullius in verba* ("On the word of no one"). It represents the birth of the modern era, with its call to escape the shackles of the past while recognizing the historical rootedness of all knowing; it acknowledges the importance of carrying on inquiry without an a priori commitment to an informing tradition.

The same can be said for the interpretation of the Bible. The modern era can be characterized by an increasing willingness to regard the biblical materials as in some sense the product of human efforts and, therefore, writings with which people might responsibly disagree. Indeed, Johann Salomo Semler (1725–91) counselled an approach to reading the Bible famously captured in the motto, "Like any other book" – a motto that would open the door to questioning its truthfulness. Eventually, the discipline of biblical studies that emerged from those seventeenth and eighteenth century beginnings would identify the aims and methods of academic study of the Bible in ways that allowed scholars to explore the biblical materials without committing themselves to whether they agreed or disagreed with these texts.

In short, the era when modern science began to emerge was marked by a mammoth shift in how we know what we know. There was a wholesale move away from dependence on past authorities and traditions. "Probability", "belief", and "credibility", concepts used by philosopher-theologians engaged in exploration of the world, became categories for natural scientists as well.

Andreas Vesalius (1514–64) of Padua, author of *De Humani Corporis Fabrica* (1543), based on careful dissection of human bodies.

The Reformers introduced a discipline of literal interpretation of both the world and the Bible, eschewing the medieval use of metaphors – such as the lion being used as a metaphor for Jesus.

READING THE BIBLE "LITERALLY"

Second, and closely intertwined with this first observation, was a shift in hermeneutics itself. The sort of biblical interpretation championed by the Protestant Reformers, with their focus on "literal interpretation", opened up the possibility for new ways of viewing the order of nature.

An interesting example is provided by the semiologist Umberto Eco. He observes that, in the medieval encyclopaedia, everything that exists is profoundly an expression of God, God's character, and God's purpose. This included words on the page but also creatures in the world, which then served as a mural of the divine plan at work in history. In this widely shared understanding of the world, everything that is was seen as a metaphor of God. Objects and creatures of the natural world were interpreted analogically, even allegorically, as though their purpose was to point beyond themselves to God and God's overarching intentions for his creation. Consider the lion walking through the forest: is it not potentially a figure both of Christ and of the antichrist? Observing that the lion erases his tracks with his tail, some found in the lion a figure of Christ whose work is to cancel every trace of sin. At the same time, following a medieval interpretation of Psalm 21, the dreadful jaws of the lion could serve as a metaphor of hell and, thus, of the antichrist. If the whole world is a book written by the hand of God, then all of nature serves metaphorically to reveal the Divine Author.

The English naturalist John Ray (1627–1705) wrote that in his work, he had "wholly omitted what we find in other Authors concerning *Homonymous* and *Synonymous* words, or the divers names of *Birds, Hieroglyphics, Emblems, Morals, Fables, Presages* or ought else pertaining to *Divinity, Ethics, Grammar*, or any sort of Humane Learning". In other words, Ray was concerned to distance himself from the convention that living things were symbols with an underlying meaning, choosing to concentrate instead on "only with what properly relates to their Natural History". This represents an approach in line with the re-evaluation of the Bible and its interpretation which led to and flowed from the Reformation.

In the pre-modern church, interpretation of the world proceeded along the lines of interpretation of the Bible, that is, in accordance with the traditional theory of the four levels of interpretation: the literal, the allegorical, the moral, and the analogical. However, when interpreters began to cast off this fourfold method of understanding in favour of the literal sense alone, it followed only naturally that the cosmos, too, would be examined along different lines. In effect, new emphases in hermeneutics, worked out explicitly with reference to the Bible, also pressed for fresh ways to make sense of the world.

The literalist mentality of the Protestant reformers gave a determinate meaning to the text of scripture and at the same time precluded the possibility of assigning meanings to natural objects. Literalism here means that only words refer; the things of nature do not. In this way the study of the natural world was liberated from the specifically religious concern of biblical interpretation, and the sphere of nature was opened up to new ordering principles.

Peter Harrison, *The Bible, Protestantism and the Rise of Natural Science* (1998)

The combination of these two points is important. Jewish and Christian writers in the first few centuries of the Christian era were not blind to what we might call scientific problems of the Bible; they had hermeneutical resources for addressing those problems. We might go so far as to say that, because of their commitment to the authority and relevance of the Bible, they had to have interpretative protocols for dealing with tensions between scientific discovery and the their understanding of the Bible. Jewish historians of the first century identified Abraham as the father of astronomy and mathematics, in part to counter ideas that Israel's Scriptures were lacking in terms of their scientific awareness. Early opponents of the Christian movement tried to use empirical observation to disprove scientific claims of the Bible. In the second century, Celsus concluded that Noah's Ark would have been too small to support the number of animals claimed to have been rescued from the flood. But Christian intellectuals drew on especially two interpretive tools to counter those attacks.

First, Origen (185–254) and his heirs interpreted problematic texts in an allegorical way. For Origen, such texts did not refer so much to literal realities as to inner, spiritual phenomena. Second, church fathers and Jewish interpreters developed theories of "accommodation". According to this perspective, God *accommodated* his description of natural events into language, concepts, and principles that could be understood by ancient people. In short, the question was never whether the Bible was applicable for understanding the world known to us through our five senses but rather how biblical texts might best be understood to shed light on the world God had made.

One more observation which may be difficult for us to grasp: these alternative readings of biblical texts did not contradict "literal" interpretation for those who sought to understand them. Today, we tend to think of "literal" in historical, real-world terms. Many of us have been trained to think that biblical texts are capable of only one meaning. We might be surprised, then, to learn how little earlier interpreters were concerned with only one "true" meaning, but were committed rather to exploring the many ways in which the one God might speak in and through these texts. Our

modern definitions of "literal" would not have been assumed. Indeed, to read the Bible "literally" for some past interpreters would have been not the world of events recounted by these texts but the nature of God and life before God.

> *The literal sense was never restricted to a verbal, philological exercise alone, but functioned for both Jews and Christians as a "ruled reading" in which a balance was struck between a grammatical reading and the structure of communal practice or a "rule of faith"* (regula fidei).
> **Brevard Childs, "Toward Recovering Theological Exegesis" (1997)**

In spite of the way the debate is sometimes understood today, the history of biblical interpretation is not the story of ongoing battle between literal and non-literal interpretations of the Bible.

SCIENCE, THE BIBLE, AND CHRISTIAN THEOLOGY

Why should Christians account for science in their understanding of God's world? This is an important question because of the ease with which some dismiss the findings of science when they seem to contradict the plain teaching of the Bible. When confronted with scientific data that seem to compete with the witness of the Bible, they reply, so much the worse for science. When science and Christian belief stand in tension, then Christian belief must trump science. And others simply deny that true knowledge of God is available through the natural world. In fact, the Bible and theology speak against such dismissing of science.

The Noah's Ark Centre in Hong Kong, based on one particular interpretation of the story of creation – and a failure to use non-biblical information.

"Science" itself is not easily defined, but generally refers today to the disciplined, systematic examination of the universe by means of evidence derived from one or more of the senses – seeing, touching, hearing, smelling, and tasting – and/or through their logical entailments. In this view, "science" has no room for God. By definition, does not a single-eyed focus on nature rule out the supernatural? This way of thinking, it is argued, locates God outside the scientific arena, although it does not completely rule out the possibility that science can tell us something about God, God's character, and God's ways. Accordingly, the combination of God's two books – the Bible and the natural world – was a regular fixture among many proponents and practitioners of the new science that emerged in the 1600s.

In the preface to his 1664 publication, *The Anatomy of the Brain*, Willis likened his dissection table to "the most holy Altar of Your Grace" – "Your Grace" being a reference to Gilbert Sheldon, Archbishop of Canterbury, to whom he dedicated his work. Willis goes on to identify his research as an examination of "the Pandects of Nature, as into another Table of the Divine Word, and the greater Bible: For indeed, in either Volume there is no high point, which requires not the care, or refuses the industry of an Interpreter; there is no Page certainly which shews not the Author, and his Power, Goodness, Trust, and Wisdom."

An anatomy lesson for artists, by the school of Pietro Longhi, early 18th century.

If God made the world, it is only to be expected that something of God's character (and thus his power, goodness, faithfulness, and wisdom) would be on display in creation. Consequently, for contemporary theologian Alister McGrath, there are two modes of knowing God – the natural order and the Bible – with the second clearer and fuller than the first.

For our predecessors, this way of construing the significance of the natural order is rooted in the apostle Paul's "natural theology", which comes into sharpest focus in the first chapter of his letter to the Romans. There, he writes:

> *For what can be known about God is plain to them, because God has shown it to them. Ever since the creation of the world his external power and divine nature, invisible as they are, have been understood and seen through the things he has made.*
> **Romans 1:19–20**

The significance of Paul's statement is underscored by comparing two other texts – the first from the Old Testament, the second from a Jewish writing of the first century BC, called the Wisdom of Solomon or simply the book of Wisdom:

PSALM 19:1–6	WISDOM 13:1–7
The heavens are telling the glory of God; and the firmament proclaims his handiwork. Day to day pours forth speech, and night to night declares knowledge. There is no speech, nor are there words; their voice is not heard; yet their voice goes out through all the earth, and their words to the end of the world. In the heavens he has set a tent for the sun, which comes out like a bridegroom from his wedding canopy, and like a strong man runs its course	For all people who were ignorant of God were foolish by nature; and they were unable from the good things that are seen to know the one who exists, nor did they recognize the artisan while paying heed to his works; but they supposed that either fire or wind or swift air, or the circle of the stars, or turbulent water, or the luminaries of heaven were the gods that rule the world. If through delight in the beauty of these things people assumed them to be gods, let them know

• •

with joy. Its rising is from the end of the heavens, and its circuit to the end of them; and nothing is hid from its heat.

how much better than these is their Lord, for the author of beauty created them. And if people were amazed at their power and working, let them perceive from them how much more powerful is the one who formed them. For from the greatness and beauty of created things comes a corresponding perception of their Creator. Yet these people are little to be blamed, for perhaps they go astray while seeking God and desiring to find him. For while they live among his works, they keep searching, and they trust in what they see, because the things that are seen are beautiful.

Psalm 19 goes on to speak explicitly of the law, decrees, commandments, and ordinances of God, perhaps implying what is transparent in the opening of Wisdom 13 – that creation puts God and God's character on display, although this knowledge of God is available only to God's own people, Israel. Gentiles lack the intellectual categories for making sense of what they see, with the result that they make the beautiful things of the world into gods. Paul makes a similar complaint (see Romans 1:21–23), but only after observing that some knowledge of God is universally available – to Gentiles as well as Jews. What is more, from Paul's words "God has shown it to them", we are to understand that it was actually God's purpose that humanity would find his fingerprints, so to speak, in their observations of the natural world. Even if God's self-disclosure reaches ultimate expression only in God's Son, Jesus Christ – who "is the reflection of God's glory and the exact imprint of God's very being" (Hebrews 1:3), God has nonetheless spoken through all that he has created, so that God's handwriting is visible through study of the created world.

Jesus speaks similarly, of course. Are not the lilies of the field a lesson about God's gracious care for his people? Are not the wild birds? (Matthew 6:25–34). Or consider

The beautiful Sea of Galilee. God has revealed himself in a "book of works" (creation) as well as in his "book of words" (the Bible).

the account in Acts of Paul's missionary address among the people of Lystra, where he characterizes rain and fruitful harvests as testimony to God's goodness (Acts 14:16–17).

In short, for Christians, science must be taken seriously for the simple reason that the theology of creation demands it. God is knowable only because he has chosen to reveal himself. The natural world is one means of access to God's self-disclosure, but it does not give decisive access to God's character and purpose. For this, it is necessary to turn to Jesus: "Whoever has seen me has seen the Father" (John 14:9). The Bible itself tells of the God of Abraham, Isaac, and Jacob; the God who liberated Israel and who raised Jesus from the dead. And yet this same God has borne witness to himself through the world he has created. Study of God, or theology, thus encompasses exploration of any and all testimony to God's character and plan, every means by which God has chosen to reveal himself to humanity. This includes God's two books: the testimony of the Bible and the testimony of science. And if God has borne witness to himself especially in the Bible and in the universe of his own creation, it is important to remain always open to the possibility that the understanding of God may be sharpened, even corrected, through ongoing exploration of these means of communication.

THE ROLE OF SCIENCE IN BIBLICAL INTERPRETATION

That the Bible and science are inseparably related is true for at least three additional reasons.

- We are simply incapable of coming to the Bible without bringing our assumptions about the nature, purpose, and function of the world. Readers of the Bible, ancient and modern, have inevitably read it from within their own scientific worldviews. This is true even though, across times and cultures, our understandings of "science" have changed considerably.

- Second, ancient scientific views can be found in the Bible itself. The biblical writers drew on scientific views present in their world in order to speak to the significance of God and God's engagement with the world.

- Third, contemporary scientific investigations sometimes help us to see the world of the Bible in ways more at home with the biblical writers themselves.

Each of these three considerations points to a single, inescapable conclusion – not *whether* science will be taken into account but rather *which* science? *Whose* science? Can certain scientific perspectives on the world parade as "timeless truths"?

ANCIENT COSMOLOGY

The Old Testament's theory of the physical universe (that is, its "cosmology") shares much in common with the thought world of other peoples of the ancient world. This common understanding of the structure and constituent components of the universe is known to us because of numerous texts from ancient Mesopotamia and Egypt, as well as several texts in the Old Testament.

Although there were differences between the Mesopotamian and Egyptian cosmologies (we have no clearly articulated Canaanite cosmology), the common elements portray a tripartite division of the whole universe. First a domed sky was considered the domicile of the most important deities. Sometimes this "firmament" or the dome was itself divided into as many as three compartments. Above the dome were cosmic waters that needed to be held back from flooding the earth. Second, the earth was considered home to gods and humans, and sometimes also divided into three levels. Finally, the underworld was the residence of more deities, some of them malevolent, and in most cases, the place also of the human dead. This last point is one of the differences for the Egyptians, who nevertheless envisioned a universe of three discs with two spaces between them: the sky, the earth, and the underworld.

In common with this general picture, the ancient Israelites perceived the world as a flat disc-shaped earth with mountains at its ends supporting a multilayered sky, or domed firmament. The sun, moon, and stars crossed this firmament in regular and predictable patterns. The firmament had chambers through which the water above it came down as rain. Below the visible flat earth existed a second level of earth, the netherworld, abode of the dead. There was more water under the earth, and water around the whole making up the cosmic seas, so that the inhabited world was a bubble in cosmic waters.

In the Bible, this cosmology is expressed most clearly in the creation account of Genesis 1, where God fashions the dome on Day Two as "Sky" to separate waters above from that below (1:8) and on Day Three, the dry ground as "Earth" and the collected waters beneath the dome as "Seas" (1:10). Thus in Genesis, the phrase "the heavens and the earth" (1:1) and its reverse order "earth and

The Creation, as depicted in the German Bible of 1534, translated by Martin Luther.

sky" (2:4) is a figure of speech by which a single object is referred to by its parts, denoting all observable cosmic phenomena, the universe, for which there is no separate word in biblical Hebrew. In the flood story of Genesis 6:9–9:29, we learn that the Sky-dome has windows, which together with gushing springs from the sea beneath combine to produce the catastrophe: "… all of the springs of the deep sea erupted, and the windows in the skies opened" (7:11, CEB). In a similar way, the threefold compartments of the universe may be in view in the Bible's ban on idol-making: "You shall not make for yourself an idol, whether in the form of anything that is in heaven above, or that is on the earth beneath, or that is in the water under the earth" (Exodus 20:4; cf. Deuteronomy 5:8). This ancient cosmology is only indirectly indicated elsewhere in the Bible, in a few passages such as the resuscitation of the prophet Samuel by the medium at Endor, where the deceased prophet is perceived as rising up out of the earth from the netherworld beneath (1 Samuel 28:8, 11, 13, 15). Elsewhere these concepts are only implicitly perceived as a general worldview.

These convictions about the universe should not be dismissed as "primitive" or "unenlightened". Rather they were ancient cosmologies that analysed the phenomenological world for answers to life's biggest questions. Those questions found satisfactory answers in the role and purpose of God (or the gods) in creating the universe for human habitation. Contemporary scientific cosmologies have a different perception because modern science intentionally limits itself to the physical and mechanical features of the universe. These differences are not so much contradictory as complementary because of different purposes. Science today addresses the *how* of the physical, while the cosmologies of ancient science also addressed the *why* of the functional.

WE BRING SCIENCE TO THE BIBLE

Biblical interpreters inescapably read the Bible from perspectives shaped by their scientific
views. This is true whether acknowledged or not, making it often difficult to sort out
whether a particular interpretation of a biblical text comes from reading a scientific view
out of the Bible or into it. Indeed, in the history of Christian theology, it has sometimes
been the case that traditional and church-supported views of what the Bible says have
been confused with the teaching of the Bible itself. Having heard a certain interpretation
of a biblical text for so long, we cannot imagine that it might faithfully be read in any
other way. This might remind us of the tension we sometimes find in the Gospels, where
both Jesus and his contemporaries assume the importance of Israel's Scriptures but find
themselves locked in debate concerning how best to read those scriptures.

Today, we easily recognize that the debate of the 1600s over whether the universe
circled the earth was actually a debate between competing scientific descriptions of the
universe. This was a case in which one scientific view had become so intertwined with
the church's understanding of the Bible that calling that scientific view into question
seemed to be nothing less than calling the Bible into question. It seems obvious to us
now that the Bible does not teach that the stars and planets rotate around the earth.
However, on the basis of that scientific view, certain biblical texts were read in just that
way (for example Psalms 19:5, 6; 96:10), and these were exploited in support of the
traditional science. The result was that, for many, the Christian faith itself seemed to be
undermined by scientific discovery.

A more contemporary example concerns the nature of the human person. Among
Christian theologians today we can find two general positions. The traditional view is
that humans have bodies and souls, with the soul identified as the essential person; this
is called body–soul "dualism". The second broad position is also an ancient one, one
that has been championed throughout the history of the church, but it has remained
a minority position. This is some form of "*monism*": the view that human capacities
and distinctiveness can be explained without recourse to a second entity like a soul or
spirit. The scientific evidence points strongly towards a monist perspective because the
empirical evidence increasingly supports a tight, mind–brain link. Most scientists today
– and particularly neuroscientists – hold to some sort of monist position. In contrast,
most contemporary Christians, clinging to the church's tradition, assume a dualistic view
of the human person, despite the scientific evidence.

This assumption is far from universal. For example, Wolfhart Pannenberg (1928–) is
a theologian for whom the relationship between theology and the natural sciences has
long been particularly important. He judges the evidence as having shown that study of

"If your eye is healthy, your whole body is full of light…" – what might this mean? On one level, we see how Jesus' message trades on the well-known use of the language of darkness and light, sight and blindness, as metaphors of salvation, knowledge, and ethical life. Elsewhere, for example, Paul's commission is to "open eyes" and to turn people "from darkness to light" (Acts 26:18). But this observation does not yet address the primary problem with which this text confronts us. Instead, we need to know that, in one important strand of first-century Roman ophthalmology, the eyes were regarded as the channels through which the body's own light would leave the body. This view was called "extramission", which contrasts with "intromission", namely, that the eye receives rays and serves as the first stage in the processing of visual stimuli. Plato (fourth century BC) and Galen (second century AD) were among those who held to a theory of extramission, while Aristotle (fourth century BC) is a representative of those who thought this view highly improbable and who embraced intromission instead.

In extramission, the eye is like a flashlight. A good eye emanates good light whereas a bad light emits bad light (or no light at all). According to this physiology, Jesus' claim, "Your eye is the lamp of your body", identifies the eyes as sources of light in that they direct the body's light outward. The critical question, then, is whether the eyes are sick or healthy, for this tells us whether a person is full of darkness or full of light. Drawing on the metaphorical use of eyes and light for ethical behaviour and using an obsolete ophthalmology, Jesus can identify a sick eye as a signpost to inner darkness and a healthy eye as evidence of inner light.

In short, Jesus' saying makes perfect sense within an ancient, flawed physiology, and this illustrates for us how biblical texts – and not only biblical interpreters – are implicated in scientific understanding.

SCIENCE IN THE SERVICE OF BIBLICAL INTERPRETATION

Finally, there are occasions in which contemporary science gives us valuable background and interpretative patterns for biblical texts, while not denying that contemporary science can also obscure biblical texts. In the previous example, contemporary science of the eye gets in the way of our reading of Jesus' words. This is because we bring our scientific knowledge with us to the text, expecting our knowledge to be reflected by the text. Actually, investigation of health and healing in the Bible gives us a good example of how contemporary science can be both a hindrance and a helper in biblical interpretation.

Throughout the Bible, both Yahweh, the God of Israel, and Jesus are depicted as healers, and salvation itself is portrayed in terms suggesting human recovery and human flourishing. This claim may seem obvious, but the prevalence of these themes encourages

Christ Healing the Blind, by El Greco

special care in understanding how best to read texts related to sickness and health. For example, our usual categories of "healing" may be stretched when we read a text like Exodus 15:26: "I am the Lord who heals you" (see also, for example, 2 Kings 5:7; Isaiah 57:19). This is because Yahweh's self-attribution comes immediately after the Lord rescues Israel from Egypt, rather than in the context of a more typical healing story.

Even in the modern West, "healing" and "sickness" can be difficult to define. For example, if "sickness" refers to an unwanted condition or the impairment of normal bodily functions, who decides what is "unwanted" or "normal"? To a degree not often recognized, "sickness" is in the eye of the beholder, so the identification and **aetiology** of sickness, and the therapeutic interventions it warrants, are typically grounded in cultural understandings of health and can therefore be shaped autobiographically. If "sickness" is any unwanted condition of self or substantial threat of unwanted conditions of self, then notions of health and sickness are tied to how a person measures human well-being.

A pathological approach like this one can demonstrate how study of healing and health in the Bible can be sidetracked by assuming the categories of Western medicine when reading ancient texts from the Near East. Western biomedical concerns are easily projected on to accounts of healing from biblical cultures far removed from our own. As a result, readers of the Bible too easily focus on a diagnosis of a presenting problem and its resolution in terms oriented toward the physical body, an approach that turns a blind eye to other definitions of "healing" and "health" assumed in and supported by the biblical materials.

We need to recognize a classification of healing independent of culture, following Robert A. Hahn's *Sickness and Healing* (1995):

- *Disease accounts* which focus on abnormalities located within the body, at or beneath the skin. The problem lies in the structure and functions of bodily organs or systems and healing requires physical or biomedical intervention.

- *Illness accounts* centred on the body but also on one's networks of relationships and interactions with the wider social environment. The body is not discounted, but placed within a larger web of meaning that includes the embodied lives of persons in community. Healing might require physical intervention, but certainly must address the nexus of relationships.

- *Disorder accounts*, without neglecting either the body or one's networks of relationships and interactions within a larger social environment, also attend to one's relationship to the world at large, experiences as unbalanced, out of order. The recovery of well-being, in this case, would be tantamount to "putting the world back together", or otherwise redressing a cosmic imbalance.

If we think of disease pre-eminently in bodily terms, healing necessarily requires bodily or biomedical intervention. People in the biblical accounts, however, tend to think of sickness in more holistic ways. The source of sickness for them sometimes lies in their social environments, sometimes even in the larger cosmos, rather than in the sick body itself. Accordingly, healing may entail alleviating some combination of the pressure of one's social relationships, bodily intervention, or redress of cosmic imbalances. This means that persons who tend toward a biomedical paradigm for understanding sickness and healing will generally need to expand what they allow as significant in talk about human flourishing to include concerns with relational integrity and the life of the community. This does not suggest that they should jettison concern with the body as unimportant; such an assumption would only substitute one form of reductionism for another.

An example of all this is "leprosy", a "sickness" that appears in both Old and New Testaments. In biblical accounts, "leprosy" includes a range of skin conditions and only rarely, if ever, refers to true leprosy, or Hansen's disease. This is why some modern versions translate the relevant Hebrew and Greek words as "skin disease". According to Leviticus 13–14, such skin diseases are a sign of divine curse on a person and make a person "unclean" from a religious point of view. Someone diagnosed by a priest as a leper is relegated to the margins of human community: "The person who has the leprous disease shall wear torn clothes and let the hair of his head be dishevelled; and he shall cover his upper lip and cry out, 'Unclean, unclean.' He shall remain unclean as long as he has the disease; he is unclean. He shall live alone; his dwelling shall be outside the camp" (Leviticus 13:45–46).

In the Bible, then, "leprosy" is not necessarily life-threatening, nor is it itself contagious. Biblical accounts of leprosy are not concerned with the communication of a biological pathogen; lepers are to be isolated but not on account of biomedical necessity. It is the *disorder* of leprosy that is communicable through physical contact. The contagion is not a disease-causing microorganism, but the socio-religious status of ritual impurity.

Biblical accounts of leprosy illustrate how religious, social, and physical considerations unite in a single disorder. According to the Gospels, Jesus' intervention is classified as a "cleansing" rather than a healing. This is because religious impurity is the primary presenting problem, and intervention is followed with instructions like that found in Luke 5:12–14: "Go... and show yourself to the priest...". Here, the priest has the role of what we might call a health care consultant; the priest does not heal the patient but rather certifies that the patient has been cured and mediates the former leper's return to normal relations and interactions with others.

In these examples, the interpretation of the Bible and the study of science are not separable. This means that all rigorous interpreters of the Bible should include increased awareness of the science informing the writers of biblical texts, heightened attentiveness to the scientific assumptions passed down to us in interpretations of biblical texts, and a keen recognition of the scientific perspectives we ourselves bring to our reading of the Bible. At every point, the influence of scientific understanding is unavoidable. To repeat, the question is not *whether* science will be taken into account. The question, rather, is: *which* science? *Whose* science?

THE "SPIRITUAL BODY" (1 CORINTHIANS 15:35–57)

One important way in which science and the Bible can work together is that science can help us understand and apply the Bible. This works in two ways. First, knowing the history of science and the worldviews of the ancients can illuminate the meaning of biblical passages, written as they were from within an ancient worldview. Second, contemporary scientific understanding is an important part of our worldview today. Science thus provides part of the horizon or understanding of the world, self, and community within which the church must grasp, apply, and live out the meaning of the Bible for today. The apostle Paul's fascinating argument about resurrection and the spiritual body is a good example of both ways in which science helps us understand the Bible. Paying attention to ancient science, that is, to the astronomy and natural philosophy of Paul's day, brings clarity to his viewpoint on what he refers to as the *soma pneumatikos*, often translated as "spiritual body".

In the physics of Paul's age, every earthly thing was composed of a mixture of the four basic elements: earth, air, fire, and water. At the centre of the cosmos, under the heavens or sky, the earth was a place of change, generation, death, and corruption. But the astronomy of the time taught that the universe itself was eternal. Sun, stars, and moon all moved forever in majestic spheres around the earth. They were made up of a fifth element or "quintessence" called "ether". Above the sphere of the moon, everything was made of ether. Aristotle taught that ether was divine, eternal, immutable, and incorruptible. Jews and Christians added another sphere to the heavens, beyond the sun, moon, and stars. For them, God and the angels dwelt in the highest heaven, a sphere beyond even the farthest stars.

This ancient world picture should be kept in mind when we interpret what Paul has to say about heaven and heavenly bodies in 1 Corinthians 15. Paul begins with a question: "How are the dead raised, and what kind of body do they come with?" This question sets up the entire passage on the *physis* (nature) of the body in resurrection.

Since Paul uses the word "body" for plants, seed, and humans, it must mean something like "substantial object". Paul's point in 15:36–38 is that there are different kinds of bodies that God has created, not just one kind. Plants and animals are created by God to have the kinds of bodies appropriate for their environment. Each kind of body or flesh is well suited for life in its proper place (vv. 40–41).

"And thus it is with the resurrection of the dead", the apostle now claims (v. 42). Paul sets up a series of antitheses that describe the different kinds of bodies we have in this life and in the next life after resurrection. Our mortal bodies are corruptible, dishonourable (especially as dead corpses), weak, and "soulish" or physical. Our resurrection bodies will be glorious, powerful, "spiritual", and incorruptible (the same word Aristotle used for ether). They will, in fact, be heavenly bodies, as verses 47–50 indicates. In the resurrection of the dead there is both continuity and discontinuity. The very same person has a new and transformed body, fit for heavenly and immortal existence.

Paul now contrasts the bodies of the first and second Adam, as archetypical human beings. "The first man," he tells us, "was of the earth – dust" (v. 47). Our earthly bodies must perish, as Adam's did. The second Adam (Christ) is "a man of heaven". This phrase does not indicate that Jesus was from heaven. He is of heaven, in the sense that he is made of the very stuff of the heavens, just as Adam was made of the stuff of the earth (dust). Paul presses home his point in verse 50: flesh and blood (the substance of our moral bodies) cannot inherit the kingdom of God. Only heavenly bodies are fit to live in the heavens!

Grasping the meaning of this text today, and living out this promise, we will of course alter the larger world picture of Paul's day, exchanging it for a modern, scientific one. Faithful biblical living and thinking requires this of us. Yet while the assumptions behind this text will need to change, the main point is just as true as ever. For Christians, our resurrected bodies will be like the immortal body of the Risen Christ. We have no idea what substance is best fitted for that future, eternal life. But Christians know the promise of God, and can rest assured that our resurrected bodies will be fit for eternal life with him.

CONCLUSION

Perhaps the most basic problem between scientific understanding and biblical reasoning is simply that the natural sciences concern themselves with observable phenomena, with data accessible by means of the natural senses, and so with natural causes, whereas the Bible has as its most characteristic, pervasive claim that the cosmos rests in the hands of the God who by definition is other than the natural world.

This is not a new problem. The father of Methodism, John Wesley, lived in an age of unprecedented scientific discovery, when phenomena that had belonged to the realm of the mysterious were increasingly being explained in terms of the natural sciences. When commenting on Jesus' commission to his followers that they should "cast out devils" (Matthew 10:8), Wesley noted that someone had said that diseases ascribed to the devil in the Gospels "have the very same symptoms with the natural diseases of lunacy, epilepsy, or convulsions", leading to the conclusion "that the devil had no hand in them". Wesley writes:

> *But it were well to stop and consider a little. Suppose God should allow an evil spirit to usurp the same power over a man's body as the man himself has naturally, and suppose him actually to exercise that power; could we conclude the devil had no hand therein, because his body was bent in the very same manner wherein the man himself bent it naturally?*
>
> *And suppose God gives an evil spirit a greater power to affect immediately the origin of the nerves in the brain, by irritating them to produce violent motions, or so relaxing them that they can produce little or no motion, still the symptoms will be those of over-tense nerves, as in madness, epilepsies, convulsions, or of relaxed nerves, as in paralytic cases. But could we conclude thence, that the devil had no hand in them?*
>
> *Explanatory Notes upon the New Testament* (1755)

Reading Wesley's comments in the mid eighteenth century, we might forget that serious study of the central nervous system and its relationship to human behaviour is barely a century old. Nevertheless, Wesley had made an avocation of studying medicine and anatomy, so was in a remarkable position to account for the importance of science for biblical interpretation and for Christian mission. In this tradition, Methodists have always emphasized health care, especially for the poor, a commitment that goes right back to the clinics Wesley set up in the eighteenth century. In terms of biblical interpretation, here his solution is openness to the truth of both faith and science.

John Wesley (1703–91) preaching

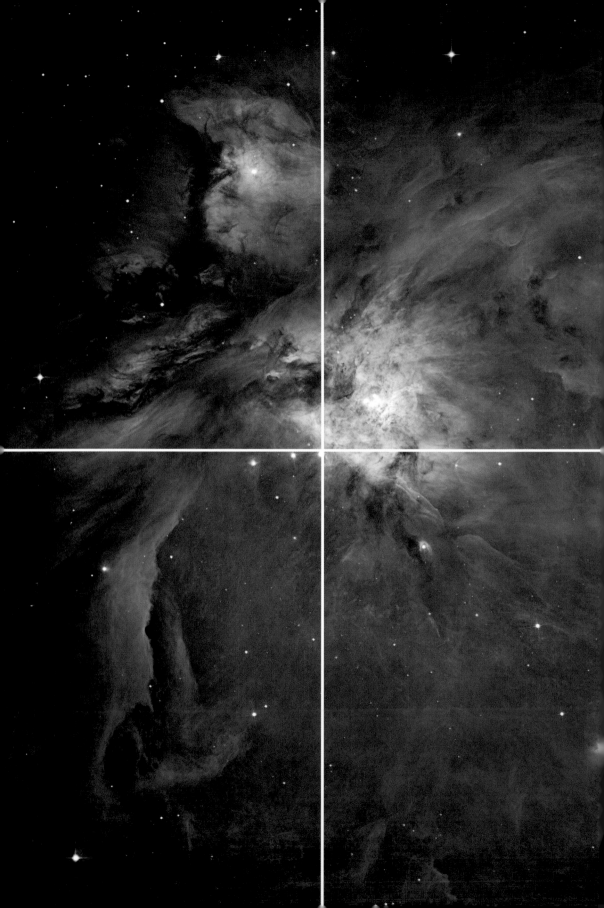

Physical and Earth Sciences

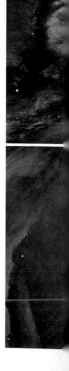

FROM NEWTON TO EINSTEIN: RELATIVITY

THE CLOCKWORK UNIVERSE

With Christiaan Huygens's building of the first successful pendulum clock in the seventeenth century, the world got reliable time but also started to be describable as a reliable and predictable place. The clock became the image of an understandable and mechanistic universe. Just as you could see the workings of a clock and in this beautiful and simple mechanism describe the passage of time in the world, so the physical sciences for 200 years following the invention of an accurate clock were thought to describe a universe that was beautiful, ordered, and simple to understand.

It was an image that was matured in the scientific work of a premature child born on Christmas Day 1642, the year of Galileo's death. In 1665, the plague drove that child, Isaac Newton, by then a Cambridge student, back to his family home for nearly two years. These months were tremendously productive for the young Newton, leading to his detailing of the binomial theorem, differential and integral calculus, and the composite nature of white light. Rising above even these magnificent

Huygens' clock, 1656

discoveries was his universal law of gravitation, which stated that the gravitational force between two bodies depended on the mass of the bodies and the distance between them. This law when applied to the motion of the planets gave a simple and powerful way of describing their movement. For Newton this was a reflection of the order given to the creation by its Creator.

But questions remained. For example, how did the gravitational force act? Was it due to active principles associated with but not inherent in matter, or was it a direct expression of God's continual activity? Where did the planetary orbits originally come from? Did they need God to start this whole system off, and then keep correcting the orbits back to their original paths? More importantly, Newton wondered about the stability of the fixed stars in the sky. If this was a universal law of gravitation, why did the stars not fall into each other? Does God hold them in place against the attractive force of gravity? In this case, the Divine Watchmaker would have created a wonderful mechanism, but one which he would have to continually correct or wind up.

To Newton's contemporary, the philosopher Gottfried Leibniz (1646–1716), this spoke of a second-rate clockmaker rather than the God of perfection. If God was such a perfect Creator, then the universe should not need his continual intervention. This argument was reinforced scientifically in Laplace's *Système du Monde* (1796), which showed that on the basis of better observations Newton's system did not need the "hypothesis of God".

Laplace's reply to the Emperor Napoleon when asked about the place of God in his science, that he had no need of that hypothesis, is often quoted. It was not a denial of God, but a recognition that there was no need for a sort of treadmill operator in the universe envisaged by him.

Just as the physical sciences were revealing a perfect clockmaker who created the universe with reliability and intelligibility, they were at the same time causing problems about the Creator God. Where was God in all of this? If the perfect clockmaker was not needed to wind up the mechanism, how could divine involvement in the universe be seen? How could the universe be self-sufficient but under his control? The legacy of this view became one of the strongest arguments against miracles. There was no need for God to poke his fingers into the mechanism of this clock through events which could not be described by the laws of science. And if God did not work in such a way, what do we make of the miracle stories of the New Testament? The miracles became seen as myths through the conclusions of Strauss, Bultmann, and a generation of nineteenth- and twentieth-century biblical scholars, stories created by the early church to express belief about Jesus but not real historical events.

Isaac Newton (1642–1727), physicist, mathematician, alchemist, and theologian.

Thus in the hundred years or so between Huygens and Laplace, the issues that would characterize the relationship of the physical sciences to faith were crystallized. The extraordinary order and beauty of the world would lead to a natural theology in which many would see the design and purpose of God. At the same time, God would be seemingly pushed out from direct involvement and specific action in the world. These issues would be severely questioned by relativity and quantum theory, but it is fair to say that the Newtonian mechanistic worldview remains powerful both in the popular and indeed the theological mind.

A RELATIVE REVOLUTION

At the end of the nineteenth century there remained a major problem for physicists. Maxwell had united electricity and magnetism in an elegant theory showing that light could be understood as a wave motion of electric and magnetic fields. However, light travels through a vacuum, so there had to be some medium to propagate these waves:

the ether. If it was there, how could it be detected? In a classic experiment in 1887, Albert Michelson and Edward Morley attempted to show that the speed of light would be different in two directions due to the Earth's motion through this postulated ether, but they found that the speed of light did not vary at all.

Then entered Albert Einstein. In an imaginative insight, he saw that talk about an ether was unnecessary. The speed of light was the same however and wherever you measured it. The concept of absolute time was abandoned; one's measurement of time depended on one's own motion. Clocks travelling at speeds close to the speed of light would appear to run slower than those at rest. Other surprising consequences were that as speed increases, so mass increases and length contracts. These effects only become obvious at speeds close to the speed of light, so we do not notice them at an everyday level. However there is clear experimental evidence that Einstein's theory of special relativity is a good description of reality. In such a picture, time is not totally divorced from space; the two are to be talked about together in a framework called "space–time".

Albert Einstein (1879–1955): "Science without religion is lame; religion without science is blind."

Einstein then went on to take gravity into account in his General Theory of Relativity. This suggested that space–time was not fixed and permanent, but that the mass and distribution of matter in the universe determines the geometry of space and the rate of flow of time. His prediction of the curving of space–time was confirmed experimentally.

This is a very different picture of the world to the one that we see in the world of everyday experience. In fact, relativity is one of the ways that, in the words of John Polkinghorne, "the tyranny of common sense" has been exploded. This is very important for Christian faith. T. F. Torrance is only one of a number of theologians who have pointed out that because we cannot perceive the structure of space–time by our senses, it encourages a humility towards surprising aspects of our experience of the universe as a whole. Moreover, relativity supersedes the Newtonian model of the absolute nature of space and time, which theologically had led to the mechanistic view of the universe. We will return to this later.

In the Einsteinian picture of the world, time is not isolated but is only seen in relationship to space, how you measure it, and the mass of the bodies around it. It is not difficult to move from there to the suggestion that time has to be seen in relationship to God. Much thinking about God has set up time as an isolated ontological concept and then asks how God can "intervene" or be "timeless". Perhaps the relationship between God and time is much more organic, that is, the very existence of time depends on the sustaining creativity of God.

A majority of modern philosophers and theologians have found the explanations concerning God's relationship with the world required by **atemporalists** (see p. 104–105) unsatisfactory. The concept of divine atemporality, coupled with a particular notion of immutability make the atemporalist account of divine action highly problematic. An atemporal God must do whatever he does all at once and for all eternity. To allow an act to begin or end would violate God's immutable nature by introducing change. Divine atemporality would also introduce problems in conceiving the Triune God as Being-in-Communion because, as some theologians have argued, interpersonal relationships inherently involve temporality. As a consequence, most scholars conclude that the concept of divine temporality is not only more philosophically coherent but also more faithful to the accounts of divine action in the Bible.

Does this mean that all time is relative? In Einstein's theories of relativity, space and time are linked, but the equations themselves do not distinguish between past and future. Does this mean that our psychological experience of a flow of time, allowing us to distinguish between past and future, is simply an illusion? It is here that many scientists have recognized that there are good arguments for an arrow of time. The second law of

GOD AND TIME

• • • • • • •

In Psalm 90:3, the psalmist speaks of the eternity of God: "Before the mountains were born or you brought forth the earth and the world, from everlasting to everlasting you are God." Divine eternity is not only an essential doctrine of the Christian faith, it is a doctrine that provides comfort and assurance to the believer. However, it is also fraught with difficulties. How should we understand the relationship between God and time? If God created time, he must in some sense transcend time. But how could a God outside of time possibly interact with his temporal creation? Our understanding of the relationship between God and time must shape our concepts of omniscience, immutability, divine simplicity, creation, providence, and the incarnation.

From the fourth to the fourteenth centuries, theologians generally held the view that God is timeless. This meant that temporal concepts could not be applied to the being of God. In Patristic theology, this conception of divine eternity was influenced by Neoplatonic philosophy, which makes a distinction between Being and Becoming. While the realm of Becoming is mutable and temporal, the realm of Being is immutable and eternal. In medieval theology, the concept of divine atemporality can be traced to Boethius (480–525), who in *The Consolation of Philosophy* crafted its classic definition: "Whatever includes and possesses the whole fullness of interminable life at once and is such that nothing future is absent from it and nothing past has flowed away, this is rightly judged to be eternal." According to this view of eternity, God transcends time altogether.

The medieval theologians that advocated divine atemporality effectively espoused a static view of time – that there is no ontological difference between past, present, and future because all moments in time coexist. This understanding is becoming popular among modern metaphysicians for at least two reasons. The first is the influential thesis of the Cambridge idealist John Ellis McTaggart that time does not exist ("McTaggart's Paradox"). The second is the prominence of a particular philosophical interpretation of the Special Theory of Relativity (STR). While philosophers are generally not persuaded by McTaggart's conclusion that time does not exist, they are in agreement that time cannot be defined by properties of pastness, presentness, and futurity (A Theory). They favour the static view of time defined by relations of earlier than, simultaneous with, and later than (B Theory).

Opponents of the static view argue that the passage of time is a real and inexorable feature of the world that can never be reduced to mental perception. These philosophers advance a dynamic theory of time (A Theory) which takes tense very seriously. They maintain that there is a fundamental distinction in saying that x is P and x was P. This means that the present and the past have different ontological statuses from the future. While the present is real, and the past has been real, the future is not yet real. The most serious challenge to this theory of time comes from a particular interpretation of STR that maintains that the passage of time cannot be an objective feature of the world because there is no such thing as absolute simultaneity. Philosophers of the dynamic theory of time make one of two responses to this challenge. They can either (1) deny the theory of relativity, or, more promisingly (2) argue that the relativity theory does not entail a rejection of absolute simultaneity.

The dynamic theory of time requires a different view of divine eternity to the classical understanding. In the late Middle Ages, theologians such as John Duns Scotus (c. 1266–1308) and William Ockham (1285–1347) paved the way for conceiving God's being as temporal. Thus although God is unchanging, he endures through time. Scotus's understanding of contingency serves as the foundation for the concept of dynamic time, while Ockham's reflections on the problem concerning divine foreknowledge and human freedom led to the idea that God is temporal.

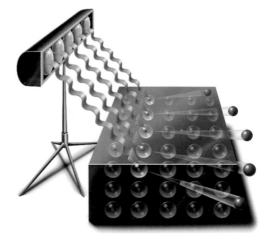

thermodynamics states that the disorder in a closed system, characterized by a property known as **entropy**, increases with time. Moreover, the universe expands in size and increases in complexity with time. This allows us to make a distinction between the universe now in terms of its structure and the universe of the past. But how does this arrow of time emerge from Einstein's description? Some argue that it may emerge from the so-called measurement problem of quantum theory, or perhaps that it emerges from the cosmic expansion, or from the self-organization of complex systems where order emerges from disorder.

There is little ground to doubt the reality of time. Indeed within the Christian tradition there is the strong sense of the linear flow of time from creation to new creation: the universe was viewed to have a definite beginning in the sovereign acts of God; God revealed himself to the people of Israel at specific times in their history; and such events as the death of Jesus were unique and could not be repeated. Augustine argued against the idea of cycles of time on the basis that Jesus could die only once.

Yet relativity shows us that the nature of time may be subtler and more complex than we often assume. The God of the Bible is one who is not limited by time but acts within time, supremely in becoming a human being in Jesus. Theologians continue to disagree on how to understand this. Some place emphasis on God's transcendence over time, while others give more weight to the biblical pictures of God responding in time to petitionary prayer and human responsibility. Some suggest that God has both eternal and temporal poles to his nature. Others use the Trinity as a way of maintaining both his eternal and temporal aspects. Yet others speculate that God is timeless without creation and temporal subsequent to it. Perhaps the solution however is more fundamental. Rather than separating time and eternity, we may need to see time as a fundamental part of eternity.

The God of the Bible is also the God of resurrection and new creation. One of the fascinating things about the risen Jesus is that he is no longer limited by space and time, appearing in rooms with locked doors, but at the same time being fully present in a form of physicality which allows him to eat fish. Pannenberg has continually stressed that the resurrection is the "unique break-in of the reality of the end-time". Not only do we need to think about how God relates to time in this creation, but how time is going to be transformed in God's new creation of a new heaven and new earth.

The photoelectric effect. Blue or ultraviolet light leads to the emission of electrons from a metal surface, but as the frequency is decreased to red light no electrons are emitted. Einstein explained this by describing light as composed of discrete quanta (photons) rather than waves. The energy of a photon was equal to the frequency multiplied by a constant. Only blue light has sufficient energy to eject electrons.

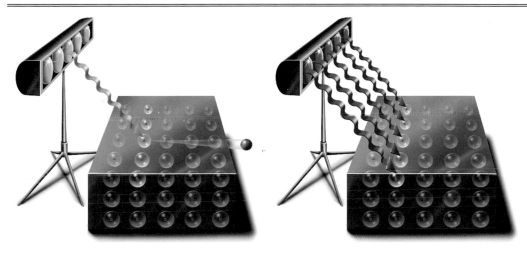

QUANTUM THEORY: SUBVERTING COMMON SENSE

A WORLD OF CLOUDS AS WELL AS CLOCKS

The clockwork world of Newton was a world that was reliable and could be pictured; it was a world of cause and effect. But it was not an easy world into which God could intervene, or would even want to interact. The divine clockmaker had set up a perfect system and apart from setting it off had nothing more to do. This became a strong argument against miracles. Why would God want to mess up the intricate world of cause and effect?

However, physics was transformed in this area in the early part of the twentieth century. Theologians have largely ignored this fact. Quantum theory is one of the most powerful theories of modern physics, and is the basis of a host of technological developments from lasers to nuclear power. Yet it explodes the Newtonian paradigm. The quantum world is cloudy and fitful. Instead of things being determined, they are uncertain, uncaused, and difficult to envisage.

At the beginning of the twentieth century, physicists were puzzled by light. In Maxwell's theory of electromagnetic radiation, there was clear evidence and a clear explanation of how light propagated as a wave. But in 1900 Max Planck showed that electromagnetic radiation from heated bodies could only be understood if the energy was in discrete packets or quanta. This was confirmed in 1905 by Albert Einstein's work on the emission of electrons when a metal surface was bathed in ultraviolet radiation. But how could light be both wave and quanta?

The problem was not confined to light. Evidence began to emerge that particles such as electrons also had wave properties. Imagine an experiment where a beam of electrons is directed at a screen which records the position of their arrival, but with a barrier in front of the screen with two slits. In this set-up, a pattern of fringes will emerge on the screen, with regions of high intensity separated by regions of low intensity in a regular pattern. It is called a diffraction pattern and is characteristic of wave motion.

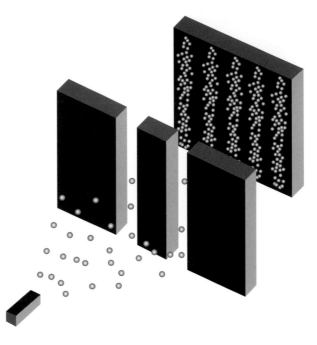

If one of the slits is covered, the electrons form a different pattern on the screen grouped around a position corresponding to the centre of the slit. What happens if we only send one electron at a time through the barrier? With one slit closed the electron hits the screen within the one slit pattern. But now open the closed slit. Amazingly the electron hits the screen within the fringe pattern rather than the one slit pattern. The electron must pass through one slit, but how does it know that there is a second slit in order to fall on the two slit pattern? The only conclusion is that the electron passes through both slits. How can that be? The quantum theory explanation is not to talk of where the electron actually is but to talk in terms of probability. You cannot say that the electron passed through one slit as opposed to the other, you can only calculate its probability. Such a situation is impossible to picture in everyday terms, and to talk of causes becomes irrelevant.

This unpicturable nature of the quantum world is expressed in Werner Heisenberg's Uncertainty Principle, which says that you cannot know precisely both the position and the momentum (that is, its velocity multiplied by its mass) of a particle. You can know one or the other precisely but not both.

Quantum theory's development has provided a very successful tool to use in understanding the nature of the micro world at the level of atoms. But how does this relate to the everyday macro world where we do see cause and effect, and where we can know position and momentum simultaneously? This is the measurement problem of quantum theory. In other words, how does the uncertain quantum world give certain answers when interrogated by our macro world? There are at least three options to answering this question.

- The "Copenhagen Interpretation" of Neils Bohr is that the intervention of macro world measuring instruments "collapses" the probability of the quantum world.

Electrons hitting a target behave differently if they pass through a single slit in a barrier from when they pass through one of two parallel slits (see text above).

Niels Bohr (1885–1962), Danish physicist who received a Nobel Prize for his contribution to the understanding of atomic structure and quantum mechanics.

• Measuring instruments themselves are composed of atoms which have quantum behaviour. What makes them different to atoms or electrons in themselves? Perhaps it is the intervention of a conscious observer that leads to a measurement. This measurement becomes definite only when the mind becomes involved. This of course has the same problem as before, since the brain is composed of atoms, but it might be argued that we still do not fully understand the relationship between mind and brain.

• The third and most bizarre option, Hugh Everett III's "Many Worlds Interpretation", is that in every act of measurement, each possibility available is realized and at that point the universe splits into separate universes corresponding to the realized possibilities. This has been popular with cosmologists, particularly those who want to apply quantum theory to the beginning of the universe, where there is no observer or measuring device. However, it means that there are countless parallel universes, indeed trillions coming into existence every second.

Another question concerning quantum theory is what does quantum theory actually tells us about the nature of reality? Here again there are differing responses. Some say that the theory is simply a computational procedure telling us nothing of the actual nature of atoms. Others such as David Bohm argued that there is some deeper explanation to the apparent randomness of quantum theory, that there is an "implicate" (or enfolded) order in the universe so that "everything is enfolded into everything". However, the majority of scientists want to hold a strong link between epistemology (what we know about the world) and ontology (what the world actually is) and therefore see quantum theory telling us that the very nature of the universe at the atomic level is cloudy and fitful.

ROOM FOR GOD TO ACT?

To view the world as an inflexible clockwork mechanism as the Newtonian worldview sees it does not describe the world as it is. But does the uncertainty of quantum theory give God space to act in the world, in a way that would be hidden and not ruled out by the mechanistic description of the universe? There have been many who claim that it does. The neurophysiologist John Eccles (1903–97) argued that quantum theory opened up an understanding of free will, while the physicist William Pollard saw God working at the atomic level. The difficulty with these suggestions is the problem of understanding how the quantum level relates to the everyday world. This remains unclear; even if God works by pushing electrons here and there, he would need to push an awful lot in order to make a meaningful difference to the world we experience.

However, quantum theory is important in understanding the providence of God. It reminds us to be very hesitant to say that something cannot possibly happen. As Bohr remarked, anyone who is not shocked by quantum theory has not understood it. This uncertainty of position and momentum, and of energy and time, dissolves our classical picture and indeed many of the apparently solid foundations of "common sense". Further, reality is not the same as simple everyday objectivity. Particles such as electrons are real but not in the sense of everyday objects. It is here that we begin to see that while our common sense may not understand the quantum world, the language of mathematics gives us understanding. As theologians such as Polkinghorne and Lonergan have suggested, intelligibility may be a clue to reality.

It is worth noting that some, such as the Californian physicist, Fritjof Capra in *The Tao of Physics*, have argued that the uncertainty and connectedness of quantum theory affirms a view of the world closer to Eastern religions rather than Christianity. This has been popular in some circles (particularly among "New Agers"), but has little support among physicists and theologians. While the pictures of the quantum world do resonate with some Eastern thinking, quantum theory itself is a mathematical and universal law, which relates strongly to the Judeo-Christian view of a faithful Creator who is the source of the order of the universe.

CHAOS: UNCERTAINTY AT THE EVERYDAY LEVEL

John Polkinghorne has argued that if there is room in the physical world for our own exercise of free will, then surely God must enjoy similar room. He then goes on to locate this space, not within the quantum world, but within chaotic physical systems. These systems have a great advantage for this purpose over quantum systems in that their effects are felt at the everyday level. Therefore, Polkinghorne argues that it is here that God has freedom, and that God's activity is unable to be directly seen.

Chaos has helped us to see that Newton's laws themselves are not able to predict the future in the way we thought. The full implications of chaos theory have only been brought out in the last few decades, mainly due to the advent of computers able to do high speed calculations. When we look for problems to solve we begin with the easy ones and work up towards the difficult ones. When Newton applied his new theory of gravitation he chose a reasonably simple system consisting of two bodies, such as the Earth's motion around the Sun. It is simple because you can get an exact answer.

Unfortunately most of the rest of the world is not that simple. Most systems in the world are extremely sensitive to the circumstances around them, so much so that the slightest disturbance will make them act in a radically different way. This means that after a short time a system becomes essentially unpredictable. This is the reason why weather forecasts can be relatively good in the short term, but get much worse the further ahead you want to predict. The atmosphere is partly chaotic. The laws of physics can be known, but this extreme sensitivity to initial conditions means unpredictable results. This has become known as "the butterfly effect" after a lecture entitled, "Predictability: Does the Flap of a Butterfly's Wings in Brazil Set off a Tornado in Texas?" given by the scientist Edward Lorenz in 1972.

John Polkinghorne (1930–), mathematical physicist and Christian apologist

When the dynamics of a system is chaotic, its behaviour can only be predicted if the initial conditions are known to infinite precision. This means that for finite beings there is an uncertainty to some systems within the everyday world even if the laws of physics are known.

Therefore, is it right to pray for rain? Yes it is, according to Polkinghorne. This is because the weather system is a chaotic system showing this openness to the future. Is it right to pray for summer to come before spring? The answer is no, for the seasons are determined by the simple non-chaotic system of the Earth's rotation about the Sun. This may seem attractive in some ways for the defence of miracles. However, if we go down this road the risk is that you see God being able to work only in chaotic systems and not in other ways. Furthermore, the biblical writers see miracles as signs of God's activity. If God's work is "concealed" in chaotic systems, are miracles really a sign?

Such a view still has the danger of falling into the trap of seeing scientific law

as prescriptive rather than descriptive. It is saying that in chaos the laws are less prescriptive. As with quantum theory, chaos does not give an easy way to understand miracles. But in a similar way, it is a clear reminder that the problem of God violating the Newtonian worldview is not such a severe problem as it was the nineteenth century. These developments have undermined one of the strongest arguments against miracles. If the final picture of the relationship of God to particular actions in the physical world is still somewhat unclear, at least these actions are not ruled out by a now outdated worldview which has more to do with philosophy than science.

In the biblical sense, in miracles God is not overriding the order in the world. The scientific laws are regularities of the way God sustains the universe. The unusual phenomena which amaze us may be part of a deeper unity, or they may be, from the human standpoint, deviations from what is regular, while for God they are changes to the regular ordering of natural events.

GOD'S ACTION IN THE UNIVERSE

Christian theology has at its centre a God who not only relates to human beings but also a God who acts. God's action in the world is seen not only in creation, but also in the Exodus and in the cross. But, how does God act in the world? This is not an easy question to answer. Alongside the ways in which science describes how God relates to the universe, there is also the problem of evil: why does God not act more often in preventing suffering? There is also much discussion and indeed controversy among theologians as to interpreting the biblical witness over how much God knows and controls the future.

Within the dialogue of science and theology a number of positions have been held:

1. The "working in the mind" God

Rudolf Bultmann suggested that God does not act in any particular physical way, but achieves his purposes by working through the person of faith as he or she encounters God's word. God changes things by changing our minds on certain issues. But the biblical story is much more than that. Of course, the Bible does speak of God changing minds and working his purposes out through human beings, but the resurrection is not based simply on the belief of the early church that Jesus was alive. That belief was based on an empty tomb and resurrection appearances. A further difficulty of this view is that even a model of God changing a person's mind implies some particular interaction of God with the physical world.

2. The "sit back and watch" God

Maurice Wiles has argued that God's action is limited to one great single act which caused and now keeps the universe in being. Rather like a producer who leases a theatre on Broadway and then lets the actors improvise a drama without interfering in any way, God creates the universe, sustains it, but never intervenes. The attraction of this position is that God is not directly responsible for evil in the world. It is true that if God is at work in the world, part of the expression of this will be found in the reliability and beauty of the laws of nature, and this can be seen as a reflection of the faithful, sustained acting of God. However, the God who does nothing particular in the universe makes it difficult to see how God can be spoken of in terms of personal relationship and makes it impossible to understand the resurrection in terms of historical event.

3. A "persuasive" God

Process theology has its origin in the philosophy of Alfred North Whitehead. It developed in the twentieth century and has been embraced by a number of leading thinkers (such as Ian Barbour) in the science–theology dialogue. It suggests that each event in the universe has a psychic pole and a material pole, and God works as an agent at the subjective level, exercising power by persuasion or lure rather than coercion. It has many critics: is there any evidence that the physical world has such a nature? How are the psychic and material poles connected? It is difficult to see how God can do anything of importance at such a level. Is God reduced to a passive deity like Wiles's creator?

4. An "open" God

Thinkers such as William Vanstone and Jürgen Moltmann have been influential in suggesting that God sets limits on himself and gives to human beings, and indeed the universe, a degree of freedom to explore its own potentiality. This is termed **kenosis**. Within evangelical theology this has provoked one of the major controversies of recent years. Clark Pinnock has championed "openness theology" where God creates a world where the future is not yet completely settled and takes seriously our response. There are significant similarities here with process theology, but with a greater stress on God's transcendence and a claim to be motivated more by the Bible than by philosophy. Pinnock argues this primarily from the biblical images of God as a free personal agent who acts in love, cooperates with people, and responds to prayer.

A mechanism for such openness has been explored by John Polkinghorne in the context of chaos theory. He argues that chaos means that the universe is inherently open to the future, unpredictable, and undetermined. This gives a "space" for human freedom and also provides a "free-will process defence" for natural evil, in that the openness that the universe has in exploring its potential can sometimes be for good and sometimes for evil. Polkinghorne suggests that God is at work in the flexibility of these open systems as well as being the ground of law. God's particular activity is real, but it is hidden.

In response, some have asked whether chaos implies just a limitation on our knowledge rather than a genuine ontological openness in the universe itself. We might not know the future, but is an infinite God bound in this way? Moreover, should God be confined to such "gaps" of scientific prediction? Is God's activity so self-limited to chaotic systems and in a way that is hidden?

5. A "bodily" God

"**Panentheism**" has been a popular image of God's action in the world, especially championed by the biologist Arthur Peacocke. It uses an analogy between God's action and our action but attempts to assimilate God's action in the world to our action in our bodies. So Peacocke views the universe as a child in the "womb" of God. This leads to difficulties. How do we "act" in our own bodies? Further, if the universe is in some way God's body, then does God become vulnerable as the universe changes with time? Panentheism seems to threaten God's otherness and freedom, while also compromising the world's freedom to be itself.

6. A "double agency" God

Rather than describing in scientific terms the causal joint of God's action, Austin Farrer and more recently John Houghton have argued that we cannot conceive of God's way of acting in terms of our own, and therefore the causal joint between God's action and ours will always be hidden. Each event in the universe will therefore have a double description, so-called "double agency". The event can be spoken of in terms of the providential action of God while at the same time having a full natural description in the laws of nature or the action of human agents. Objections to this view centre round whether freedom is at all real in this picture, and whether it is simply a retreat into mystery in the face of difficult questions.

COSMOLOGY AND THE ORIGIN OF THE UNIVERSE

UNDERSTANDING THE BIG BANG

Progress over the centuries in cosmology and cosmogony – the exploration of the structure and origin of the universe – has involved a number of important elements. Belief in order in the universe as described by mathematics began in the Greek culture, was strengthened by the Christian worldview, and led to laws such as Einstein's theories of relativity. These laws have enabled scientists to probe back in time in both the physical and biological spheres. Observation, again encouraged strongly by a Christian worldview, took a leading role in determining how good the models were.

The Big Bang model of the origin of the universe is built on observations linked to Einstein's General Theory of Relativity. It describes the universe back to an age when it was only a fraction of a second old. At that stage, 13.7 billion years ago, the universe was an incredibly dense mass, so small that it could pass through the eye of a needle. From that point it expanded very rapidly in what is commonly called the Big Bang.

Within the first 1,000 seconds of the expansion, hydrogen and helium atoms are formed. Over the next billions of years clouds of hydrogen gas collapse under gravity to form galaxies of 100 billion stars. Stars continue the process of creation as they progress from their birth to their death. The energy they produce is due to burning of hydrogen into helium and other elements such as carbon, oxygen, and nitrogen. When stars exhaust their fuel, they shed these elements into space to be used for the next generation of stars. Thus, on this picture, the carbon that forms human beings is literally the "ashes of dead stars".

The evidence for this is helped by the fact that we can look back in time. Light travels at a finite speed of 300,000 kilometres per second. Therefore, when we look at the most distant galaxies, we see them as they were over 10 billion years ago, because it has taken that length of time for their light to travel to us. This means we can check our "models" of what we think the universe was like 10 billion years ago against our observations of what it was really like. However we can never get right back to the start.

This is where cosmologists try to give the best reconstruction or "model" of what happened billions of years ago on the basis of various observations. Early in the twentieth century, the astronomer V.M. Slipher observed that the light from other galaxies displayed a phenomenon called redshift, which occurs when light is emitted by an object moving away from an observer. Edwin Hubble then found that the further away the galaxies were, the faster they were moving away from us. This was the first piece of evidence that the universe was not static, but expanding. And if it is expanding, it must have expanded from somewhere. This fitted well with Einstein's geometric description of the law of gravity. As we have seen the mass and distribution of matter in the universe determines the geometry of space and the rate of flow of time. This complex interaction of matter and space–time could be described by a set of equations whose solution gave the geometry of space–time and showed how bodies moved within it. However, they were so difficult that they could only be solved in a few simple cases. One of these was for a uniform distribution of structureless points freely floating in space–time, which is in fact a good approximation to the universe: taken as a whole, the clusters of galaxies have a relatively uniform distribution. The Dutch astronomer Willem de Sitter and the Russian mathematician Alexander Friedmann confirmed that they showed the universe was not indeed expanding.

Image of the Antennae Galaxies from the Hubble Telescope.

Arno Penzias (1933–) and Robert Wilson (1936–) received a Nobel Prize for their discovery of cosmic microwave background radiation, evidence that there had been a Big Bang.

The next piece of evidence came in 1965 when Arno Penzias and Robert Wilson, attempting another experiment altogether, detected microwave background radiation, an "echo" of the Big Bang. Observations by the Wilkinson Microwave Anisotropy satellite have confirmed this conclusion, but have also shown that we have still much to understand about the universe. It seems that over 90 per cent of the universe is in the form of dark matter and dark energy, and we are far from clear what this matter and energy is.

Then in the 1980s it became possible to measure the amount of helium in the universe. This is a good test of theoretical models of the Big Bang. Once again, observation was in good agreement with predictions.

STEPHEN HAWKING AND QUANTUM GRAVITY

Professor Stephen Hawking, Lucasian Professor of Mathematics and Director of Research for the Centre for Theoretical Cosmology at the University of Cambridge is one of the most famous scientists of recent years. Hawking achieved international fame in 1988 with his book *A Brief History of Time*. Diagnosed with a rare form of motor neurone disease while a young man, he now has to communicate via a voice synthesizer into which each word has to be laboriously entered. Hawking has worked on a vast range of questions from black holes to the very beginning of the universe, where his work has provoked headlines about whether God is necessary as the Creator of the universe.

What Hawking does is to suggest a possible way of uniting quantum theory and gravity to describe the beginning of the universe. He thinks that such a theory can explain how the "blue touch paper" of the Big Bang lights itself. The core of Hawking's theory is that once upon a time there was no time. Hawking argues that the universe does have a beginning, but it does not need a cause. In the theory the notion of time melts away. Hawking's universe emerges from a fluctuation in a quantum field. No cause as such is necessary.

It must be stressed that Hawking's thinking on this is not fully accepted by

THE ORIGIN OF THE BIG BANG

Cosmology uses its knowledge of the physical laws to reconstruct a model of what happened in the past and has been extremely successful. It can describe what the universe was like billions of years ago – indeed it can describe what the universe was like when it was only a very small fraction of a second old, that is, 10^{-43} second. Here the great theories of the twentieth century, general relativity and quantum mechanics, break down. It is extremely frustrating to scientists who want to understand the whole story of the universe by describing its initial conditions.

Some have seen this as evidence for a Creator God. Do we need God to "fix" the initial conditions of the universe? If science is unable to describe the initial moments, is this where God comes in to set the universe off? Others, including Stephen Hawking, take a different view. They believe that relativity and quantum theory can be combined

the rest of the scientific community. There are other proposals on how to deal with the problem of the laws breaking down, and it remains difficult to know whether quantum theory can be applied to the whole universe. Most importantly, Hawking actually does not have a full theory; he makes his suggestions on the basis of this is what the theory would look like if he had a full theory. In a more recent book, *The Grand Design*, he proposes that current work on a fundamental theory called M-theory may provide this. However M-theory itself is highly contentious. Hawking's friend and erstwhile mentor, Roger Penrose, has described it as "a collection of ideas, hopes, aspirations… enjoying no observational support whatever".

into a unified theory, quantum gravity, which will have the capability of describing the initial conditions of the universe without recourse to God as an explanation.

If a unified theory is discovered, does God become redundant? The argument that the Big Bang needs God to start it off is a temporal form of the cosmological argument and has been used in different contexts for centuries. It has, however, a number of weaknesses. Augustine pointed out many years ago that the universe was created with time, not in time. Therefore to ask the question what came before the universe is attempting to use the concept of time before it came into existence! In addition, the argument derives from a notion that the universe is a thing or event. Now it is easy to say every thing has a cause, but is the universe a thing or event? Surely it is the totality of all events and things. To argue that everyone has parents does not mean that humankind has a mother.

The design argument, which argued from design in the natural world to a designer, flourished in the scientific revolution during the eighteenth century, and was expressed in the work of John Ray, the Boyle Lectures, and the Bridgewater Treatises, reaching its classic expression in William Paley's *Natural Theology* (1802). Paley's image of walking across a field and finding a watch, so intricate in design that it necessarily implied a designer of the watch, became a standard way of interpreting the intricacy of the biological world. Darwin, though, gave an alternative explanation to design in the natural world, and the crude design argument was largely rejected. It is therefore remarkable that there has been a revival of the design argument among physicists, many of whom have no religious axe to grind, on the grounds that the laws and circumstances of the universe need to be just right in order to give us a universe of structure and intelligent self-conscious life. For example, Paul Davies has argued that science pushes us to see an intelligence within (or behind) the universe.

The argument depends on the extraordinary fine-tuning of numbers fundamental to the universe, such as the ratio of the electric force to the gravitational force; how firmly atomic nuclei bind together; the ratio of energy needed to disperse an object compared to its total rest mass energy; and the number of spatial dimensions in the

More importantly, such an argument risks two major theological mistakes. The first is the "God of the gaps" (see pp. 38–39). Christians have a recurring tendency to insert God as the missing explanation if they perceive a gap in science. Newton needed God to occasionally reposition the planets in his theory of how gravity described their orbits; when understanding of the orbits grew, science filled in this gap. As scientists explain more and more about the universe, there is a temptation to look for unexplained gaps in the knowledge of the natural world in order to find space for God. But this "God of the gaps" is always in danger of becoming

universe. If any of these numbers were only slightly different to what they are we would not be here.

A theoretical explanation is that the anthropic principle selects this universe out of many: we see this fine-tuning because we are here. In other universes where these numbers were different, there would be no one there to see them. There is debate as to whether such "other universe" speculation is metaphysics rather than physics proper. Can we know that "other universes" are there by the passing of information from one universe to another, or do we accept their existence on the basis of the prediction of theories which solve other problems to do with our early universe? Such speculation cautions us against

resurrecting the design argument in this form. As long as we lack physical evidence for other universes, it remains metaphysical speculation. A strong possibility must be that there is a creator God. Anthropic balances certainly do not prove the existence of a creator, but they do provoke questions and, for some, pointers to the existence of a creator.

Archdeacon William Paley (1743–1805)

irrelevant as science fills in more of its own story. In contrast, the Bible understands that the whole universe is the result of God's working. He is as much at work in the first 10 to 43 seconds as at any other time. A scientific description of that moment in time does not invalidate it as being any less the activity of God than any other event. The work of Hawking and others on quantum gravity can close the gap of the initial conditions of the universe, but the God of the Bible does not need to shelter in such gaps.

Charles Coulson, the Oxford scientist who many years ago criticized the "God of the gaps" approach (pp. 38–39), wisely wrote: "When we come to the scientifically unknown, our correct policy is not to rejoice because we have found God; it is to become better scientists."

Attempts to prove the existence of God often lead to a picture of God closer to deism rather than the God of the Bible. Deists believe in a god who set the universe off and then went away to have nothing more to do with it. Nothing could be further from the God of the Bible. Creation is not a single initial act, but the bringing into being and moment by moment keeping in being of the whole universe.

> *The waning of Deism can be attributed primarily to its own inherent weaknesses. The Cosmic Designer, who started the world-machine and left it to run on its own, seemed impersonal and remote – not a God who cares for individuals and is actively related to man, or a Being to whom prayer would be appropriate. It is not surprising that such a do-nothing God, irrelevant to daily life, became a hypothesis for the origin of the world or a verbal formula which before long could be dispensed with completely.*
> Ian Barbour, *Issues in Science and Religion* (1966)

The search for an explanation for the first moments of the universe should caution biblical Christians to stay away from trying to attempt a proof which leads to a deistic god of the gaps. God is the creator and sustainer of every moment in the history of the universe.

POINTERS TO GOD FROM THE UNIVERSE?
One of the fascinating elements of the thinking of cosmologists in recent decades has been the way that the science of the origin of the universe has led to a range of philosophical and theological questions. While science has been extremely successful, the universe it has revealed seems to pose questions which go beyond science. It has led even non-believing scientists such as Paul Davies and Fred Hoyle to wonder if there is a deeper story to the universe.

Fred Hoyle (1915–2001), proponent of a "steady state' universe with no beginning.

First, why the universe? Gottfried Leibniz asked many years ago why there is something rather than nothing. This was not to resurrect the cosmological argument about a first cause but to recognize that the purpose and meaning of the universe lie beyond science. The Christian answer is straightforward: Christians believe in a personal God.

Second, where do the scientific laws themselves come from? If the universe emerges as a quantum fluctuation, where does quantum theory itself comes from? What determines the pattern of the world and how is it maintained? This is not a "God of the gaps" question, since science itself assumes these laws. Once again, the Christian will argue the Creator God is a natural answer.

Third, why is the universe intelligible? Why do our minds resonate with the mathematics of the universe expressed in the laws of physics? A number of physicists find the beauty, simplicity, universality, and intelligibility of the laws of physics themselves to be pointers to this universe being created. In Einstein's words, "the most incomprehensible thing about the universe is that it is comprehensible."

Fourth, why is the universe so carefully balanced to bring forth life? The discovery of many **anthropic** balances in the circumstances and laws of the universe making possible the emergence of intelligent life has been a striking feature of recent cosmology. While this cannot become a proof of the existence of a creator, some of these balances are so extraordinary that for many people they point to some kind of purpose in the universe. Fred Hoyle, when he calculated the fine-tuning which makes possible the creation of carbon in the nuclear furnaces of stars, said, "Nothing has shaken my atheism as much as this discovery".

Fifth, why is the universe so awe-inspiring? Dramatic photographs of the universe taken by the Hubble Space Telescope engender a sense of the finite nature of human beings in such a vast universe. This sense of awe has often led into worship. The psalmist exclaims, "The heavens declare the glory of God" (Psalm 19:1). This can sometimes be intimidation at how little we know, but can make us wonder expanded by the insights of modern scientific knowledge. Physicists often get this sense of awe in their work. Most of science is mundane, boring, pressured, and beset with failure, but there are moments when a few elegant laws are glimpsed underneath the complexity of the universe. This can lead to what John Habgood, one-time physiologist and then Archbishop of York, called "Woor lookatdat" moments. Indeed it can be argued that the design argument has power not because of its logical force but by its emotive power keying into people's awe at the universe. This reaction constantly recurs.

These insights do not prove God but may point the way towards him.

THE SEARCH FOR EXTRATERRESTRIAL INTELLIGENCE (SETI)

The search for extraterrestrial intelligence (SETI) has its origins in part in a Christian view of creation. The historian Colin Russell has suggested that a common feature of the many speculations about other worlds in the seventeenth century was an insistence on God's ability to create life anywhere he wished and that the universe existed not just for the sole benefit of human beings but to exhibit his glory to all. The cosmologist E.A. Milne went even further, "Is it irreverent to suggest that an infinite God could scarcely find the opportunities to enjoy himself, to exercise His godhead, if a single planet were the seat of His activities?"

The scientific jury is still out on this question of whether there is other intelligent self-conscious life within the universe. New observational techniques have led to the identification of hundreds of planets outside our Solar System. This has strengthened the view that there may be planets around a large number of the 100 billion stars in each of 100 billion galaxies. It therefore becomes possible to argue that there must be other planets able to sustain life elsewhere in the universe. On the other hand, biologists clearly point out that the evolution of self-conscious life depends in a very delicate way on many aspects of the laws of physics and the circumstances of the Earth. Finding evidence of primitive life on the surface of Mars (and assuming it could be shown that this was not contamination from the Earth) might tell us that life itself may be emerging elsewhere in the universe – although without necessarily implying that all amoebas will inevitably turn into accountants! Indeed the lifeless surface of Mars today is a reminder that things have to be just right for intelligent life to develop, even if the building blocks for life might be present in abundance.

While the SETI programme continues looking for signals of other civilizations, the continued silence of the heavens is not encouraging. The physicist Fermi in the 1950s suggested that if the universe were giving birth to many civilizations then "if they existed they would be here". While some will argue for UFOs and alien abductions to be good evidence, the vast majority of the scientific community is unconvinced.

However, what might the discovery of extraterrestrial intelligence mean for religion and Christian faith in particular? Paul Davies, struck by the anthropic balances that make life possible, believes that there are as yet undiscovered principles of complexity, organization, and information flow consistent with the laws of physics but not reducible to them, and these principles lead to intelligent life. If this turns out to be the case, Davies feels that atheism would seem less compelling and something like design more plausible. Nevertheless, he does think that the discovery of extraterrestrial intelligence would somehow undermine what he sees as Christianity's claim that humans have a special and exclusive relationship with the Creator. If we are not alone,

then we are not special. Davies might be right in seeing this in some expressions of Christianity, but it is not true to the traditional Christian position. Russell points out that the popularity of the speculation about other worlds in the seventeenth century was a significant indicator of the ascendancy of biblical values over those of Aristotle. The reason for this is that position and status were closely associated in the Aristotelian universe: we were special because the Earth was placed at the centre of all things. In contrast, the Bible does not link status with place. The dignity and worth of human beings comes from the gift of relationship with God. Such a relationship can be special without being exclusive. Therefore extraterrestrial intelligence does not pose a problem to Christian belief that men and women are special in the eyes of God. It may even increase the sense of awe at how great this God is, who creates with such diversity and extravagance.

Would the success of SETI undermine the central Christian claim that God has become a human being in Jesus to communicate with human beings and to save them from sin? Christian faith is based on a particular revelation at a particular time to a particular people, while being universal for all time and all people. Christians have thought about this in terms of other cultures and faith communities, and a few have tried to extend this to SETI. The speculations have followed two separate paths. Some have said that the revelation of God in Jesus is once for all for the whole universe, which would imply that Christians need to become cosmic missionaries. Others have taken a different view. The theologian E. L. Mascall argued that if salvation was what God was all about, then he would make sure his creatures knew about it. Mascall stresses that salvation has to be achieved through incarnation That Jesus became a human being means that it is doubtful that his saving work would be for different types of beings: he would need to become incarnate in alien flesh. In deciding between these two views one needs to proceed carefully. Christian faith understands God in human flesh as both showing us what God is like, and also saving us from sin. C. S. Lewis was right to ask the question that if aliens do exist, and if they are intelligent, will they have sinned like human beings?

Some of these questions may not be answerable until and if SETI is successful. Even so, we can note that some of the fascination with SETI reflects some religious themes: Are we alone in the cosmos? Is the purpose of the universe tied up with the existence of intelligent life? What is the nature of human beings in relation to the rest of creation? And where is the hope that, in the words of Sir Fred Hoyle, "we are going to be saved from ourselves by some miraculous interstellar intervention"?

C. S. Lewis (1898–1963): "I believe in Christianity as I believe that the sun has risen: not because I see it, but because by it I see everything else."

THE HISTORY OF THE EARTH

The best estimate for the age at which interstellar material fused to produce the Earth is 4,567 million years, a time accurate to within 2 million years (and, incidentally, an easy date to remember since it is comprises sequential numbers 4567). This is only one-third of the age of the universe since its formation in a Big Bang. During the preceding nine billion years the processes of star formation and explosions created all the elements which eventually formed our solar system.

Within a short period of its emergence and following a phase of heavy bombardment by meteorites, the earth settled down into something resembling its current structure: a dense, solid inner core made primarily of iron with substantial amounts of nickel plus smaller amounts of other elements. Surrounding the inner core is a still molten outer core with similar composition. This outer core is crucial to the existence of life on earth: it produces the magnetic field which forms a shield around the earth and protects it from much of the solar radiation which would otherwise make life as we know it impossible; second, it provides the heat which powers the movements of the tectonic plates and ultimately drives the earthquakes and volcanoes which are crucial for recycling the nutrients on which all life depends.

Surrounding the core is a thick layer known as the mantle. This has a markedly different composition, made up of silicate rocks rich in iron and magnesium. Although solid, it is hot enough to flow on geological timescales, thus allowing plate tectonics to occur. Sitting on top of this mantle is a relatively thin crust, mostly 5 to 40 kilometres in depth. This crust concentrates many of the elements on which life depends including, crucially, carbon. It is rather like the scum that floats to the surface on the top of jam when it is being cooked in a saucepan.

Covering the solid earth are the hydrosphere (the water layer), which now covers more than two-thirds of the globe, and the atmosphere. Water, along with

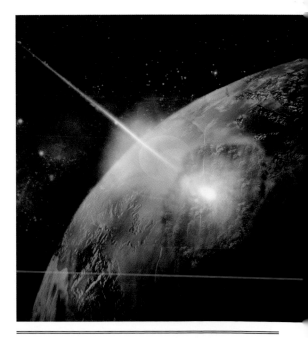

The newly formed Earth was bombarded by meteorites

carbon is the most important requirement for life. All biological life exists in these thin layers. Viewed from space, if the Earth were to be shrunk to the size of a billiard ball, it would appear smoother than that billiard ball (even including all the mountain ranges), and the zone in which life is found would be only a few hundredths of a millimetre thick.

Yet life has existed in this seemingly fragile, wafer-thin biospheric zone for many millions of years. The oldest mineral grains so far found on Earth, called zircons (which are very hard and are often used as cheaper replacements for diamonds in jewellery) are 4,400 million years old. The oldest known intact rock assemblage is found in Arctic Canada and is only a little younger, at 4,300 million years. Already at that time there were signs of water present at the surface of the earth. Despite the unlikelihood of preservation from such a long time ago, there is evidence that life existed on Earth almost as soon as the environmental conditions made it possible to do so, with some indications from 3,850 million years ago and microbial fossils in rocks 3,500 million years old.

Ever since then, the conditions on Earth have remained favourable for life, despite the Sun's heat output having increased by about 30 per cent and the rate of the Earth's rotation having slowed by a factor of four or five. This survival is remarkable because life can tolerate only a relatively narrow band of environmental conditions. If the temperature of the Earth's surface were

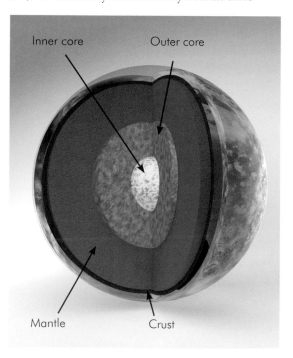

Inner core   Outer core

Mantle   Crust

Above: The oldest rock known on Earth on the shore of Hudson Bay, formed from ancient volcanoes and dated at 4.3 million years of age.

Cross section of the Earth

to increase to more than 100 °C, all the water would boil off and that would be the end of life as we know it. At the other extreme, if it were not for the greenhouse effect of carbon dioxide and water in the atmosphere, the Earth's surface would be more than 30 °C colder and would be a barren, icy waste. We can take this either as an amazing coincidence or as an example of God's providence in continually

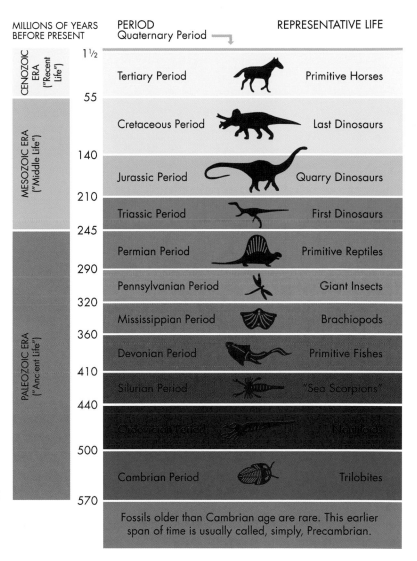

MILLIONS OF YEARS BEFORE PRESENT	PERIOD Quaternary Period →	REPRESENTATIVE LIFE
CENOZOIC ERA ("Recent Life")		
1½	Tertiary Period	Primitive Horses
55		
MESOZOIC ERA ("Middle Life")		
	Cretaceous Period	Last Dinosaurs
140		
	Jurassic Period	Quarry Dinosaurs
210		
	Triassic Period	First Dinosaurs
245		
PALEOZOIC ERA ("Ancient Life")		
	Permian Period	Primitive Reptiles
290		
	Pennsylvanian Period	Giant Insects
320		
	Mississippian Period	Brachiopods
360		
	Devonian Period	Primitive Fishes
410		
	Silurian Period	"Sea Scorpions"
440		
	Ordovician Period	Nautiloids
500		
	Cambrian Period	Trilobites
570		

Fossils older than Cambrian age are rare. This earlier span of time is usually called, simply, Precambrian.

upholding and sustaining the world as a place fit for life (Hebrews 1:3).

There was a long interval between the first signs of life and the appearance of multicellular animals on Earth some 575 million years ago. During this time there were slow changes in the atmosphere, particularly an increase in the amount of oxygen through plant photosynthesis. It may have been this increase in oxygen which eventually allowed large animals to appear. As far as we can tell from the geological record, the processes on Earth were much as they are today, with volcanic activity, earthquakes, mountain building and erosion, floods and droughts all occurring. However, the earth was certainly dynamic in its development, with periods when it was much hotter than at present, and others when ice spread widely. There were also occasional episodes of mass extinctions, where up to 95 per cent of the species alive at the time were wiped out. One of the most recent of these was some 60 million years ago when dinosaurs became extinct and mammals prevailed in their place.

Table of the genealogical descent of *Homo* species & Neanderthals

Despite living organisms having existed on Earth for such a long time, humans have been present for only a tiny portion of its most recent history. To put this into perspective, if the history of the Earth were to be compressed into one year, modern *Homo sapiens* would have been present for only the last 15 minutes before midnight on New Year's Eve. This has no theological significance in itself. But taken in conjunction with the understanding that has emerged over recent years that the conditions in the universe are finely tuned to make it possible for life to exist on Earth – the anthropic principle – it does give reason to pause for thought and for Christians to marvel at the creativity and sovereignty of the Creator God. It also provides a humbling perspective on the position of humankind in the time frame of the universe, given that the long history of the universe and then of the Earth itself was all part of making the world a place where humans could not only exist, but thrive.

Over the past few thousand years, the history of the Earth is marked most strongly by the influence of humans. We now have more impact on the Earth than any earlier geological processes have. We move more rock, sand, and gravel per year than all the normal geological processes put together, including river, glacier and mountain erosion, volcanic eruptions, wind storms, and the action of the waves and currents in the seas. We have become agents of mass extinction, causing species to go extinct at a rate estimated as about a thousand times above normal. And we are causing climate change at a rate far faster than anything known from the geological record, affecting the biosphere, storms and rainfall patterns, sea level and on the melting of glaciers and ice caps, to say nothing of the effect on the poor and marginalized people of the world.

Temperatures have varied considerably throughout the Earth's history. At the moment glaciers are retreating almost everywhere, showing a rising global temperature.

DATING METHODS

The basic method of geological dating is to use the layering of a rock sequence to define the order in which they were formed: unless they were disturbed subsequently, younger rocks lie above older ones. Rock units of the same age can be correlated around the world if they carry some unique identifier which changes through time. For example, fossils can be used to "tag" the age of that rock, indicating that is the same age as all others around the world which carry the same fossils. It has limitations: dating by fossils is only useful for the last 10 per cent of the Earth's history and only tells the relative age of a rock layer in the global sequence, and not its absolute age.

One way to calculate the absolute age of a rock is to use known cyclic changes, such as annual tree rings, and then to count these cycles back in time starting from the present. Tree rings, have been counted back from beyond 8400 BC. Annual layers are also found in coral growth rings, in lake sediments, and in snow layers such as those accumulated on the Greenland and the Antarctic ice caps. In the Antarctic a 3,190-metre (10,500 feet) ice core has reached 740,000 years old. Counting annual layers in the uppermost ice is unambiguous, but at greater depths, the ice becomes compacted and errors in counting annual layers increase from about 2 per cent at 11,000 years to 10 per cent at 150,000 years ago. Changes in the Earth's orbit cause long-term cyclicity in climate patterns, known as Milankovitch cycles on timescales ranging from 19,000 to 413,000 years. Identification of these cycles by their rhythmic climatic effect on ancient sediments allows precision dating back to 30 million years. Irregular cyclic changes in the earth's magnetic field allow volcanic rocks, which includes almost all the seafloor, to be dated back 170 million years.

Climatic conditions in the past can be determined from ice cores.

Radiometric dating is the most useful method for dating older rocks. It relies on the fact that many atoms have unstable nuclei ("parent" nuclides) that decay spontaneously to a lower energy state ("daughter" nuclides); because this radioactive decay involves only the nucleus of an atom, the rate of decay is independent of physical and chemical conditions such as pressure, temperature, and chemical binding forces. This makes them ideal chronometers. In its simplest form, radiometric dating involves measuring the daughter/parent ratio of an isotopic system with a known decay rate. The best way to protect against untrustworthy dates is to use two or more different decay systems on the same rock, or to use decay systems of three different isotopes which allow checks to be made for internal consistency.

Well over 40 different radiometric isotopic systems are in current use for dating rocks. Half-lives of commonly used isotopic systems cover a wide span: 106,000 million years for samarium-147 to neodymium-143; 18,800 million years for rubidium-87 to strontium-87; 1,260 million years for potassium-40 to argon-40; and 700 million years for uranium-235 to lead-207. Shorter time periods are best investigated using cosmogenic isotopes generated in the atmosphere, such as 1.52 million years for beryllium-10; 300,000 years for chlorine-36; and 5,715 years for the well-known carbon-14. In most cases, decay rates are known to within 2 per cent, and uncertainties in the dates derived from radiometric decay are of a similar magnitude.

The span of half-lives makes it possible to date rocks by choosing an appropriate isotopic decay system, although the precision of the measurement limits reliable ages to a maximum of five or six half-lives. The best-known technique using carbon-14 is useful for archaeological and recent geological studies, but is of no use for dating the demise of the dinosaurs (60 million years), or the age of the Earth. The most accurate methods in current use for dating geological rocks are uranium–lead and argon-40–argon-39 methods. These both rely on two different decay systems, which enables internal consistency checks to be made that no isotopes have been gained or lost.

THE END OF THE UNIVERSE AND NEW CREATION

SCIENTIFIC PESSIMISM ABOUT THE FUTURE

When it comes to the future of the universe, science is pessimistic. Alongside the destruction of the Earth's environment by pollution and global warming, there is a small but significant possibility of an impact of a comet or asteroid which would cause catastrophic environmental conditions for human beings. However, even if we avoid an asteroid impact, the Earth will not last forever. In another 4 to 5 billion years the Sun will come to the end of its available hydrogen fuel and will begin to swell up as a red giant. Its outer layers will absorb the Earth, and the Earth will be no more.

If these scenarios are not bleak enough, the universe itself seems destined to futility. Studies on distant supernovae, confirmed by recent observations from the Wilkinson

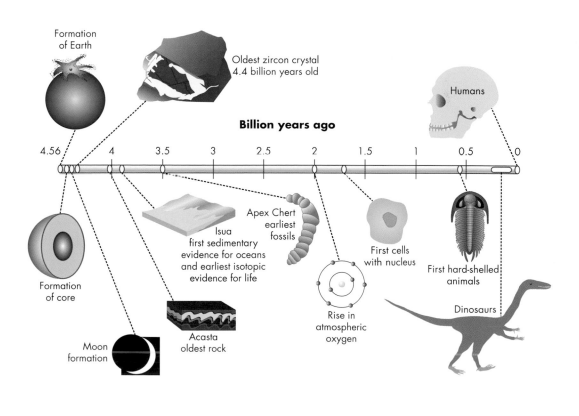

Chart of the history of the Earth

HISTORICAL UNDERSTANDING OF THE AGE OF THE EARTH

Early attempts to date the Earth range from Zoroaster's sixth century BC belief in an age greater than 12,000 years, to the assertions of the Chaldean priests that the Earth emerged from chaos two million years ago. Throughout most of the Christian era, the Bible was used as the source of credible information about the age of the Earth. In AD 169, Theophilus of Antioch used biblical chronologies to calculate an age of 5529 BC for the creation of the universe. He was the first of many to use this method. Bishop Ussher's (1581–1656) date of 4004 BC for Adam is only one of many similar calculations, although its influence has been exaggerated by later writers: only a handful of theologians in the seventeenth and eighteenth centuries adopted a strict 24-hour day chronology for Genesis 1.

The stretching of Earth history resulted from scientific discovery. On the assumption that the Earth was spun off from the Sun, Isaac Newton calculated that it must have had to cool for at least 50,000 years before it was sufficiently cold to allow life to exist. He thought that there must be an error in his logic, because it was so different from the church's teaching.

Count Buffon carried out experiments on the cooling of spheres and in 1774 reported a minimum age of 75,000 years. Newton's contemporary, Edmund Halley, believed the Earth was much older than the traditional date of 4.3 million years on the basis of the salinity of seawater, derived from salts transported from rivers. At the end of the eighteenth century, James Hutton argued that the slow processes of geological erosion meant that it was even older; he introduced the notion of "deep time". Such conclusions were entirely empirical and not intended to challenge biblical understanding, but they inevitably led to strains in the conventional interpretation of God's creating work.

Between 1770 and 1800, the main controversy was not whether the Earth was 6,000 to 8,000 years old, but whether it was around 100,000 or many millions of years. By the time Darwin wrote *The Origin of Species* in 1859, the idea that the Earth was millions of years old was well established, not least by clerical geologists such as William Buckland and Adam Sedgwick who dominated geology at Oxford and Cambridge. The conservative Anglican view of the time is well expressed by Revd Richard Main writing in 1862: "Some school-books still teach to the ignorant that the earth is 6,000 years old... No well-educated person of the present day shares that delusion."

By the end of the nineteenth century, Lord Kelvin (1824–1907), the leading physicist of his day and a Christian firm in his belief in the existence of design or divine order, calculated the Earth's age from the time it took to cool as 98 million years, with a range from 20 to 400 million years. His arguments were mathematically sound and seemingly superior to the geological estimates. But many geologists were unhappy, believing that Kelvin's figure simply did not provide sufficient time to produce the geological strata they walked over and hammered. Their answer came from the discovery in 1896 by Henri Becquerel of radioactivity and its recognition as a heat source in radium by Pierre Curie in 1903. Kelvin had known nothing of radioactive processes, which is why his estimates based on cooling of the Earth and the Sun were more than an order of magnitude too small. Once the heating caused by the decay of radioactive elements was factored into the calculation, the age of the Earth required to explain its present temperature increased immensely. Rutherford quickly became a leader in the new field of radioactivity, and as early as 1904 he suggested that the decay of helium trapped in minerals might provide a way of calculating geological ages. From then on it was just a matter of improving the estimates as more rock samples were examined and better instrumentation became available. By 1953, Patterson determined an age for the Earth of 4,550 million years, a figure which has hardly changed since.

Archbishop James Ussher of Armagh (1581–1656), best known for his biblical chronology.

Microwave Anisotropy Probe satellite, have revealed that we have still much to understand. It seems that over 90 per cent of the universe is in the form of dark matter and dark energy. Dark matter is a form of matter which we only know is there because of its gravitational effects; we cannot see it directly. It is most probably in the form of some new type of particle, which is currently the object of searches at the Large Hadron Collider. The dark energy is responsible for the accelerating expansion of the universe, but apart from that little more is known about it. There are a number of current theories as to its

THEOLOGICAL PERSPECTIVES ON THE AGE OF THE EARTH

The problem with reconciling the scientific age of the Earth with the biblical account is not in the period since Genesis 2 onwards, which is easily accommodated within 10,000 years or so, but in the assumption that the six days described in Genesis account for the entire history of the universe are six 24-hour days. One approach has been to treat the six days not as literal 24-hour periods, but as long periods of time. Another is to assert that the Earth only appears to be very old. Although science cannot address such a suggestion, it raises immense theological problems, because if true it would mean that God purposely designed a universe to deceive us. That does not sit easily with everything else God tells us about himself in the Bible.

The most fruitful approaches take seriously the literary genre of the Genesis passages dealing with the six days of creation. Indeed, Augustine, Origen, and other early church fathers were already interpreting Genesis figuratively in the early centuries AD. It is anachronistic to press scientific meanings onto Genesis. The central aim of the Genesis text is to explain God's purposes in his creation and his own relationship to it. The theological narratives of early Genesis proclaim that the universe was created by a loving, personal God, in an orderly fashion, that he was pleased with it, and that one of his main objectives was to make it a place in which humans could live fruitful lives and have loving relationships with him. The biblical evidence of a purposely created universe, taken together with the scientific evidence for its evolution over billions of years into a place fit for human habitation, reinforce the message that humankind is not the accidental product of a meaningless universe.

nature and origin but as yet no general agreement. The implication is that the universe will expand forever into "heat death" and become a cold lifeless place full of dead stars.

For Nobel Prize-winning physicist Steven Weinberg, "the more the universe is comprehensible the more it seems pointless". However, this is only one understanding. Some physicists have suggested that this universe may be one of many and therefore the demise of this universe needs to be seen in the context of "endless fertility" of new universes. Others are more **anthropocentric**. Freeman Dyson has been impressed by the ability that

The Large Hadron Collider is a massive particle accelerator below the Alps near Geneva, designed to explore the deep structure of space and time.

intelligent life could have in manipulating the environment of the Earth. Extrapolating forwards, he concluded that the combined resources of natural and artificial intelligences should be able to maintain some form of life in the universe over the next trillion years. His idea is that biological life could adapt through genetic engineering to redesign organisms that could cope in such a universe. Consciousness would then be transferred to new kinds of hardware that would be able to cope with the ultra low temperatures of a heat death universe. For him, "life and intelligence are potentially immortal".

THE BIBLICAL FUTURE

Do the world and humanity have any purpose? Are they moving towards some kind of fulfilment or *eschaton* (final end)? The monotheistic religions deny that time and history are cyclical. Judaism, Islam, and Christianity believe that humanity was created for a purpose and we are moving towards a final end when God himself will bring a new heaven and new earth redeemed from sin, evil, and their consequences. The world and humanity would be as they were meant to be. For the Jesuit scientist Teilhard de Chardin, this was the "omega point" of final fulfilment. The prophetic writings of Isaiah and Revelation offer idyllic accounts of the unity of nature, harmony between humanity and the animal and material world with God as the central focus of worship. Faith must be based on evidence as well as hope; it provides a view of the future which purely scientific accounts cannot pretend to offer. Our human condition leads us to ask the big ontological questions: Why do we exist? What are we doing here? Where are we going, if anywhere?

When we come to the question of how the Bible discusses the future we are presented with a range of different kinds of literature which have been interpreted in a wide range of ways. Despite this, it is possible to look at the bigger picture throughout these writings, and to relate the hope for human beings to hope for the whole universe.

Central is the idea of new creation. While the original creation is seen to be good because of a good God, another biblical theme should be put alongside the Genesis emphasis. This is that God's purposes go beyond this creation to a new creation characterized by "a new heaven and a new earth" (Revelation

Frank Tipler is another who has speculated on the future of human intelligence. His belief is that consciousness might be transferred to computers. As computers expand across space, information processing would increase. He argues that it is possible that a point will be reached when an infinite or maximum amount of information will have been processed, and "life" will have expanded everywhere in the universe. Such scenarios are not possible within an accelerating universe, but they do illustrate in the context of the end of the universe, the belief that science could be the ultimate saviour.

21:1). Jesus told us "Do not be anxious about tomorrow; tomorrow will look after itself". He repeatedly warned his followers to be prepared for the coming of "the kingdom". His last words on earth were, "Go to all nations". And Peter wrote that "the heavens will disappear with a great rushing sound, the elements will be dissolved in flames, and the earth and all that is in it will be brought to judgement". It is obviously possible to interpret these texts as meaning that we should forget this world; they could imply that the more faithful we are in proclaiming Christ's saving work at all times and in all places, the sooner Christ will come again in glory and take us all to be with him in heaven. Ronald Reagan's Secretary for the Interior James Watt notoriously said, "My responsibility is to follow the Scriptures which call upon us to occupy the land until Jesus returns… we will mine more, drill more, cut more timber". He was reflecting a premillennialist or dispensationalist position once widespread among evangelicals (not least because of the popularity of the "Scofield Reference Bible Notes"). This interpretation remains common in North America, but is less influential in Europe. A key text is where Peter writes about the heavens disappearing and the elements melting. But just before this, he tells us "the first world was destroyed by water, the water of the flood" (2 Peter 3:6). Now it is apparent that the first world was not destroyed by Noah's flood, or we would not be here; what happened is that God purged the earth through the flood, and it is reasonable to assume that he will use fire to purge our current world – indeed Paul explicitly says he will (1 Corinthians 3:13). Moreover, we will not "go up" to heaven; the new Jerusalem will come down from heaven, so that the dwelling of God will be with his fellow creatures. Eventually heaven and earth will not be separated, but in being renewed, will be integrated with each other. The great claim of Revelation 21 and 22 is that heaven and earth will finally be united.

It is this biblical emphasis that challenges many of the secular futurologies around today. To those who say that the future hope is about a heaven where our souls float up to a kind of ghostly other worldly existence, the theme of new creation emphasizes the importance of the physical in the purposes of God. To those who want to preserve this creation for as long as possible, new creation says that God's purposes go beyond this creation to something better.

Whatever the circumstances, creation is not limited to its own inherent possibilities. Christians believe that there is someone greater than the universe who can give hope, a hope focused and indeed evidenced by the resurrection of Jesus Christ. For them, the evidence of the empty tomb, resurrection appearances, and transformation of the disciples point convincingly to a God who raised Jesus from the dead, able to give hope even in the face of death. Further, Paul in 1 Corinthians 15 sees the resurrection of Jesus as the first-fruits of what will happen, not just to the followers of Jesus but to the whole universe. The empty tomb means the transformation rather than replacement of the body (see pp. 94–95). The implication is that God's purposes for the material world are that it should be transformed, not discarded. At the same time, the resurrection opposes the view that this universe is an end in itself, for there is new experience in the resurrection. In trying to describe the appearances of the risen Jesus, the Gospel writers struggle with this continuity and discontinuity. He is the same Jesus for they see the marks of the nails, but he is also different, no longer constrained by space and time. He eats fish with the disciples but also appears in rooms where the doors are locked.

What this might mean to the physicist is intriguing. Will the new creation have space and time not associated with experiences of limitation or decay? Will the atoms of the new creation be different from the atoms of this creation

or will it simply be our relationship with the material that is different? Whatever the answer to these questions, C. S. Lewis was surely right to see the new creation as more real and exciting than this creation. It is this life that is the "shadowlands" and the next will be in full colour.

Martin Rees, UK Astronomer Royal, has commented: "What happens in far-future aeons may seem blazingly irrelevant to the practicalities of our lives. But I don't think the cosmic context is entirely irrelevant to the way we perceive our Earth and the fate of humans."

The pessimism of science poses the old question of why we are here. The Christian response is one of hope. The resurrection of Jesus is a clear signal that God's purposes for good cannot be defeated and one day both believers and the whole universe will be transformed into a new creation. It is in the light of that hope that Christians are called to share in the transformation by trusting in God's power and sharing with him the work of mission, whether it is caring for the environment or sharing hope with others.

How certain is the future? *The Incredulity of St Thomas*, painted by Benjamin West (1738–1820).

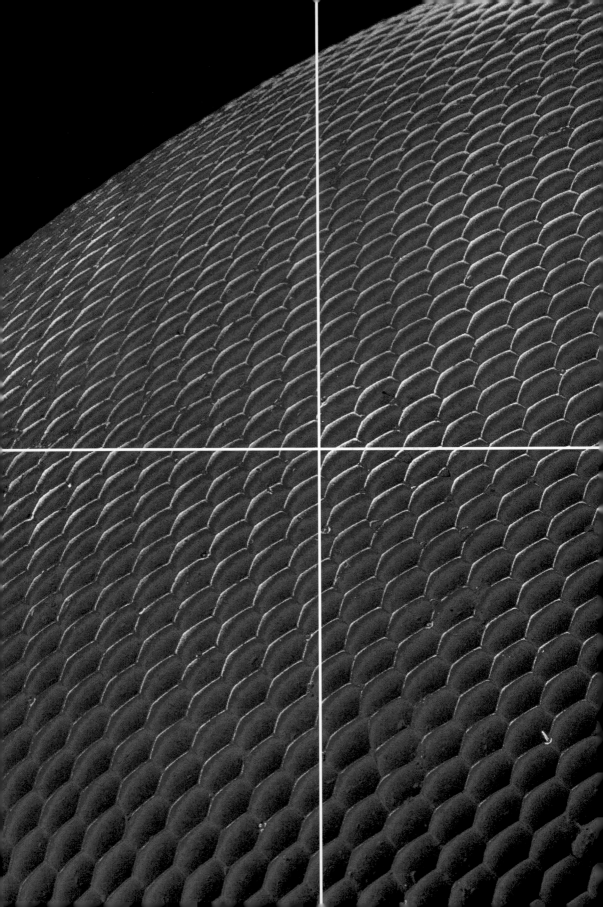

Life Sciences

Until the middle of the twentieth century, the biological sciences tended to be regarded as the poor relation of the physical and highly quantifiable "exact sciences". The real problems for Christians seemed to concern determinism and how to find God in a mechanistic universe; the problems raised by biology centred around evolution, and were either ignored or treated by denying evolution. This changed radically with the elucidation in 1953 of the structure of DNA (Deoxyribose Nucleic Acid) and the revolution in molecular biology that followed. Further developments in analytic and measuring techniques have transformed biology into a quantitative discipline and reduced the speculative elements in tracing evolutionary processes.

LIFE ON EARTH

Direct knowledge about the history of life on Earth comes from studying its remains in the rocks, the vast majority of which are fossils. For centuries fossils were assumed to be the remains of creatures drowned in Noah's flood, but this explanation became increasingly implausible with the discovery of fossil seashells in rocks high on mountains and the recognition that fossils are not randomly distributed but are laid down in discrete geological strata. During the latter half of the

Above: James Watson (1928–) and Francis Crick (1916–2004) discovered the double helix structure of DNA in 1953.

Opposite: The compound eye of a bee, made of thousands of individual units (ommatidia).

Fossil of an extinct ammonite

eighteenth century, there grew a general acceptance that the Earth was much older than the traditional 6,000 to 10,000 years and that some rocks were younger than others and had been laid down in strata on top of older ones (pp. 136–37). In the eighteenth century, the French naturalist, the Count Buffon, identified several epochs of geological history with humans appearing only in the last of them. This challenged the assumption that the history of the Earth and of humans was effectively coextensive. By the 1830s the distribution of fossils in such strata had been worked out in detail, giving a progressive stratigraphic sequence, although the absolute timings of the different features were not known until methods using radioactive decay became available in the early decades of the twentieth century (see pp. 133–34).

All the major invertebrate groups are represented in the Cambrian Period which lasted about 54 million years (Ma), from a beginning about 543 Ma ago. It was long thought that the Cambrian represented the beginning of life on Earth, but many groups of Pre-Cambrian fossils are now known. The Cambrian fossils are the remains of animals which include a much higher proportion of hard shells than in previous times, and are therefore more likely to leave traces in the rocks. Fish fossils first appear in the Ordovician Period (488–446 Ma), land plants in the following Silurian (446–417 Ma), amphibians and vascular land plants in the Devonian (417–370 Ma), reptiles and widespread forests, which are the source of coal, in the Carboniferous (370–320 Ma). The subsequent period (Permian, 300–252 Ma) ended with a major extinction of marine animals, marking the end of the Palaeozoic Era, the time of ancient life.

The following Tertiary Era was the time when dinosaurs were in abundance. It is divided into Triassic (250–200 Ma), Jurassic (200–148 Ma), and Cretaceous Periods (148–68 Ma), ending with another major extinction event and the disappearance of most of the dinosaurs. The next era is the present one, the Cenozoic, the age of mammals, with two parts: the Ice Age (Pleistocene) Period (2.6 Ma to 12,000 years ago), then our current Holocene.

The earliest known fossil hominids (comprising the great apes and humans) date from Africa six to seven million years ago; the earliest hominins (members of the human family), *Homo erectus*, also came from Africa, between 1.5 and 2 million years ago. A number of *Homo* species have been described; our own species (*H. sapiens*) first appeared (also in Africa) only 200,000 years ago, very recently in the 3.8 billion year history of life.

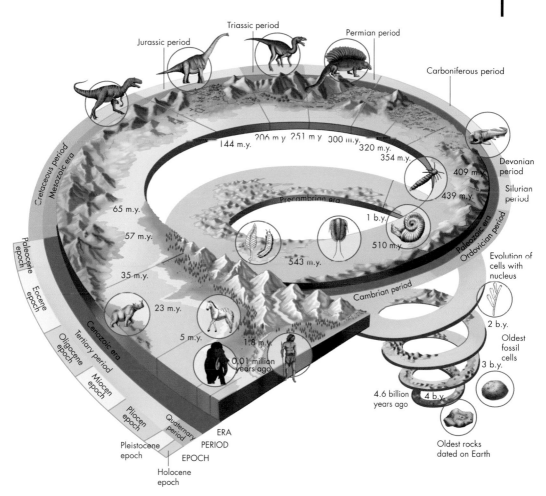

ORIGIN OF LIFE

We can only speculate about the origin of life. In 1907, a Swedish chemist, Svante Arrhenius proposed *panspermia*, the notion that life came from outer space, as microorganisms drifted between planets. This idea still persists, strengthened by the discovery that fairly complex molecules are sometimes found in debris from space. Notwithstanding, a considerable amount of effort has been put into finding ways in which life may have originated on Earth. Charles Darwin suggested one possibility in a letter (1871) to his friend Joseph Hooker. He proposed that life may have begun in a "warm little pond, with all sorts of ammonia and phosphoric salts, lights, heat, electricity, and so on, present, so that a protein compound was chemically formed ready to undergo still more complex changes… At the present day such matter would be instantly devoured or absorbed, which would not have been the case before living creatures were formed."

This idea was taken up in 1924 by Aleksandr Oparin (writing in Russian) and independently in 1929 by J. B. S. Haldane. They suggested that the early seas might have functioned as Darwin's "warm soup", containing relatively simple inorganic compounds (ammonia, methane, hydrogen sulphide, carbon monoxide, phosphate radicals) which did not immediately break down as they would nowadays because the atmosphere at the time was thought to be oxygen-free. In due course, these simple chemicals might have combined in various random ways under the influence of energy from sunlight or lightning. This hypothesis was tested in 1952 by Stanley Miller and Harold Urey at the University of Chicago. They passed an electric current through a sealed vessel containing methane, ammonia, hydrogen, and water. After a week they found 11 of the 20 commonly occurring amino acids (the building blocks of proteins) in their solution. In 1961, Joan Oró, a Spaniard working with NASA, found bases which form nucleic acids in a similar experiment where hydrogen cyanide was in the solution. Much debate surrounds these experiments. We cannot be certain of the exact nature of the early atmosphere. More importantly, we do not know how the simple organic molecules turned into self-replicating systems. Claims have been made that juxtaposition in bubbles or on clay could have catalysed their assembly. Such systems may have been helped by the sort of extreme conditions found in volcanoes or deep sea vents or by radioactivity. We have to acknowledge that all we can do is to speculate. But at least it is fair to say that most people regard the speculations as plausible.

Once self-replicating life had appeared, further developments were less speculative. A major step must have been the association of some of the primitive molecular components in a mutually beneficial way (*endosymbiosis*) to form a cell. Grouping of such cells would allow some clusters to adopt specialized functions. A progression of this nature would be almost inevitable, particularly in situations where nutrients were limiting and hence efficiency at a premium.

CREATION IN THE BIBLE

The Bible is unequivocal that God is the creator of all things. We are told that "In the beginning God created the heavens and the earth" (Genesis 1:1). The psalmist affirmed that "To the Lord belong the earth and everything in it... for it was he who founded it" and "the Lord is maker of heaven and earth, the sea and all that is in them" (Psalms 24:1–2; 146:5–6). Paul proclaimed to the Athenians, "The God who created the world and everything in it... he is the universal giver of life and breath" (Acts 17:24–25); John recorded the heavenly beings crying, "You are worthy, O Lord our God, to receive glory and honour and power, because you created all things; by your will they were created and have their being" (Revelation 4:11).

THE ORIGIN OF LIFE

Around 4 billion years ago, the Earth's environment became conducive to life. The earliest (indirect) evidence for life is found about 3.8 billion years ago, but the evidence for fossil cells becomes unequivocal by 3.5 to 3 billion years ago. Cellular life emerged on earth remarkably quickly in terms of geological time.

The basic building blocks of life are carbon-containing chemicals. Many of the meteorites that arrived on Earth in its early history are thought to have been rich in carbon – as are some of the meteorites that reach the Earth's surface today – including significant amounts of amino acids, the building blocks of proteins, together with compounds related to sugars and lipids (fats). It is not impossible that life itself hitched a ride to earth from some other planet, but there is no evidence for this. The challenge is to work out how the basic chemical building blocks were gradually built up into self-replicating living systems. Since this happened around 4 billion years ago and since replicating systems simpler than cells are very unlikely to have left any fossil traces, this is not easy. The first single-celled living entities are likely to have eaten any earlier life forms, thereby deleting the path leading to their own formation. We have a few possible pieces of the jigsaw of life's origin, but most of the jigsaw is missing.

Possibly relevant is the way that amino acids adhere to clays, resulting in the formation of small protein-like molecules. Proteins now provide the structural and functional components of all living things. The DNA that encodes genes is similar to another information-containing molecule, RNA. Clay surfaces can also catalyse the synthesis of small RNA molecules. RNA is of particular interest because it is not only self-replicating, but also has the ability to act as a catalyst. Catalytic forms of RNA are known as ribozymes, and still function in cells, most notably in the ribosomes that catalyse protein synthesis. This has led to the idea of an early "RNA world" being involved at the start of life.

Two further challenges were involved before an independently self-replicating system (= life) could come into being. The first is to compartmentalize the system so that it retains its own integrity. Small lipid vesicles that can contain mixtures of RNA and proteins known as "liposomes" may provide some clues. The second challenge is how the RNA

• •

might acquire its specific sequence of chemical genetic "letters" that will enable some continuity in the information conveyed to the next generation. Further clues in this case come from the finding that amino acids prefer to bind to certain RNA molecules rather than others, so the RNA code, which eventually became a DNA code, may have been "chosen" by the amino acids.

Much of the current research is being carried out by NASA in the USA with the aim of helping to find if there is life on other planets. Discovery and characterization of life on even one other planet could potentially greatly assist in our understanding.

Does our present ignorance about the origin of life have any theological significance? It is difficult to know why this should be so. The Christian doctrine of creation points to God as the ground and source of all existence. Christians do not believe in a God of the gaps who acts as a lazy "plug" for our present ignorance. Neither is there anything in the Bible that suggests that the origin of life was some special miracle inaccessible to normal scientific enquiry. All that scientists can investigate and describe is God's good creation; indeed there is nothing else to investigate. There is no particular reason why our current ignorance about the processes whereby life came into being should reflect on God's creative handiwork one way or another. When Darwin published *The Origin of Species* in 1859, nothing was known about the mechanism of inheritance. Now a mere 150 or so years later we know in great detail how genetic inheritance occurs by means of DNA. There is no reason to doubt that the same will be the case once the mechanistic processes for life's origin become considerably clearer than at present, even though that may take a further 150 years.

In acknowledging and accepting God as Creator, we must also note two important truths:

- Very rarely in the Bible are we told anything about the mechanisms that God uses to carry out his work; and

- It is a massive logical error to assume that knowing one cause of an event means that we know all its causes.

As long ago as the fourth century BC, Aristotle pointed out that there were differences between material, efficient, formal, and final causes (roughly the matter, cause of change, essential nature, and purpose of a thing) (pp. 181–82). We rarely separate all four causes in this way, but we commonly distinguish proximate from ultimate causes. For example, the proximate cause of a cup of tea would be to heat water to boiling point, the ultimate cause would be slaking one's thirst; the proximate cause of a disease might be a pathogenic agent in the blood, the ultimate cause would be exposure to the infection via an infected needle or a droplet infection. It is legitimate to concentrate on a particular cause for the purpose of analysis or experiment; that is the normal practice of science. On the other hand, it is unhelpful and probably positively confusing to insist that the cause in question is the only relevant one.

When we are concerned about the action of God in the world, it is entirely consistent to acknowledge him as the author of an event and at the same time recognize a scientific agent as the efficient or proximate cause. This is what the astronomer Johannes Kepler meant when he examined the conclusions of his studies and rejoiced that he was "thinking God's thoughts after him". In exactly the same way, we can worship God as Creator of all things while at the same time exploring the method(s) that he might have used in his creating work. Charles Kingsley (author of *The Water Babies* and Professor of Modern History at Cambridge University) responded to *The Origin of Species* in this way: "I have gradually learnt to see that it is just as noble a conception of Deity to believe that He created primal forms capable of self development... as to believe that He required a fresh act of intervention to supply the lacunas [gaps] which he himself had made".

DARWIN AND EVOLUTION

Traditional understandings of God's creative work as described in the early church fathers and Jewish commentators tended to focus on figurative and symbolic interpretations. The Reformation was associated with a reaction against explicitly symbolic interpretations of the Bible so that the early chapters of Genesis were seen more as literal history, for example in Luther's writings – that God had made the universe by divine fiat in a space of six frenetic days about 6,000 years ago. In the absence of knowledge about the age of the Earth, of fossils, or of relationships between different animals or plant groups, there was no reason to think otherwise. Archbishop

Charles Darwin (1809–82), painted the year before his death.

Ussher's much-quoted calculation (which still appears in older Bibles) that creation took place in 4004 BC, was based largely on the genealogies in the Bible, particularly Matthew 1:1–17 and Luke 3:23–38. Ussher's date was in fact similar to many others. Early church commentators believed that Adam was created during the sixth 24-hour period after the beginning and that Jesus would come in the 6,000th year. The Ethiopian church dates

"DAYS" IN GENESIS

Genesis 1 describes God's work as taking place in six days. The obvious meaning of "day" is a period of 24 hours, but there are other possible interpretations:

- They may represent long periods of time, perhaps geological epochs. This has been a common understanding from earliest days. Both Origen and Augustine argued that the Genesis days can have no relationship to human days.

- The Scottish divine, Thomas Chalmers, suggested that the six days were days of reconstruction, not of creation. He argued that a catastrophe happened between the creation of the heavens and the earth (Genesis 1:1) and the formless and empty world described in Genesis 1:2. Indeed, there might have been a series of catastrophes, perhaps corresponding to the mass extinctions revealed in the fossil record. The days of reconstruction would have no connection between either the original creation or the fossil record, and therefore (it is argued) there can be no conflict with science. This "gap theory" was incorporated by Scofield into his "annotated Bible" and achieved wide circulation among evangelicals. However it depends on reading the verb in Genesis 1:2 as "the earth *became*", which is wrong. Also it requires the verb "make" in Genesis 1 (and Genesis 2:2 and Exodus 20:11) to have the meaning "remake". There is no justification for this.

- Philip Wiseman has argued that, since "the Sabbath was made for man" (Mark 2:27; clearly the Creator did not need a day of rest), it was intended for human rest, and so "it is only reasonable to suppose that what was done on the 'six days' also had to do with mankind". If so, then obviously God was not creating the earth and all life, because there

creation to 5493 BC; in the eighth century AD, the Venerable Bede dated it to 3952 BC; Luther thought it was in 3961 BC. All these dates have to be regarded as suspect, not least because comparison of the genealogies used in their computation shows that some omit individuals named in others. The dating of creation is a matter of how best to interpret the Bible, just as is the meaning of how to understand the "six days" of God's creative work.

were no humans when they were being created. He then suggests that the implication of the repeated phrase "God said" was that God was recounting what he had done in times past. The six days therefore become "days of revelation". However, like the "gap theory", this idea has exegetical problems, because the world translated "made" in Exodus 20:11 cannot mean "made known".

- Finally, Genesis 1 may be an ancient hymn. Augustine held this view. There are two triads of days, with similarities between days 1 and 4; 2 and 5; and 3 and 6. Corresponding to light in day 1 are the luminaries of day 4; the creation of the expanse of the sky and the separation of the waters (day 2) corresponds to the birds and fish (day 5); and the appearance of dry land and vegetation (day 3) corresponds to the land animals, together with the gift of food (day 6). Medieval tradition distinguished the work of separation (days 1–3) from the work of adornment (days 4–6).

It is often claimed that the Hebrew word (yom) translated "day" always means a 24-hour period in the creation accounts. This is not so. Yom is used in several different senses in the Genesis story: in 1:5 it refers to the "light" as day; in 2:4 it describes "the day that the Lord God made the heavens and the earth"; in John 5:17, Jesus is recorded as saying "My Father is always at his work to this very day", referring to the seventh day of the creation week. We must avoid attempting to make the text concordant with any particular interpretation of the creation story. It describes the relationship of God to his creation, not merely what God did in six days. The crown of creation is not humankind on the sixth day, but the Creator himself on the seventh. The Bible links the Sabbath with the whole of creation (Exodus 20:11).

The biblical record of creation is to be regarded as a dramatic narrative, providing a graphic representation of those things which could not be understood if described with the formal precision of science. It is in this pictorial style that the divine wisdom in the inspiration of the writing is to be signally exhibited. Only a record presented in this way could have met the needs of all time.
Ernest Kevan, *New Bible Commentary* (1953)

When we consider our world and contemplate the fact of our existence, it is natural to reflect on why there is something rather than nothing. We look for explanations for where we and the world come from, and how the world and humanity came into existence. The Bible sets the context, opening with "In the beginning God created the heavens and the earth" (Genesis 1:1), stating that the world has a specific origin and purpose given by a supernatural, transcendent, divine being. This act of creation was from nothing (*ex nihilo*), and we are told nothing about any pre-existent material. The material reality and beginning of the world are totally dependent for its being and sustaining on God. Likewise, the created order of everything in the world including animal and human life was brought into being and is sustained by God. Genesis is not meant to be a modern scientific account, but is rather a timelessly graphic way of explaining the fact, purpose, and process of creation. Indeed, modern scientists themselves offer differing accounts of the beginning of the world and humanity, recognizing that without actual observation, we can only offer likely hypotheses. We have no direct experience of absolute beginnings (or, for that matter, absolute endings).

From the time of Aristotle, scientists believed that the world made sense. It had meaning and purpose. This **teleology** (the study of the end, goal, or purpose) of each particular thing and of everything as a whole meant that we could understand, react to and prepare for what happened in the world. Ancient science asked what the purpose of a thing was and then enquired if that purpose was being fulfilled. This led to natural philosophy (or natural law) explaining what was natural. If something did not fulfil its function then we could try to restore proper functioning – as in medicine, where we try to put right whatever is wrong with the body and its functioning. Behind this is a "Principle of Sufficient Reason" (originally propounded by the German mathematician, Gottfried Leibniz) that there is a good reason why something is as it is or acts as it does. If it failed to fulfil its function, that, too, was for some good and discoverable reason. This is exemplified by heredity: our genetic framework and its interaction with the world and environment allow us to understand who we are, what we do, and what is happening to us and why. We do not yet know what all genes do or how they interact with each other and the environment, but we are confident that there is some point to our genetic structure and its interaction, even if we do not know what that purpose is.

In the "Enlightenment" of the eighteenth century, more and more was discovered about causation in the physical world. All this brought about no insoluble problems, so long as God could be seen as the First Cause and Designer. This was encapsulated in the writings and influence of Archdeacon Paley. In his *Natural Theology* (published in 1802) he developed his analogy of God as a divine mechanic. He argued that a watch could not have happened by chance; it must have been designed. This was a powerful argument and was widely accepted, but it removed God from everyday involvement with the world and relegated his involvement to its beginnings. In theological terms, it was deism, not theism.

Darwin described Paley's logic as "irresistible". He wrote about his time as a student at Cambridge that "The careful study of these works [Paley's writings]… was the only part of the Academical Course of the least use to me in the education of my mind". But scientific discoveries were already causing tension with Paley's ideas. As knowledge of the Earth's animals increased, it became increasingly less credible that they were all descended from animals that had survived a great flood in Noah's Ark. Perhaps there were "multiple centres" of creation. Even more problematic was the effect of a long Earth history on the adaptation of organisms to their environment. A creator could presumably design an organism perfectly fitted to a particular environment, but such perfection would disappear if the environment was not constant. Adjusting to changes in climate, to the physical structure of the Earth's surface, or to predators and competitors is possible only if organisms can adapt. One of the explanations for the different fossil faunas of different geological strata was that they might represent previous creations which had disappeared, perhaps under God's judgment.

The alternative was that changes had appeared in the animals since they were first created, in other words that the changes observed in the fossil record were evolutionary changes. Charles Darwin's grandfather held the latter view, but the best-known proponent of evolution was a French biologist, Jean-Baptiste Lamarck, who put forward his ideas in a book, *Philosophie Zoologique*, published in 1809. Lamarck believed that there was a progressive increase in perfection from the simplest organisms to its peak in humankind; he argued that over a long period of time, one species would become transformed into another "higher" one. This got over the problem of species extinction, which was becoming increasingly contentious in the late eighteenth century as it became clear that organisms found as fossils were not still surviving in a yet undiscovered El Dorado; on the other hand, it seemed to contradict the notion of a perfect world created by God. By the mid nineteenth century, very few Bible scholars believed that the Genesis 1 creation story was a literal account.

Charles Darwin's Paleyian ideas were challenged during the five years (1831–36) he spent sailing around the world as naturalist on board the surveying ship, HMS *Beagle*. He saw how animal species replaced one other along the length of South America and how fossils often resembled – but differed in details from – similar living forms. Notwithstanding, he still retained a "traditional" belief in a world more or less as it was at its creation. The trigger that changed his views about this seems to have been a conversation in March 1837 with John Gould, the ornithologist at the London Zoo, to whom Darwin had entrusted the bird specimens he had collected while on the *Beagle*. Gould's finding that the mockingbirds on the Galapagos were an entirely new group wholly confined to those islands, forced Darwin to re-think his earlier assumption of a static world. He made a note for himself, "the Zoology of Archipelagoes will be well worth examining, for such facts would undermine the stability of species".

HMS *Beagle* as she would have appeared off the Galapagos Islands, 17 October 1835.

The vegetarian finch (*Geospiza crassirostris*), one of the fourteen species of related finches found only in the Galapagos Islands.

Darwin first put his ideas about evolution on paper in 1842. By 1844, he was sufficiently sure of himself to write a 200-page "Essay" which later formed the core of *The Origin of Species*, published in 1859. Its starting point was a Paleyian belief that the creator used laws in his creating work. Darwin invoked a very simple mechanism, based on three facts and two deductions. He began with the observation that virtually all species have a large potential for increase in number (think of the number of acorns produced by an oak tree or the masses of frogspawn laid by every female frog), but (second observation) numbers remain roughly constant. The inference from this is that there must be a *struggle for existence*, with only a proportion of young surviving. The existence of such a struggle is essentially an ecological deduction and one understood in Darwin's time. It forced itself on Darwin's awareness when in 1838 he read "for amusement" Thomas Malthus's *Essay on the Principles of Population*, which set out the spectre of the human population outstripping its food supply, leading to the weak and improvident succumbing in a struggle for resources. Darwin's genius was in linking this ever-prevalent struggle for existence with a third fact: heritable variation. If only a small proportion of a population survives the struggle, the likelihood is that it will include an increased proportion of those with any trait that gives them some advantage in their survival. Over the generations, those carrying such a trait will increase at the expense of those lacking it. There would be a genetic change in the population, amounting to *natural selection* for the trait in question.

The fact of evolutionary change was rapidly accepted. It made sense of so many data: of comparative anatomy and physiology, of classification, of geographical distribution, of fossil relationships. The *Origin* received an effective imprimatur in 1884 when Frederick Temple (soon to become Archbishop of Canterbury) declared "[God] did not make the things, we may say; no, but He made them make themselves". Ironically in the light of future history, Darwin's ideas were assimilated more readily by conservative theologians than by liberals, apparently because of the stronger doctrine of providence of the former. Many of the authors of *The Fundamentals*, a series of booklets produced between 1910 and 1915 to expound the "fundamental beliefs" of Protestant theology and which have led to the word "fundamentalism" entering the language, were sympathetic to evolution. Princeton theologian B. B. Warfield, a passionate advocate of the inerrancy of the Bible, argued that evolution could provide a tenable "theory of the method of divine providence in the creation of mankind".

This is not the place to describe the scientific debates about evolution. There have never been any serious doubts among scientists since Darwin that all life is descended from one (or very few) original forms. On the other hand, Darwin's proposal that the mechanism whereby adaptation comes about by natural selection has been more contentious; it did not fit easily with conventional notions of progress or improvement. Even worse, the rediscovery of Mendel's results in 1900 and the subsequent explosion of the science of genetics seemed to show that the physical basis of heredity could not be the basis of the variation expected by Darwinism. Mutations studied in the laboratory tended to have a large effect, to be deleterious, and to be inherited as recessive traits. The Darwinian expectation was that evolution progressed through small steps produced by favourable variants. In a book surveying the state of evolutionary biology published in 1907 for the Jubilee of the *Origin*, Vernon Kellogg referred to "the deathbed of Darwinism".

Into this apparent void, an extravagance of speculative theories poured – more metaphysical than scientific: Berg's *Nomogenesis*, Willis's *Age and Area*, Smuts's *Holism*, Driesch's **entelechy**, Osborn's **aristogenesis** and **orthogenesis**. Invention was rife. A common feature was some form of inner progressionist urge or *élan vital*.

Jean Baptiste Lamarck (1744–1829)

Right: The Galapagos Islands
Below: The Islands are the result of volcanic action under the surface

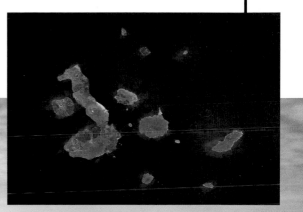

A book *L'Evolution Créatrice* (1907) by a French philosopher, Henri Bergson, was particularly influential in this respect. Unfortunately three standard and still-read histories of biology (by Nordenskiöld, Rádl, and Singer) were written during this time of "Darwinian eclipse", perpetuating the idea that evolutionary theory is an illogical mess and that Darwinism is effectively redundant. This conclusion is emphatically wrong. The work of R. A. Fisher, J. B .S. Haldane, and Sewall Wright in the 1920s brought together genetics, palaeontology, and comparative studies into a "neo-Darwinian synthesis"; this rehabilitated Darwin's original thesis and has proved resilient in the face of further discoveries – notably challenges produced by the "molecular revolution" of the 1960s and 1970s. There are ongoing and proper debates about the ways in which evolutionary change has come about, although there is little dissension that by far the most important mechanism of adaptation is natural selection.

THEOLOGICAL ISSUES ABOUT EVOLUTION

There are three issues for Christians about evolution:

1. Naturalism

A recurring unease on the part of Christians when thinking about evolution as understood by scientists is that it seems to have no place for God; it can be seen to operate entirely by scientifically investigable processes. The Divine Watchmaker could indeed be reduced to a blind watchmaker. In fact, this is no different from the situation with almost all parts of life – answers to prayer, miracles, guidance. Christians do not expect to find indisputable signs of divine involvement, but by faith they accept that God is at work. How God should be envisaged as operating in the world is discussed elsewhere (see p. 55). There is no problem here specific to evolution, but it is an area which repeatedly leads to religious believers proposing some form of metaphysical agencies to "explain" certain stages (in contrast to others) in the whole process – from unease among Darwin's contemporaries to the overt antagonism towards evolution of proponents of Intelligent Design, leading to the notion that "design" is required to supplement "natural processes" (see p. 184).

2. Chance

A common criticism of natural selection (as distinct from evolution itself) is that it is dependent on randomly occurring mutation. However, this criticism misunderstands the evolutionary process. Darwinian evolution does not depend on chance if we consider the overall process: adaptation results from the selection of advantageous variants, and this is a deterministic process. The accusation of chance arises because the origin of inherited variation is random, depending on mutation or, much more significantly in sexual organisms, on the **phenotypic** expression of new variants through recombination. While it is true that adaptation relates to survival and the possibility of gene transmission rather than long-term purpose, it is wrong to claim that "Darwinian evolution" is an entirely fortuitous process. Indeed the range of viable options for any trait is so limited that whenever variants appear and are subject to selection, successive changes over time may lead to the appearance of progress. Natural selection is the only known scientific mechanism which fits organisms to their environment.

3. Waste and suffering

A major stumbling-block for Darwin himself was animal suffering. He wrote to Asa Gray, Professor of Botany at Harvard, who was a Christian, "I own that I cannot see, as plainly as others do & as I shd wish to do, evidence of design & beneficence on all sides of us. There seems to me too much misery in the world. I cannot persuade myself that a beneficent & omnipotent God would have designedly created the Ichneumonidæ [parasitic insects] with the express intention of their feeding within the living bodies of caterpillars, or that a cat should play with mice."

God declared his creation to be "Good… very good". However, that was his judgment, not ours (Isaiah 55:8); it referred to his own assessment of his achievement, and did not refer to a final state of perfection. We can be confident of this, because creation was explicitly committed to us to till and nurture it (Genesis 2:15). For some, the widespread occurrence of conflict and death in the natural world mars God's work and is seen as the direct consequence of God's curse on Adam and Eve following their disobedience as recorded in Genesis 3. This explanation fails as soon as it is accepted that there were many millions of years of life on Earth before the appearance of humankind, and these years inevitably included death on a large scale. There are many fossils of animals which lived long before humans appeared but who had disease (such as dinosaurs with rheumatic joints). No changes in the fossil record have been detected at the time humans appeared which can be attributed to sin. The commonest explanation of animal disease is that it is an inevitable consequence of the way that the natural world works. Mutations are necessary to produce the wonderful variety of the world, but they may also produce disease. It is worth noting that pain is a positive protective mechanism. If we did not feel pain, we would expose ourselves to all sorts of hazards.

Adam and Eve were not themselves cursed, but their disobedience had consequences for them both (that childbirth will be painful and that "love and cherishing" will become "desire and domination"). The serpent was cursed and condemned, but the other "curses" are manifestations of a failure of relationship, describing human existence without God. The couple hide to escape from God, the blessing of communion becomes fear, and work becomes toil. The condemnations of Genesis 3 reflect a disjointedness in creation, which Paul links to Adam's sin, calling it "frustration" (Romans 8:20). The result has been described as the discord produced by an orchestra when it has no conductor to direct it. The consequences of the "fall" arise because of the break in relation between humanity and its creator. The Psalms sing of God's creation as we now have it, and the awesome beauty of creation celebrated in the concluding chapters of Job is a warning against any interpretation that the natural world itself was changed.

It has been argued that all suffering is somehow redemptive. After all, Christ reconciled *all things* to the Father through the cross (Colossians 1:20), but such interpretations are not very compelling. It is difficult to escape the conclusion that physical death is an integral and inevitable part of the way that God has made creation. We should beware of overstressing death because of our own experience of it; certainly it is improper to extrapolate our experience to the non-human creation. The Book of Job ends with God reminding the suffering Job that he must not put his puny human interpretation on the facts of creation. It is God who gives the lions their prey (Psalm 104:21). Apocalyptic passages such as those describing wolves lying down with lambs or lions eating straw (Isaiah 11:6; 65:25) must be interpreted carefully; Daniel 7 and Revelation 12 describe God's work, but there are few who would interpret passages like these literally. The essential fact for the Christian is that Christ on the cross provided an answer to death and suffering, not a reason for it.

Adam and Eve and the Serpent, by Andrea Mantegna (1431–1506)

HUMAN EVOLUTION

The biggest evolutionary challenge for Christians concerns human evolution. Anxious to minimize controversy, Darwin steered clear of this in the *Origin*. He included only one mention of the subject, "I see open fields for far more important researches… Much light will be thrown on the origin of man and his history". However, he could not ignore the topic altogether, and 14 years after the *Origin* appeared, he returned to it with *The Descent of Man*.

Darwin knew almost nothing about human fossils. The first Neanderthal fossils were only described in 1856. But since that time, many putative hominoid and hominid fossils have been discovered, to the extent that it is fair to claim that *Homo* has a better fossil record than almost any other genus. Unfortunately the credibility of the record has been marred in popular understanding by over-imaginative reconstruction of particular finds, notably the Piltdown debacle, but also by many fanciful attempts to portray human ancestors as either hulking brutes or mere variants of modern individuals. The image of human fossil history for many is probably the much-reproduced frontispiece of T. H. Huxley's book *Man's Place in Nature* (1863), showing a parade of modern skeletons from a gibbon, through a series of stooping apes, to an upright man ("A grim and grotesque procession" as Darwin's critic, the 8th Duke of Argyll called it). Notwithstanding and recognizing many uncertainties, there is now general agreement among specialists that *Homo* originated from an *Australopithecus* stock in Africa, with the first fossils classified in the genus *Homo* occurring between 2.0 and 1.6 million years ago; they are named *Homo habilis*. About 1.8 million years ago, a new form of *Homo* appeared in eastern Africa, *H. erectus*. It persisted in Africa for more than a million years, but also spread out of

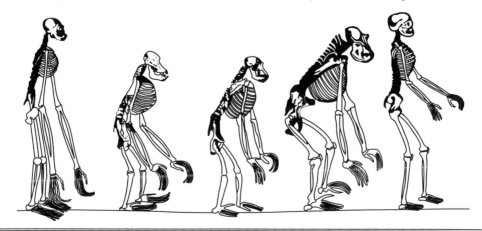

The skeletons of apes (gibbon, orangutan, chimpanzee, gorilla, and human) as illustrated by T. H. Huxley in his book *Man's Place in Nature*. All the species share a common ancestry, but it is incorrect to assume that these adult forms represent an evolutionary sequence.

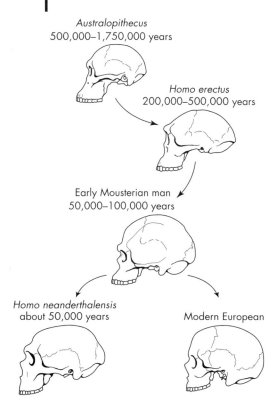

Australopithecus
500,000–1,750,000 years

Homo erectus
200,000–500,000 years

Early Mousterian man
50,000–100,000 years

Homo neanderthalensis
about 50,000 years

Modern European

Africa into Asia. It had a brain size (or more strictly, cranial volume) of 800–900 ml, about a third greater than *H. habilis* and a less projecting face. From 200,000 years ago, the earliest fossils regarded as anatomically modern humans (brain c. 1100–1300 ml) began to occur in Africa, and then much later in other parts of the world after the "great trek" out of Africa that is thought to have occurred around 60,000 years ago. The Neanderthals appeared c. 200,000 years ago in Europe and south-west Asia. They are now regarded as a sub-species distinct from *H. sapiens*, and coexisted with the latter until disappearing 30,000 to 40,000 years ago.

Developments in molecular biology have driven the recognition of our genetic closeness to the other primates. An earlier calculation that humans and chimps share 98.4 per cent of their genes has been refined to 96 per cent now that both genomes have been sequenced. About 35 million single-nucleotide changes (the "letters" of the "genetic alphabet") separate us from our nearest living relatives, representing about 1 per cent of the genome. The proteins directly coded by genes are highly conserved between chimps and humans: 29 per cent are identical and the rest differ by only two amino acids on average. We have one less pair of chromosomes than all other apes (23 pairs instead of 24), but the difference is a result of simple end-to-end fusion between two separate elements of the ape chromosome set.

Further evidence of a common descent comes from the study of ancient repetitive elements (AREs), which arise from nucleotide sequences that are copied and inserted into other parts of the genome, usually without functional consequences. Mammalian genomes contain large numbers of AREs; they make up almost half the human genome. Interestingly, they often occur in precisely corresponding places in the mouse, chimpanzee, and human genomes, which is what one would predict if mice, chimpanzees, and humans share common ancestry. In view of the fact that AREs are mostly non-functional and are inserted more or less randomly, it is virtually impossible to devise alternative explanations.

Skulls of some of the putative ancestors of modern humans.

The Rift Valley, which runs for many miles across eastern Africa, has yielded many fossil hominid skeletons.

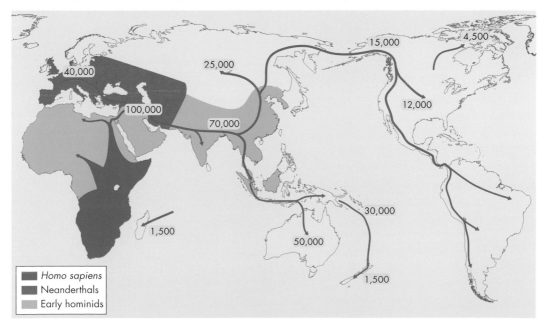

Map showing the timing and extent of the movements of the early humans from an origin in east Africa. The numbers show the time when different parts of the world were colonized.

"Jumping genes" multiply in the genomes of all organisms; humans are no exception. This diagram shows the times when one sort of such genes (Alu inserts) were incorporated into the genomes of apes; the numbers indicate the number of genes at each stage. Data of this nature enable the relationships of different groups to be ascertained.

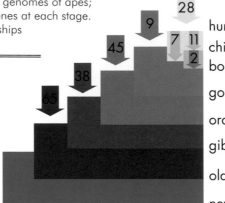

Retroviral insertions provide yet another argument for the common ancestry of the great apes and humans. Retroviruses convert their RNA genomes into DNA, which becomes stably integrated in the DNA of a host cell. When the infected cell is a germ cell (egg or sperm) the retroviral DNA may be passed on to the offspring and become a permanent part of their genome, in which case it is called an *endogenous retroviral insertion*. These can be recognized in descendants of the host cell and can be used as markers to trace ancestry as is shown in the diagram above. There are abundant similar data, providing very strong evidence for the common ancestry of humans and apes, as well as confirming in considerable detail the "family" or phylogenetic tree, drawn up on the basis of genetic (that is, DNA) resemblances.

Even though the resemblance between the human and chimpanzee genomes is striking, the two species are obviously very different. Many of the distinctive human features (brain size, hairlessness, prolonged adolescence) can be attributed to a change in development rate (*neoteny*) in the human line, which could be genetically simple – perhaps the result of mutation in a single (or very few) genes. Several studies have brought to light genes that differ between us and chimpanzees; some of these seem to be particularly involved in brain development.

One trait which is universally accepted as highly important in humans is the complexity of language – without denying the sophistication and complexity of communication in many non-human groups. A major difference between ape and human is not the ability simply to make meaningful sounds, but to control those sounds precisely. A possibly significant change in the human line is in a gene called *FOXP2 (Forkhead box P2)*, which codes for a protein which acts to control genes affecting the development of grammar, speech production, non-verbal intelligence, and the regulation of movement of the mouth and face, plus cerebellar development. This gene is highly conserved: mice and non-human primates differ in only one out of its 715 amino acids, whereas the gene is identical in humans and Neanderthals. Intriguingly, two nucleotide changes on the long arm of chromosome 7 (the same section as involved in the determination of some autism) carried by 15 out of 31 individuals in three generations of a human family produced a complex of symptoms, including an inability to speak intelligibly. Interestingly, *FOXP2* is also implicated in sound communication in other species including mice and songbirds. Studies on lower animals indicate that the *FOXP2* protein occurs in many brain regions and even in tissues outside the brain such as lung and gut

A thorough understanding of the evolution of linguistic abilities will take many further decades of research, and the same is true of the inheritance of altruistic behaviour. Darwin did not know how selection might have acted to produce such self-sacrificing cooperation. He wrote in the *Descent of Man*, "He who was ready to sacrifice his life, as many a savage has been, rather than betray his colleagues, would often leave no offspring to inherit his noble nature". One answer to this problem would be if a group rather than an individual is the target of selection, but such a process seems highly improbable from all that we know about biological fitness and gene transmission. It was left to J. B. S. Haldane to show a possible way forward, pointing out that if individual unselfishness (even to the extent of self-sacrifice) had an inherited basis and helped near relatives, then "altruistic genes" could be selected and would spread within families as a result. In this way, there could be situations where cooperation (or unselfishness) is an advantage to a group of individuals, even if particular individuals are disadvantaged. Haldane's argument was formalized in 1964 by W.D. Hamilton as "inclusive fitness", often called nowadays "kin selection"; it was popularized with broader applications by E. O. Wilson as "sociobiology".

Sociobiological ideas have been extremely important in biology, and have stimulated an immense amount of research. They have also provoked much dissent, particularly as they apply to mammals (especially humankind) because of the implication that behavioural choices are programmed (or determined) by genes. In this respect, it is important to emphasize the big difference between animal cooperation, or biological altruism as it is sometimes called, and human altruism of the kind described by the New Testament Greek word *agapē*, which involves actions of unmerited love seeking no reward.

Are the differences between human and apes merely ones of degree or is there a real qualitative difference? This is probably unanswerable from a scientific point of view, but

J. B. S. Haldane, one of the originators of the "neo-Mendelian synthesis"; he pioneered many developments in evolutionary biology, including the possibility that altruism could evolve.

theologically there is a simple solution: to regard the biological species *Homo sapiens*, descended from a primitive simian stock and related to living apes, as having been transformed by God at some time in history into *Homo divinus*, biologically unchanged but spiritually distinct. There is no reason to insist that this event took place at the same time as the emergence of the biological form we call *H. sapiens*. Genesis 1:27 describes the creation of humankind as a *bārā* event, a specific act of God, characterized by "being made in the image of God", which would not in itself involve a genetic or anatomical change in an existing creature. This event does not imply that something was added to human existence; rather it should be seen to mean that humans have become such that their very existence is intended to be their relationship to God. In the creation accounts in Genesis, only "the man" is addressed directly by God (Genesis 1:28).

Did humanness (that is, the acquisition of the *imago Dei*) emerge gradually or was it an instantaneous transformation by God? Does the distinction matter? Genesis 1 uses two different Hebrew words to describe God's creative work: *yasah*, which has the sense of modelling from previous material, as a potter moulds clay, and *bārā*, which is used to refer to the creation of matter (v. 1), the great sea monsters (v. 21), and humankind (v. 26), and which is always used in the Bible to refer to God's creative activity. It would be dangerous to build too much on this use of words. Both refer to a divine work, and there is no clear demarcation in the Bible between God's works in nature and his works in history; he is sovereign in both. But the meaning is indisputable. Humankind in his or her entirety is made as a creature in God's image. The creation of humankind is something far different in the biblical text from the creation of the rest of the world.

WAS ADAM AN INDIVIDUAL?

Did God make a single person (or pair) in his image, or did his image appear in a group of individuals? There are five possibilities:

- It could be that the Genesis text describing Adam (or "the man": the proper name Adam without the Hebrew definite article first appears in Genesis 4:25) is intended to be entirely theological, with no connection between the theological and biological narratives.

- Possibly a spiritual awareness emerged gradually as the human lineage developed, with the early chapters of Genesis retelling this process in a form that could be understood in the Middle Eastern culture of ancient Israel.

- Perhaps God in his grace chose a couple (or even a small group) of Neolithic farmers and revealed himself to them in a special way. Being an anatomically modern human was necessary but not sufficient for the special relationship willed by God. This transformation changed the biological species *Homo sapiens* into *H. divinus*, one capable of relationship with God.

- A watered-down version of Paley's deism is to postulate that God created progressively, intervening miraculously at various stages. This idea of progressive or episodic creationism is espoused by those who accept the great age of the Earth but seek to introduce a creator acting in special ways during the process.

- Those who hold to a "young Earth" and treat the Genesis account as literal history hold to a historic Adam with no biological relationship with any other form.

One complication in this debate is that the word translated "Adam" may be taken to mean either a single person or collective humanity. Most interpreters understand it to mean the latter, but the denial of a "historic Adam" is unacceptable to many. Indeed, contemporary "creationism" stems from the cry "No Adam, no Fall; no Fall, no Atonement; no Atonement, no Saviour", a rationale originally raised by an English atheist, Robert Blatchford. This theological debate about Adam needs to be recognized as entirely separate from the scientific debates about Darwinism – a fact which goes a long way to explaining the bewilderment and expressions of irrelevance from most scientists when challenged about evolution. But the exegetical need for a historic Adam is demanded by many theologians. Conservative commentators point out that the "one man" (Adam) is critical in Paul's argument in Romans 5. Twelve times in Romans 5:12–19 the word *one* appears; repeatedly Paul refers to the one man Adam (and to one sin of that one man) and opposes to him (and it) the one man Jesus Christ (and his unique act of grace). The one man and his sin and the one Saviour and his salvation seem inseparable in Paul's thought. John Stott argued strongly for it: "Scripture clearly intends us to accept their [Adam and Eve's] historicity as the original human pair: the biblical genealogies trace the human race back to Adam, Jesus himself taught that 'at the beginning the Creator made them male and female' and then instituted marriage, Paul told the Athenian philosophers that God had made every nation from 'one man', and in particular, Paul's carefully constructed analogy between Adam and Christ depends for its validity on the equal historicity of both." (It has to be recognized, however, that the word "man" does not appear in the Greek text of Acts 17:26.)

The assumption that a "historical Adam" is scientifically incredible and dependent on a naive literalism is actually the result of a confusion about the nature of humanness in relation to the creator. The "*imago*" which differentiates humankind from all

The Bible consistently refers to the unity of humankind and our common status as sinners in terms of solidarity rather than heredity. The one possible exception to this is Genesis 3:20, where the woman is described as "the mother of all the living". However, "Eve" means "life", and it seems likely that this description of her is a reiteration of the promise of salvation through her (Genesis 3:15) and not an anthropological statement.

Ancient texts contain numerous references to humans being created out of a variety of materials, including the tears of a god (Egypt), blood of a god (Atrahasis), and, most commonly, clay (Mesopotamia). Only in Genesis are humans treated as individuals.

In Genesis 2:18–24 we are told that God created woman out of the side of "the man" to be a partner and counterpart, described in Matthew Henry's often quoted *Commentary*, "not from the feet to be trampled on or from the head to be his lord". The Hebrew text describes the woman as literally, "a help opposite him". The conservative commentator Gordon Wenham has commented on Genesis 2:21–25: "the whole account of woman's creation has a poetic flavor: it is certainly mistaken to read it as an account of a clinical operation or an attempt to explain some feature of man's anatomy. Rather, it brilliantly depicts the relation of man and wife... Here the ideal of marriage as it was understood in ancient Israel is being portrayed, a relationship characterized by harmony and intimacy between the partners."

The creation of Eve from the rib of the sleeping Adam, part of the fresco painted by Michelangelo on the Sistine Chapel ceiling.

other animals (Genesis 1:26, 27) is as intrinsic to humanness as eye colour or memory, but it is wrong to assume that it is inherited or transmitted like a Mendelian trait. If it was initially conferred on an individual, there is no reason why it should not spread by divine fiat to all other members of *Homo sapiens* alive at the time; in this sense, Adam would be the federal head of humanity, and all men and women born after him would be his spiritual descendants.

Humankind-made-in-the-image-of-God (*Homo divinus*) is a creature in relationship with God. Sin may disrupt this relationship but does not destroy it, just as a child of human parents remains their child even if it becomes alienated from them. Although the creative acts of God are described throughout Genesis 1 as divinely driven processes ("Let there be…"), in Genesis 1:26 (only) the text is explicitly personal: "Let us make human beings…"; in verse 29 God addresses the newly created humans as "you". The "image of God" means that we are sufficiently like God that we can have an intimate relationship with him: we are told that God walks in the garden with Adam and Eve, and he speaks to them personally and in a different way to the rest of creation. The woman was created as an equal partner to Adam because "it was not good for the man to be alone".

HISTORIC FALL?

A common understanding of the story of the "fall" (a term not used in the Bible) described in Genesis is that the "temptation story" in Genesis 3 is merely a way of describing the advent of self-awareness; the eating of the fruit which led to "the opening of the eyes" of our first parents is taken to refer to the development of conscience and the possibility of moral choice. In these terms, the "fall" becomes an upward leap into true humanness rather than a descent into moral turpitude. Julian Huxley used to speak of us of having moved from the biological phase of evolution into what he called the "psychosocial phase"; C. H. Waddington described it as the "sociogenetic phase". Teilhard de Chardin's idea of progress towards "omega point" expresses a similar notion.

Social Darwinians inspired by Darwin's contemporary, Herbert Spencer, thought that they had discerned a purpose in the development of life, and that tended towards the survival of the fittest. Weaklings fell by the wayside as they failed to adapt to changing conditions and the environment; only the strong survived. Spencer's ideas were welcomed by more cold-blooded manufacturers as justifying ruthlessness toward their workers. In recent times, given our moral concern for the weaker and helpless, evolutionary ethicists suggest that the goal and purpose of evolution may

Herbert Spencer (1820–1903)

be rather "the intensification of consciousness". Biologists like Stephen Gould and Steve Jones argue that we have now evolved to the point that we are able to choose our own goals and direct life towards fulfilling them. Concern for the needy, poor, and sick can replace the traditional drive for the powerful to succeed, often at the expense or obliteration of those less fortunate. It is almost trite to point out that there is no evidence whatsoever that we are improving morally in any respect.

But the real problem of positing an "upward fall" is the damage it does to the biblical metanarrative. The most often repeated description of Christ's accomplishment in redemption is that he "delivered us from death" ("You once were dead because of your sins and wickedness… but God brought us to life with Christ when we were dead because of our sins", Ephesians 2:1, 5; "Although you were dead because of your sins… he has brought you to life with Christ", Colossians 2:13; "We know we have crossed over from death to life", 1 John 3:14; it is implicit in Jesus' conversation with Nicodemus about being "born again" recorded in John 3:1–14). In the context, "death" cannot be physical death (Adam and Eve had all their children after being expelled from the garden), nor can it be simply a figure of speech (as in the Parable of the Prodigal Son: "My son was dead"); it must mean spiritual death in the sense of being separated from God – the fate Adam and Eve suffered when they were banished from Eden.

The language and imagery of "death" might imply that physical and spiritual death are the same, but the biblical text makes some clear distinctions. The death from which Christ saved us is not simply spiritual insensitivity or blindness, nor is it merely a liability to physical mortality; it is a severance of relationship with God, the source of life. Interestingly William Buckland suggested as early as 1837 in his Bridgewater Treatise that human death ought to be distinguished from animal (biological) death. The deciding factor for him was the vast numbers of previously living organisms represented only by fossils. Distinguishing between biological and spiritual death could be regarded as importing a dualism into humanness, but it is a very weak version of dualism; in no way does it represent "body" and "soul" as separate entities as in the classical dualism of Plato or Descartes. There is a dualism in Paul's thought, but it is one between filial obedience and disobedience. This gives independent support to the understanding of death as a lack of relationship between us and God; it is the broken relationship which spells death.

The most relevant New Testament commentary on the consequences of "the fall" described in Genesis 3 is in Romans 8:19–22, where the created universe is said to have been "made subject to frustration" and to be "groaning as if in the pangs of childbirth". It is a difficult passage. The starting point is the recognition that the "fall" is not primarily about disease and disaster, nor about the dawn of self-awareness. This reinforces the interpretation that it is a way of describing the fracture in relationship between God and the human creature made in his image. The rupture means that we rattle around in our space, as it were, producing disorder within ourselves, with our neighbours, and with our environment (human and non-human). Paul's argument is that this discord will continue until our relationship with God is restored and we become "at peace with God through our Lord Jesus who has given us access to the grace in which we now live; and we exult in the divine glory which is to be ours" (Romans 5:1, 2) – words which condition and explain the state of nature which Paul uses later in the same section of Romans (8:19–21).

Adam and Eve expelled from Paradise

From beginning to end, the Bible speaks of our interdependence with the rest of creation. Sometimes we are given direct commands about how we should deal with it, as when we are told to "have dominion"; in other places, the instructions are implicit (recognizing the perils of a journey, the care needed for a farm or a flock of animals, the mastery we may expect over wild animals or fierce weather). We are told that sin led to Noah's flood and also to drought (Leviticus 26; Deuteronomy 28); the food laws regulated hunting; a very positive attitude to creation is expressed in the Wisdom Literature. Scientifically, we are learning more and more how much we depend upon "creation's [nature's] services". We cannot avoid interacting with creation; we are a part of it as well as apart from it. But running through the Bible is a parallel theme: that this is God's world, that he has made a covenant with us which he has promised to uphold, and that both creation and ourselves were reconciled to God by Christ's death on the cross.

CREATION CARE

For many Christians this world is little more than a preparation for our personal eternity. This should not be so. We are called to care for creation. The very first commandment given to our first parents was to "have dominion" over the rest of creation. This command is often taken as justifying unrestrained human plunder of the natural world. But this interpretation is wrong: the word translated "dominion" certainly implies "kingly rule", but the Hebrew model of kingship was of a servant (Psalm 72) not an oriental despot. Moreover the command was given in the context of humanity "made in God's image", which implies we are made to exercise this same kingship.

As long as we refuse to accept our responsibility for creation care, so long is the world of nature frustrated and dislocated. It does not seem too far-fetched to see Adam's failure as at root a failure of stewardship, violating the very first command to the human race and hence ignoring the purpose for which we were placed on earth. At one level, eating the forbidden fruit was simple disobedience, but its significance was treating God as unnecessary and irrelevant. Thus, for Christians, it is only when we are truly fitting into our proper place as children in relation to the Father that this dislocation will be reduced. The possibility of this is, of course, the gospel: we are assured that God, through Christ, has "reconciled *all things* to himself, making peace through the shedding of his blood on the cross" (Colossians 1:20). This is where ecology and exegesis come together and indicate that the earth's curse is not a change in ecological law, but a massive failure by what a biologist would call a "keystone species" – in this case, the human species.

ENVIRONMENTAL THEOLOGY

There is a common assumption that the world's resources are effectively inexhaustible, that God always provides everything needful for humankind. This is wrong: China alone has had around 2,000 famines in the last 2,000 years; overpopulation and land scarcity have led to successive mass population movements – the Beaker Folk, Teutons, Vikings, and New World colonizers all spilled from the western seaboard of Europe. Environmental mismanagement has repeatedly produced disastrous consequences for humans: the early Polynesian population of New Zealand depended on large flightless moa for food, but managed to drive them to extinction within 600 years; introduction of rabbits to Australia, mongooses to Hawaii, and grey squirrels to Britain have all caused major ecological problems; over-extension of irrigation was a major factor in the collapse of the ancient Babylonian empire; Sicily was once the granary of Italy but less and less corn is grown there as the soil deteriorated under excessive cultivation and goat browsing; and the ecological implosion of Easter Island through human ill-treatment is well documented.

The assumption that God will provide unconditionally for humans is unfounded: the Bible is explicit that "the earth and everything in it belongs to the Lord" (Psalm 24:1; 89:11) and, crucially, that he requires us to care for them (Genesis 2:15), a relationship usually described as "stewardship". Although aspects of stewardship have been criticized on the grounds that it exalts human endeavour, the notion that we are responsible for our use of the earth's resources is robust and remains strong, whether we call it stewardship, trusteeship, co-creatorship, guardianing, or simply creation care. The Old Testament in particular is full of examples and warnings about environmental

mismanagement through poor stewardship, from either failure or neglect (such as Leviticus 18:25, 28; 25:2–6; Deuteronomy 29:22–25; Isaiah 24:4–6; Jeremiah 12:10, 11).

The mistake in assuming infinite divine provision is failing to distinguish between the gracious providence of God ("He cares even for the birds and flowers, and the winds and waves obey him", Matthew 6:25–34; 8:27) and his expectations of us (Genesis 1:28). John Calvin commented on Genesis 2:15, "that the custody of the garden was given in charge to Adam to show that we possess the things that God has committed to our hands, *on the condition that* being content with a frugal and moderate use of them, we should take care of what shall remain." He goes on to speak of what we have come to call "sustainability":

> *Let him who possesses a field so partake of its yearly fruits that he may not suffer the ground to be injured by his negligence; but let him endeavour to hand it down to posterity as he received it, or even better cultivated… Let every one regard himself as the steward of God in all things he possesses. Then he will neither conduct himself dissolutely nor corrupt by abuse those things which God requires to be preserved.*

For the author of Deuteronomy, the Promised Land in which the Israelites are told they will lack nothing (Deuteronomy 8:7–10) is not about the existence or prosperity of its inhabitants, but reflects an indissoluble partnership between land and Yahweh – never only with Yahweh as to live only in intense obedience, never only with land as though simply to possess and manage. This produced a lasting tension and dynamic for Israel: how to hold together two traditions – the Mosaic understanding which stressed obedience to Yahweh in ways which minimized the importance of the land, and the Davidic interpretation which stressed the land and neglected the Torah.

The tension between worshipping God and caring for the land will probably never go away. At times it has had disastrous results, as when the Puritans who fled to North America saw themselves as entering a Promised Land which had to be tamed and cleansed from the native "Amalekites", just as God commanded the Israelites to subdue the wilderness of Israel. The lack of concern for the environment has progressively

intensified with the secularization of society. Land has increasingly become a resource or commodity, rather than a gift or trust.

Notwithstanding, creation care often proceeds without any acknowledgment of the Creator. In this case, environmental concerns are almost always utilitarian, driven negatively by danger rather than positively by respect. In 1964, Rachel Carson's *Silent Spring* was a major wakeup call to gratuitously ignoring natural processes. A computer simulation carried out at the Massachusetts Institute of Technology and published in 1972 as *The Limits to Growth*, showed that the economic and industrial systems of developed countries would collapse in about the year 2100 unless birth and death rates equalized and capital investment matched capital depreciation

In the 1960s the debate was between proponents of "zero population growth" and those who saw salvation coming from better and more efficiently managed resources. The *Limits* study drew attention to the danger of ignoring human impact; our survival depends ultimately on our rate of use of resources and whether the resources we use are renewable or not. It was published at the same time as the first major international conference on the environment, the UN Conference on the Human Environment, held in Stockholm (1972). The Stockholm Conference is generally credited with introducing the concept of sustainability into general discourse. It declared, "A point has been reached in history when we must shape our actions throughout the world with a more prudent care for their environmental consequences. Through ignorance or indifference we can do massive and irreversible harm to the earthly environment on which our life and well-being depend." A basic concept was "development without destruction".

The Stockholm Conference stimulated a tremendous amount of concern and support for development in low-income countries, but promoted a division between "development" and "environmental protection". Environmental care was regarded as a much lower priority than attacking poverty; indeed, it was commonly regarded as a hindrance to development. In 1980, a World Conservation Strategy (WCS) was produced as a counter to these assumptions.

United Nations Conference on the Human Environment, held in Stockholm, Sweden, in 1972

The WCS had three explicit aims:

- To maintain essential ecological processes and life-support systems;
- To preserve genetic diversity; and, significantly
- To ensure the *sustainable* utilization of species and ecosystems.

The Strategy focused firmly on people: "Humanity's relationship with the biosphere (the thin covering of the planet that contains and sustains life) will continue to deteriorate until a new international economic order is achieved, a new environmental ethic adopted, human populations stabilize, and sustainable modes of development become the rule rather than the exception". Sustainability entered the international vocabulary. The revised WCS (*Caring for the Earth*, 1991) redefined "sustainable development" as "improving the quality of human life while living within the carrying capacity of supporting ecosystems".

Importantly *Caring for the Earth* called for "a world ethic for living sustainably", that everyone should "share fairly the benefits and costs of resource use, among different communities and interest groups, among regions that are poor and those that are affluent, and between present and future generations. Each generation should leave to the future a world that is at least as diverse and productive as the one it inherited. Development of one society or generation should not limit the opportunities of other societies or generations".

We can ignore our dependence on the natural world, but we cannot divorce ourselves from it. Unless we have oxygen, water, and food we are doomed. A massive Millennium Ecosystem Assessment (2005) report identified the essential constituents of human well-being as access to the basic materials for a worthwhile life (such as food, shelter, and clothing), sound health, good social relations, security, freedom of choice and action. It focused on four categories of "ecosystem services":

- *provisioning services*, such as food, water, timber, fibre;
- *regulating services*, affecting climate, flood control, disease, waste, and water quality;
- *cultural services*, providing recreation, aesthetic and spiritual benefits;
- *supporting services*, such as soil formation, photosynthesis, and nutrient cycling.

A very crude calculation suggested that the world's ecosystems contribute £20 million million every year to the world's sustenance, a sum roughly equal to twice the annual gross national product of all the nations of the globe.

How do we respond? The Christian need is to learn what God wants from us in our relationship to creation. The Bible is unequivocal that God has a job for his followers: to care for this world and nurture it as his agents (Genesis 2:15; Psalm 115:16). Humankind will be held accountable to him for its treatment of that entrusted to it (Matthew 25:14–30). For his part, God made an "everlasting covenant" to maintain "all living creatures" (Genesis 9:8–17), long before the covenant he made with Abraham and his descendants (Genesis 17:9). He led his covenant people into a "good land… where you will never suffer any scarcity of food to eat, nor want for anything…" (Deuteronomy 8:7–10). When Jesus spoke about not being anxious about tomorrow (Matthew 6:34), his stress was on God's overriding and controlling providence. In the same passage, he says God feeds birds and "clothes the grass". Throughout, the Bible has a greater emphasis on continuity of the present with the promised "New Heaven and Earth", than on discontinuity between the present and a time to come.

We must beware any interpretation which separates the two covenants; as already emphasized, Christ's death on the cross "reconciled *all things* to him [God] – *all things*, whether on earth or in heaven". In other words, salvation extends beyond humankind to all creation. For many, this world is little more than a preparation for our personal eternity. We are mere transients, and it does not matter how we treat this world ("This world is not my home, I'm just a-passing through" as an old Christian song has it). But this is a very deficient understanding of earth in relation to heaven; a proper Christian understanding of heaven is not "a place remote from the present world" but rather as "a dimension of *present* reality". Moreover, one thing Jesus repeats time and time again is that at some time in the future there will be a judgment and we will be called to account for our actions (see, for example, Luke 9:26; 10:14; 11:31, 32; 12:46; 13:28; 16:23; 19:27; 21:36).

This brings us back to Romans 8:19–22, which is the most explicit New Testament passage on what God intends to do with the cosmos. Paul's argument in Romans 5–8 (indeed in the whole of Romans 1–8) is that the renewal of God's covenant results in the renewal of God's creation. He argues similarly in 2 Corinthians 3–5. When he writes that "The universe itself is to be freed from the shackles of mortality and is to enter upon the glorious liberty of the children of God", he is completing an analogy with the exodus from Egypt and entry into the Promised Land that he has been developing in the preceding chapters; when God's people come through the waters of baptism (paralleling the passage through the Red Sea) and so are freed from sin (slavery, in parallel with Egypt), they are given, not the Torah as in Sinai, but the Spirit.

Paul's message is one of hope, just as the liberation of God's people from exile is inextricably linked by Isaiah with the rejoicing of all creation (Isaiah 55:12–13). This reading of the Bible is important, because it emphasizes the extraordinary providence (and sovereignty) of God and contrasts radically with ideas that the future of the world is built upon a sophisticated version of deism. The latter supposition (no more than speculation) is that creation continues as some sort of intrinsic unfolding. It is theologically seductive and has repeatedly surfaced in the past 100 years or so in philosophical speculation: in the *élan vital* of Henri Bergson, the **noogenesis** of Teilhard de Chardin, the panentheism of Hartshorne, Cobb, and Peacocke, Lovelock's Gaia, the "promise of nature" as advocated by John Haught, or "strong emergence" as proposed by Philip Clayton. The Victorian theologian, Aubrey Moore welcomed Darwinism because "under the disguise of a foe, it did the work of a friend". His argument was that early nineteenth-century deism had left God "throned in magnificent splendour in a remote corner of the universe… Science had pushed the deist's God farther and farther away [until] at the moment when it seemed as if he would be thrust out altogether, Darwinism appeared and… conferred upon philosophy and religion an inestimable benefit by showing that we must choose between two alternatives. Either God is everywhere present in nature or He is nowhere."

A rewarding approach seems to be to follow the long-standing tradition that God wrote two books: a book of words (the Bible) and a book of works (creation); they are explicit in Psalm 19 (pp. 57–58). The books have the same author but are written in very different languages and therefore have to be understood using entirely different approaches. Creation cannot tell us anything directly about salvation, but neither does the Bible tell us anything about the detail of normal living. This was the reason that Karl Barth (1886–1968), in particular, disparaged the study of the natural world value as irrelevant to theology. The study of the natural world is science, and importantly, any contradiction between the two books must be false. On the title page of the *Origin of Species*, Darwin quoted from Francis Bacon, "Let no man think or maintain that he can search too far or be too well studied in the book of God's words or in the book of God's works; but rather let men endeavour an endless proficiency in both." Bacon himself did much to practise what he preached, his writings motivating many of the founders of the Royal Society in the seventeenth century.

The Bible teaches that God has put us in this world to care for it on his behalf. Thus for Christians, our purpose in this life is to praise our Creator and Sustainer with our lips and lives, but also in association with all the rest of creation (Psalm 148). God sent his Son to save the *cosmos* (John 3:16). The fact that we are made in God's image does make a difference. God's Two Books should be read together (Psalm 19).

TELEOLOGY

"Teleology" is an eighteenth-century term referring to the ways in which sometimes we explain things not just in terms of prior (efficient) causes but also in terms of ends or purposes, or what are often known as "final causes". Thus, faced with a strip of steel sharpened on one edge, with a handle, we can ask about the manufacture, but also about its purpose. It is a knife, and the end is that of cutting meat and potatoes. Note that there is an asymmetry between efficient and final causes. Something always has an efficient cause, in the sense that such a cause must have existed. You cannot have a knife without someone in a place like Sheffield getting the steel and sharpening the edge. But although the knife has a final cause, cutting, it may well be that that end is never realized. Perhaps after manufacture the firm went bankrupt and all of the stock was destroyed.

It was the Ancient Greeks who first thought seriously about teleology, and they saw it as important in two areas, both of which are matters of great interest still today. Socrates (469–399 BC) argued through his student Plato, and particularly in the dialogues the Phaedo and the Timaeus, that looking at the world, we see that efficient causes only give part of the story. If we want to understand something like the existence of fingernails we have to understand how they are made but also what purpose they serve. Why do we have fingernails? For Socrates and Plato, answering this question led to the famous "argument from design" (for the existence of God). Things show order and purpose; such order and purpose cannot have come about through blind law; hence there must be an organizer or designer, namely God.

Plato's student Aristotle picked up on this, but whereas for Socrates and Plato the design took us straight into theology and a God – we have a kind of "external" teleology where order is imposed from outside – Aristotle wanted to keep things strictly within the area of science without talk of outside influences – his was an "internal" teleology. Famously, he identified four kinds of causes – material causes (from which things are made), formal causes (the plan or pattern), efficient causes (the act of making), and final causes (the end or purpose). Often today we roll the first three together, and on occasion Aristotle does this himself. The key point is that for Aristotle the world itself has this kind of built-in drive towards ends. In some respects, therefore, Aristotle was what we today would call a "vitalist", believing in forces directed towards ends or purposes.

Christians, particularly Thomas Aquinas, took over the argument from design, believing that it bolstered belief in their God. Note that this is not quite the God of the Greeks, for the older thinkers believed that the Designer worked on already-existing material whereas the Christian God creates from nothing. Hence, it is fair to say that (even if successful) the design argument can only go part-way to establishing the God of the Old and New Testaments. But this was no small thing, and at the same time, Aristotle's approach to science became the norm and final causes were seen as an essential part of the story.

This last claim was challenged strongly in the Scientific Revolution; physicists and cosmologists maintained that their understandings of reality had no need of final-cause thinking. The philosopher Francis Bacon famously likened such arguers to Vestal Virgins, decorative but sterile. However in the realm of biology things were otherwise. Particularly with the development of the microscope, it was felt that the case for final causes was pressing. The chemist and philosopher Robert Boyle stressed this point. The intricate adaptations or contrivances that organisms have to survive and reproduce simply have to be understood in terms of ends. At the same time, this scientific claim was thought still to prove the existence of a deity, and so by the end of the seventeenth century one had the happy situation whereby the naturalist-parson John Ray could study nature and at the same time burnish the existence and power of his Lord and Creator.

Towards the end of the eighteenth century, the Scottish philosopher David Hume – once memorably described as God's greatest gift to the infidel – launched a withering attack on the design argument, arguing that not only did it suggest multiple gods and multiple universes, but that the existence of evil made the nature of the Designer God highly problematic. And yet at the end

Aristotle (384–322 BC)

of his *Dialogues Concerning Natural Religion*, Hume had to concede that there had to be something that caused the design-like nature of organisms. This was a conclusion very much endorsed by the German philosopher Immanuel Kant, who (in his *Critique of Judgment*) argued that we cannot understand the organic world without a teleological perspective and concluded that since teleology is not to be found in the physical world, "we will never have a Newton of the blade of grass." Meanwhile, in the realm of theology, Archdeacon William Paley felt so unmoved by Hume that at the beginning of the nineteenth century he laid out what is generally considered the definitive exposition of the argument from design.

Charles Darwin challenged all of this. He accepted fully the Aristotelian premise that the organic world shows final causes. He simply wanted to explain them in natural (that is non-vitalistic, non-theological) terms. This he did through his evolutionary mechanism of natural selection. More organisms are born than can survive and reproduce; the winners (the fitter) will have features not possessed by the losers; and over time this will lead to change – change in the direction of adaptation or contrivance. The ends or purposes of the eye and the ear are preserved and acknowledged.

Darwin saw (truly) that his argument did not disprove a Designer God, and indeed for some years after he discovered natural selection he himself went on believing in such a god, but he realized that no longer was the argument from design compelling. To paraphrase Richard Dawkins, after Darwin it was possible to be an intellectually fulfilled atheist. But is possibility the route to necessity? Should one now be an atheist, or at least an agnostic? Dawkins thinks one should, because natural selection is produced by a struggle for existence and this seems to be incompatible with a good god. Others are not so sure, and indeed today there are those from physics trying to resuscitate the design argument by appealing to the "fine-tuning" of the basic constants of the universe. Expectedly this "anthropic" approach has its own critics, some not thinking that the universe is that finely tuned and others suggesting that there might be many universes and it just so happens that ours is the one that works and supports life.

As it happens, many believers are happy with the implications of Darwin's science for the design argument. His contemporary, the Anglican-turned-Catholic John Henry Newman (1801–90), stressed that he believed in design because he believed in God rather than conversely. In any case, the design argument favours the God of the Greek philosophers – power and omniscience – not the God of Christianity – mercy and love. Others like Søren Kierkegaard (1813–55) welcomed the end of the argument because they thought proofs are corrosive of faith, which requires a leap into the absurd – a conclusion endorsed in the twentieth century by such thinkers as Karl Barth.

Note that however the external teleology plays out in theology, internal teleology flourishes as never before in the biological sciences. Vitalism is out, but the mode of understanding that makes reference to ends or purposes is alive and well. No less than for the Aristotelian, final causes are an essential part of the explanatory toolkit for the Darwinian. It is just that now, thanks to selection, they are thought completely natural, as much a product of law-line processes as anything else in the universe.

INTELLIGENT DESIGN

The idea of "intelligent design" has a long history. It is found among the Stoic philosophers (third century BC to second century AD) who pointed to the mechanisms of the world as evidence for a "divine intelligence". The phrase itself has been deployed for very different purposes over time. In 1874 the fiery Irish physicist John Tyndall used it when giving a lecture to the British Association for the Advancement of Science in Belfast, in which he extolled the views of the atomist Lucretius and the way that "he combats the notion that the constitution of nature has been in any way determined by *intelligent design*". Less than a decade later, James McCosh, Darwinian enthusiast and committed Christian, one of the early presidents of what was to become Princeton University, told his students that "the natural origin of species is not inconsistent with *intelligent design* in nature or with the existence of a personal Creator of the world".

In a general sense all Christians believe that the universe has in some sense been designed by God, that is, it has been brought into being with particular intentions

and purposes. Certainly the observed fine-tuning of the physical constants that render life possible in the universe is consistent with such a belief, and the complex structures of living things draw attention to the wisdom of God in creation. But during the early 1990s a movement emerged in the USA known as "Intelligent Design" (spelt with capital letters to identify it as a specific movement; henceforth: ID) claiming much more for the design argument than the traditional view. Led by a lawyer from the University of California at Berkeley, Phillip E. Johnson, the movement saw its central goal as the undermining of the perceived philosophy of naturalism that, it was maintained, pervades and corrupts the scientific community.

A particular target has been Darwinian evolution, seen more as a godless philosophy than James McCosh's concept of God's means of bringing about his creative work. In fact, Phillip Johnson's campaign was sparked by reading Richard Dawkins's book *The Blind Watchmaker*; it was Dawkins's assertions about evolution as a godless process, together with what Johnson perceived as its lack of evidence, that spurred him into his anti-Darwinian crusade.

In 1996 the Discovery Institute of the Center for the Renewal of Science and Culture was established in Seattle, USA, and became the flagship of the ID movement. Those associated with the institute come from varied theological and philosophical backgrounds, including atheism, agnosticism, Judaism, and Islam, as well as Protestant and Catholic Christianity; one fellow of the Discovery Institute is associated with the Unification Church of Sun Myung Moon. The movement is distinct from traditional creationism in that it downplays the role of religious texts in deriving its beliefs and presents its views as scientific rather than religious. Overall, however, ID may be viewed as a strong form of natural theology, as the central aim is to demonstrate evidence for design in nature and therefore, by inference, the existence of a designer.

James McCosh (1811–94), Scottish philosopher and presbyterian minister who became President of Princeton University (1868–88). He argued that evolution, far from being intrinsically atheistic, could be seen as exalting the divine designer; he became the first American religious leader publicly to endorse evolution.

There is a considerable range of views among ID proponents, but all share antipathy to Darwinian evolution as the best explanation for the origins of biological diversity, including all biological complex systems. One of the most prominent intelligent designers is Michael J. Behe, a Catholic biochemist, who in 1996 published *Darwin's Black Box: The Biochemical Challenge to Evolution*. The "irreducible complexity" of the sub-cellular world had led him to conclude that intelligent design had been at work. He argued that "The result is so unambiguous and so significant that it must be ranked as one of the greatest achievements in the history of science. The discovery of [intelligent design] rivals those of Newton and Einstein, Lavoisier and Schrödinger, Pasteur and Darwin." A core idea in ID is that there are certain biological entities, such as the bacterial flagellum (a multi-component molecular "oar" that helps bacteria swim around) that is so complex that it could not possibly have come into being as a result of a gradual Darwinian process. The flagellum is seen as "irreducibly complex", meaning that it only functions if all its components are present, so displaying evidence of "design". The detection of such "irreducibly complex designed entities" in biology plays a central role in ID arguments.

In 2005, ID was tested in a court case in the US, Kitzmiller v. Dover. The trial, which attracted extensive press coverage, arose when a local school board in Dover, Pennsylvania mandated that ID be introduced into the biology curriculum in a local high school, and that an ID textbook, *Of Pandas and People*, be made available to students. The local school board lost the case on the grounds that ID is religion rather than science, and so could not be taught in the science classroom. The judge, himself a conservative Christian, condemned the school board for its "breathtaking inanity" and ruled that ID was "not science" because it invoked "supernatural causation". Teaching it therefore violated the US Constitution.

The suggestion that ID is "science" is indeed problematic. Science is about testable ideas. The claim that a particular biological entity displays "design" leads to no obvious research programme that might test this idea. This presumably explains the dearth of scientific publications arising from ID proponents. The importing of "design" language into scientific discourse is also confusing because it ends up mingling proximate causes – what science investigates – with ultimate causes (such as "design"), which science itself is unable to address.

In fact there are perfectly good Darwinian explanations for many of the entities that ID proponents claim display "design". For example, out of the ensemble of 30 to 40 proteins that make up the bacterial flagellum, there is a 10-protein sub-module known as the Type III secretory system that functions independently to inject poisons into other bacteria, a quite different function than swimming. Another sub-module of the flagellum is a chemical pump that converts energy into useful work in many bacteria. Clearly the flagellum is not irreducibly complex after all, because the complex system can be broken down into sub-modules with independent functions, which give important clues about possible incremental Darwinian pathways involved in its evolution. Each sub-module has its own selective advantage, independently of the flagellum taken as a whole.

ID is deeply problematic for Christian apologetics because it invokes a "designer" to explain present gaps in our scientific knowledge. The result is a "designer of the gaps", which can readily disappear as scientific knowledge grows and the gap is filled. The gaps in knowledge often lie not in the molecular characteristics of complex systems, but in our understanding of their detailed evolutionary histories. It is into these historical gaps that ID wishes to interject the notion of "design".

The designer god invoked by ID arguments is clearly very different from the God of the Bible who is creator and sustainer of all that exists. Those who hold to the traditional argument from design will see God's faithful purposes worked out in all the intricacy of the created order, irrespective of whether science is yet able to understand it or not. A theologically worrying aspect of ID is that it appears to generate a two-tier universe: one tier consists of the "natural entities", which science can presently understand, whereas the second tier consists of the "designed parts", which then require the supernatural actions of an intelligent designer. But the Bible simply sees everything that exists – the "single tier universe" – as being created and upheld by God. Christians have no hidden investments in scientific ignorance, because the more science can explain, the more it reveals of the wisdom and power of God in creation.

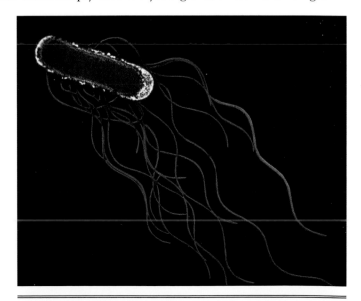

Flagella on a *Salmonella* bacterium

CREATIONISM

One of Darwin's goals in writing the *Origin* was to "overthrow the dogma of separate creations" and in this he proved highly successful. The historian James Moore writes that "with but few exceptions the leading Christian thinkers in Great Britain and America came to terms quite readily with Darwinism and evolution", while the American historian George Marsden reports that "… with the exception of Harvard's Louis Agassiz, virtually every American Protestant zoologist and botanist accepted some form of evolution by the early 1870s".

Despite occasional carping, there was no organized movement against evolution until the early 1920s Even then the so-called Christian fundamentalists failed to agree on the correct reading of Genesis. Most of them had little trouble embracing the evidence from geology and palaeontology for the antiquity of life on earth. They typically did so either by interpreting the "days" of Genesis as vast geological or cosmic ages or by following the Scofield Reference Bible in inserting a vast "gap" between the initial creation "in the beginning" and a much later creation associated with the Garden of Eden.

However, they continued to believe that humans had not appeared on earth until the creation of Adam and Eve, about 6,000 years ago. Only a small percentage of fundamentalists in the 1920s, mostly Seventh-Day Adventists, insisted on the recent creation of all life in six literal days and attributed virtually the entire geological column to the work of Noah's flood, a universal catastrophe that occurred about 2348 BC. In so doing, they were following the visions of the church's founder, Ellen G. White. The leading proponent of this view, a Canadian Adventist named

Chicago, Clarence Darrow. Like many fundamentalist leaders, Bryan, an advocate of the day-age theory, had no trouble accepting the vast antiquity of life on earth. As he explained during the trial, it made no difference to him theologically whether creation had taken place in six days or "in six years or in 6,000,000 years or in 600,000,000 years". The trial ended in Scopes's conviction (later set aside on appeal), and the anti-evolution crusade continued unabated for several more years before petering out.

Price had declined an invitation from Bryan to participate in the trial because in the mid 1920s he was teaching at an Adventist college near London. Despite his best efforts to foment an anti-evolution movement in Great Britain, he failed. Even the venerable Victoria Institute, long a haven for British creationists, repudiated his effort "to drive a wedge between Christians and scientists" in Britain. As Price reported to an American associate, "I have been somewhat disappointed in the apparent lethargy of the friends of the Bible over here, regarding the subject of evolution." It was not until the early 1930s that theologically conservative British critics of evolution, virtually all of whom accepted

George McCready Price, called it "flood geology".

Then in 1925 the state legislature of Tennessee passed a law making it illegal to teach human evolution in public schools of the state. A few months later, John Thomas Scopes, a young high school science teacher in Dayton, volunteered to test the new law. Assisting the prosecution was William Jennings Bryan, a lay Presbyterian who had run for the presidency of the United States three times as a Democrat. Opposing him was a notorious agnostic from

The Scopes Trial, Dayton, Tennessee, 1925

the scientific evidence for an old earth, founded the Evolution Protest Movement.

Until the 1960s, Price's flood geology remained a minority position among fundamentalists. That changed, however, with the publication of *The Genesis Flood* in 1961, co-authored by John C. Whitcomb, a Princeton-educated Old Testament scholar associated with the Grace Brethren, and Henry M. Morris, a Baptist who had earned a PhD in civil engineering at the University of Minnesota. Together they launched a campaign to convert Bible-believing Christians to Price's flood geology and wean them from the day-age and gap theories, which they damned as tools of Satan. In 1963 a small group of fellow believers joined Morris in forming the Creation Research Society (CRS), specifically to advocate flood geology. Nearly a decade later Morris established an Institute for Creation Research, which became the motherhouse of the movement. By this time Morris and his colleagues had renamed Price's theory "creation science" or "scientific creationism". Outsiders often referred to it as young-earth creationism, ignoring the presence of some in the inner circle who insisted only on the recent appearance of life on earth but not on a young earth.

By 1980 the advocates of Price's flood geology had become so influential among Bible-believing Christians that they successfully co-opted the label creationism for his previously marginal views. That year, after discovering that "young earthers outnumbered old earthers by more than four to one", the Evolution Protest Movement renamed itself the Creation Science Movement (CSM). At about the same time Australian creationists formed the Creation Science Foundation. One of its leaders was Kenneth A. Ham, a charismatic public speaker and former biology teacher, who emerged in the twenty-first century as the brightest star in the creationist firmament. By then he had relocated to the United States, where he eventually started his own Answers in Genesis ministry and built a $27 million Creation Museum in Kentucky.

Until late in the twentieth century, organized creationism had been confined largely to the United States, where by the new millennium nearly two-thirds of the public claimed to favour creation over evolution. Increasingly, however, it became a truly global

phenomenon, popular not only among conservative Protestants but also among pockets of Catholics, Eastern Orthodox believers, Muslims, and Orthodox Jews. Continental Europe, perhaps the most secular region on earth, at first proved resistant to American-style creationism. But conditions changed rapidly. With the demise of the Soviet Union in 1991, evangelical Christianity boomed in Russia, and along with it creationism, partly because Darwinism had been so linked to the now discredited Marxist philosophy that had undergirded Soviet hegemony. Other former Soviet-bloc countries — Poland, Hungary, Romania, and Serbia — also witnessed the spread of creationism. Sporadic outbreaks of antievolutionism also occurred in Western Europe. A poll in 2002 of European attitudes toward creation and evolution, found that 40 per cent favoured naturalistic evolution, 21 per cent endorsed theistic evolution, 20 per cent (with the Swiss leading the way) believed that "God created all organisms at one time within the last 10,000 years," and 19 per cent remained undecided. Seven years later, the first clear poll results for the UK (carried out by ComRes) revealed that 10 per cent of the population self-identified as creationists and 14 per cent as believers in intelligent design. In other words, in 2009, 150 years after the publication of *The Origin of Species*, around half the population in the land of Darwin's birth disbelieved his theory or expressed doubts.

The Creation Museum, Petersburg, Kentucky

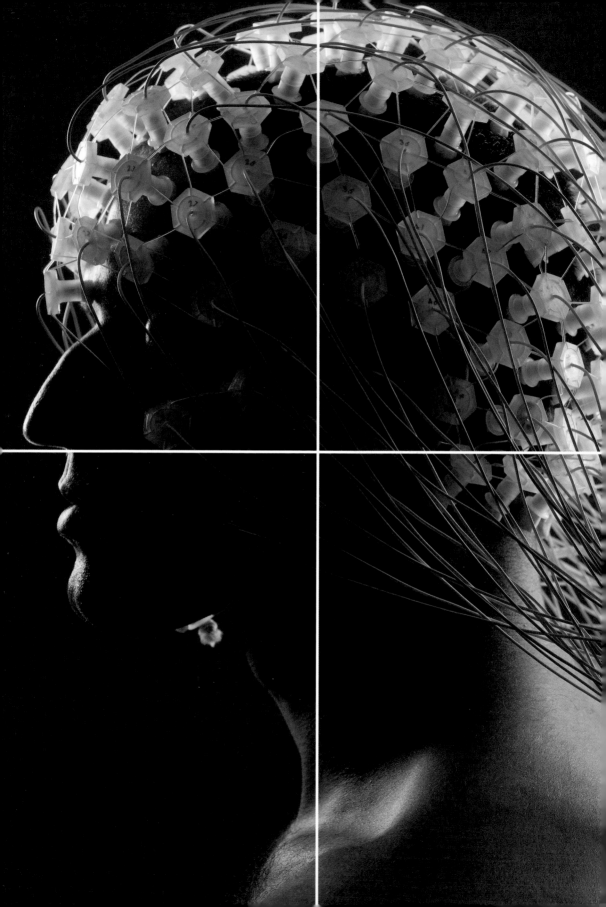

Humanity and Humanness

Both the Bible and science have a great deal to say about what it is to be a human being, but they seem to say very different things. This raises a host of questions for the Christian. How similar are we to other animals? How did we come to exist? Are we biological machines? If so, how can we be conscious?

Many different sciences contribute to an understanding of humanness. Their challenges to faith are greatest where they have to do with our origins or with our psychological and spiritual identity. The emphasis here is on our identity as it emerges from neuroscience, psychology, palaeontology, and genetics, concentrating on five main problem areas at the interface between these sciences and Christian belief.

NOTHING BUT MOLECULES AND CELLS?

Almost never can a complex system of any kind be understood as a simple extrapolation from the properties of its elementary components. Consider, for example, gas in a bottle. A description of thermodynamic effects – temperature, pressure, density, and the relationships among these factors – is not formulated by using a large set of equations, one for each of the particles involved. Such effects are described at their own level, that of an enormous collection of particles... If

one hopes to achieve a full understanding of a system as complicated as a nervous system, a bottle of gas… or even a large computer program, then one must be prepared to contemplate different kinds of explanation at different levels of description that are linked, at least in principle, into a cohesive whole…
D. Marr, *Vision* (1982)

One reason why science has sometimes been considered a threat to religious and humanistic concepts of ourselves is that attempts to explain the whole in terms of the parts have been seen as diminishing our status, even devaluing us. In these terms, my daughter is merely a mere conglomeration of cells. Your love for God, or your boyfriend, is reduced to the impersonal activity of neurons in certain parts of your brain. Because of misunderstandings such as these, opponents of science decry its reductionism. In contrast, some opponents of religion go to the other extreme and try to explain it away in terms of mechanistic science. To think clearly about these issues we need to understand the concept of *levels of discourse*, and to clarify the related idea of *reduction*.

LEVELS OF DISCOURSE

When we discuss anything at all complex, we have to choose the *level* at which we are going to talk. For example, when confronted with the message "LECTURE CANCELLED OWING TO BUBONIC PLAGUE" on the blackboard, we might start to describe the spatial positions of the grains of chalk. Let us call this level A. Or we might make a list of all the letters (level B). But we would probably be more concerned about the meaning of the message (level C). Level A is the lowest of the three, and level C is the highest. The criterion for deciding which of any level is the higher is that you can change the lower without changing the higher, but not vice versa. You could obviously move some of the grains of chalk without changing the string of letters or the meaning, but you could not change the meaning without changing the letters or the grain positions.

Clearly a description can be complete in its own terms without excluding other descriptions at different levels. The different descriptions are said to be *complementary* (see p. 54). It is possible for two descriptions at the same level to be complementary – for example, two verbal accounts or pictorial representations of an object from distinct viewpoints; but complementarity between *different* levels is more relevant in the present context. In our example of a blackboard message, the highest-level description was obviously the most relevant, but this is not always the case. For example, a car, or a computer, requires explanation at more than one level to do it justice. And so do human beings.

Three points can be made about such descriptions. There is a hierarchy of levels at which a human being or a group of humans might be considered. Descriptions at the different levels are complementary, as discussed above. One does not exclude another.

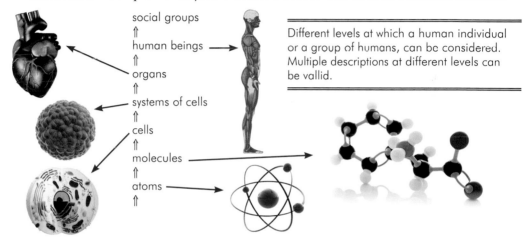

social groups
⇑
human beings
⇑
organs
⇑
systems of cells
⇑
cells
⇑
molecules
⇑
atoms
⇑

Different levels at which a human individual or a group of humans, can be considered. Multiple descriptions at different levels can be vallid.

The second point is that the significance of low-level entities is to be found with reference to the higher levels. For example, the significance of the protein molecules making up a receptor for the neurotransmitter (acetylcholine) on muscle cells is to be found at the cellular level, in the functioning of the receptor during synaptic transmission; and, still higher, at the levels of the contracting muscle and the behaving human being. The significance of a human being is to be found at still higher levels, in her relationship in social groups, for example. It would be impossible to add God and his eternal purpose for us and for the universe as a still higher level above social grouping. It is with respect to this that I believe we can all find our ultimate significance. Whether this belief is true is beyond the scope of the present text; it should at least be clear from the above remarks that looking for higher-level interpretations to give meaning and significance to lower-level phenomena is not a strange hobby for a few weird mystics, but is an intrinsic part of scientific endeavour.

The third point is that although descriptions at all the levels may be valid, and need not be rivals, different levels can still make contact. Low-level descriptions can set constraints on what is possible (or likely) at a higher level and vice versa. There can thus be tension between theories that focus on different levels, and major debates in science (and medicine) sometimes involve clashes between theories that work at different levels.

RIVALRY BETWEEN THEORIES AT DIFFERENT LEVELS: THE EXAMPLE OF SCHIZOPHRENIA

Even though multiple descriptions at different levels can all be true, and true descriptions cannot contradict each other, in real situations of incomplete understanding there are often clashes between theories pitched at different levels. A famous clash concerned schizophrenia. This psychiatric disease is characterized by a disintegration of thought processes, of contact with reality, and of emotional responsiveness. Many schizophrenics suffer auditory hallucinations or paranoid delusions, sometimes of a religious nature.

The causes of schizophrenia have been claimed to lie at many different levels. Throughout much of history (long before the term schizophrenia was invented in 1911), symptoms typical of the disease were attributed to demon possession, with treatment ranging from shamanic rituals to exorcism. In the nineteenth century, psychiatrists began to suggest that cerebral or psychological factors were the cause. Then during the twentieth century, three rival notions of the aetiology (causation) of schizophrenia, pitched at three different levels, competed with each other.

Conflicts within the psyche. As the twentieth century progressed, psychoanalysis and other psychodynamic approaches became increasingly popular as therapy for schizophrenia. These were mostly based on the belief, never clearly demonstrated, that schizophrenia resulted from unconscious or subconscious conflicts.

Interactions within the family. A new therapeutic approach appeared in the 1950s and 1960s with the rise of the family therapy movement. Its founders maintained that the main cause of schizophrenia was to be found in unhealthy communication within the family. The patient was considered to be a victim of his family's interactions, and psychiatrists started to talk about "schizogenic" families and even schizogenic mothers. Mother-blaming became fashionable. A paper published in 1965 cited earlier reports claiming that the mothers of schizophrenics were "overanxious, rejecting, restrictive… refrigerator mothers,… narcissistic, immature, married to passive, aloof men… negativistic and hostile,… domineering, nagging… devastatingly, possessively all-loving…" Theorists hypothesized that the symptoms of schizophrenia function to maintain a homeostatic balance in the family, and

Phrenologists believed that the shape of the head determine behaviour, intelligence, etc.

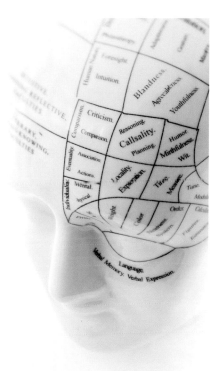

are therefore the result of schizogenic family interactions. This theory gained a considerable following in the 1960s, but subsequently lost favour. One reason was that neurobiological studies indicated abnormalities at the synaptic level. Another was that adoption studies showed that genetic factors were far more important than family interactions in the disease causation. A third was the poor success of family therapy as a treatment.

Biological psychiatry. At the end of the nineteenth century, schizophrenia (then called dementia praecox) was held by some to involve brain degeneration. A boost to this understanding came in the 1930s with the discovery that provoking a coma with insulin was therapeutic for the disease. Then, in the 1950s, several different drugs including reserpine and chlorpromazine were found to diminish the symptoms of schizophrenia. Nobel Prize winning research by Arvid Carlsson showed that the beneficial effects of these drugs were due to their inhibition of neurotransmission by dopamine. That is not to say that anomalies in dopamine transmission are the entire explanation of schizophrenia. Other factors including other neurotransmitters are also involved.

To obtain an adequate understanding of the aetiology it will be necessary to understand what causes the anomalies in the dopamine and other neurotransmitter systems. There is strong evidence that genetic factors and different pre- and perinatal stresses can predispose to schizophrenia. These stresses include viral infection of the pregnant mother, anoxia at birth, obstetrical complications, and brain trauma. A common pathway by which these different stresses may affect the brain is through generating highly reactive molecules called free radicals. The biological approach is currently dominant.

How should we relate these different approaches? A complete understanding of schizophrenia may well require

• •

taking account of neurobiological, psychological, social, and spiritual factors. A successful neurobiological account would not in itself invalidate parallel accounts at higher levels. Nevertheless, a successful explanation at one level will set constraints on what can be true at other levels. For example, the evidence for brain degeneration in adult schizophrenics went against the idea of the disease being an adaptive response to the family situation. Stressful family interactions might conceivably cause degeneration, although the (admittedly indirect) evidence for subtle brain alterations in young children who will grow up to become schizophrenics contradicts this, because the alterations occur too early. This example is simplified, but it does illustrate the fact that theories formulated at different levels can conflict if they have implications at the same level.

To summarize: in practical situations where the truth is uncertain, hypotheses at different levels can sometimes contradict each other, but there is no inherent reason why low-level ones should discredit high-level ones, or vice versa. Why then, are low-level scientific accounts sometimes thought of as discrediting higher-level religious ones? Part of the answer may lie in confusions about the nature of *reduction*.

REDUCTION

Superficially, the meaning of "reduction" (in science and philosophy) is simple: the analysis of a complex entity into its component parts; or, in more functional terms, the understanding of the workings of the entity in terms of its interacting components. But we need to go deeper than this in order to understand the difficulties. Is the whole more than the sum of its parts? It depends what you mean by "more than". Can the workings of my brain be reduced to the functioning of its component neurons? It depends on the precise sense in which you use the word "reduced".

Most philosophers of science agree that we must distinguish between different kinds of reduction. For example, Karl Popper distinguished between "reduction as a method", which he believed all scientists must welcome, and "philosophical reductionism", for which he considered there are no good arguments. Several types of reductionism have been identified. They can be simplified to three:

Behaviour – such as bird song – cannot be reduced to chemical processes, even though it may be largely inherited.

- *Ontological reduction* is essentially the question of whether life and consciousness can be understood purely in terms of physico-chemical events, or whether we need to invoke some kind of nonmaterial principle such as a "soul" or "*élan vital*" ("vital force") that interacts with the physico-chemical components. Ontological reduction would involve getting rid of such a principle.

- *Reduction by level-descent* or methodological reductionism. This concerns the choice of level for a given enquiry or discussion. Choosing a low level is reduction by level-descent.

> *I was once on the examining board for a postgraduate scholarship at Oxford University. The winning student, a biochemist, declared "Everything boils down to biochemistry in the end." "For example, the biochemistry of bird song?" asked one of the examiners, who happened to be a specialist in this area. "Yes," was the confident reply, but all the examiners agreed that the student had missed the point. Even though biochemical processes do underlie the neural functioning in bird song, and few would want to deny this or invoke any mysterious nonmaterial principle, we need to ask other kinds of questions as well: about the meaning for the birds of the sounds produced, about the temporal patterns of action potentials in neurons involved in bird song, and so on. These latter questions are not optional extras; they are not superficial preludes to the real, deep biochemistry; they are essential in their own right. Most scientists agree on this. Many levels of question need to be asked, and one of our most interesting and challenging tasks is to fit together the results from the various levels into a coherent multi-level picture. The necessity of including a particular lower or intermediate level – e.g. the ion channels involved in bird song – may perhaps be debated. But clearly the level involving the concept of bird song itself is indispensable.*

- *Epistemological reduction* is to do with predictive power. It concerns whether the theories and laws formulated in one field of science are really special cases of those formulated in some other field. If so, the former field is said to have been reduced to the latter; it is in principle no longer needed to make predictions, because the laws and theories of the latter are sufficient. For example, the kinetic theory of

gases predicts and explains the general law for ideal gases. That is not to say that the former field becomes worthless, because the reduction is never absolutely complete; a "residue" always remains. Although its laws and theories are no longer needed for prediction, its concepts and its data are still needed. And, in practice, it is usually still much more convenient to predict from the less general, higher-level theory. But, with these qualifications in mind, there is no doubt that many of the greatest achievements in science have involved epistemological reduction. During the last hundred years or so, several branches of physics have been unified by their reduction to a few theories of great generality and power, notably quantum physics and relativity. Likewise, much of chemistry was reduced to physics by the discovery that the binding properties of an atom can be explained in terms of the number of electrons in its outer orbit.

The large: a star in the Taurus constellation

CONFUSING REDUCTION AND "NOTHING-BUTTERY"

Failure to distinguish between ontological and methodological reduction can lead to what Donald MacKay called "the fallacy of 'nothing-buttery'". To illustrate this error and its absurdity, consider a particularly blatant example. You have just hung up a picture of a beautiful woman and are admiring it when your mad-scientist brother walks in. "What's that?" he asks, somewhat aggressively. "A woman," you reply. "Wrong!" he thunders, "it's just molecules, *nothing but* molecules. When it comes down to the nitty-gritty, you'll find there's nothing else. Take away the molecules, and you'll be left with nothing at all." He is, of course, denying what you never wished to assert. He is insisting on ontological reductionism, that there is not an immaterial principle hiding mysteriously between the molecules of paint. Of course not! But his confused thought blurs into the idea of reduction by level-descent, as if he had proved that the molecular level was the relevant level for talking about the picture.

Although no sane person would make such an error in the simple case of a picture, related misunderstandings can occur when referring to the brain. "It's nothing but atoms and molecules," people sometimes say. If they mean that the neurons are not being influenced by a mysterious, immaterial force, they may be right. But the danger is that their plausible ontological reduction can be confused with reduction by level-descent, leading to the false idea that molecular accounts of the brain are somehow more fundamental or true than higher-level physiological or psychological ones.

Confusion between the third type of reduction and the other two can also lead to wrong conclusions. Suppose that the development of certain parts of the brain was found to be entirely controlled by the genes, and even predictable from a complete knowledge of the information stored in the genome. While a complete knowledge of the genome will probably one day be available, this scenario is not very plausible, because in many parts of the brain development is known to be powerfully influenced by experience, never mind the enormous technical and theoretical difficulties of prediction from genetic information. But for the sake of argument let us suppose that such genetic prediction became possible some time in the distant future for certain parts of the brain. One could then state

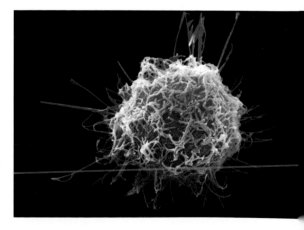

The small: a dividing HeLa cell

that the developmental biology of these parts had indeed been reduced to genetics, in the third (epistemological) sense. But it would be illogical to start talking as if there had been a reduction in sense 1 (ontological), the banishment of an unscientific concept, or in sense 2 (methodological or level-descent), the identification of a particular level (but which?) as supremely relevant. Nothing would have been banished, and descriptions of the phenomena (migration of cells, growth of axons, cell-to-cell recognition, and so on) at different levels would be needed even more than before. Without descriptions of the developmental phenomena, there would be nothing left to explain.

Christianity has nothing to fear from valid reduction. The apparent threats to our humanity and our faith are due to confused reduction and nothing-buttery.

THE NATURALISTIC APPROACH TO HUMANNESS

Science relies on naturalism, the assumption that its objects of study obey regular laws. If an experiment gives an unexpected result that doesn't seem to make sense, a scientist may assume that she has made a mistake and repeat the experiment, but she will not invoke a miracle (or demonic interference and suchlike). For most areas of study this is so routine and obvious that it does not need to be mentioned, but when it comes to the study of humanness the systematic exclusion of the divine can sometimes seem an unjustified imposition of atheistic assumptions.

A common Christian response is that God's activity is being studied, even though this may not be explicit in the scientific account. God has not been excluded, because the very scientific laws that are being studied are in fact God's laws. However this raises problems if it is made into an absolute principle. Although it is different from the deistic conception of a god who set the universe going and then abandoned it to run on its own, its implications are very similar. According to both views, all events are determined by the initial conditions of the universe and the impersonal laws of nature (and perhaps chance). It is hard to see how such a framework can allow for the loving fatherhood of God, of the indwelling of his Spirit, or of the incarnation.

The problem of naturalism became acute with the development of scientific laws and the mechanistic approach in the seventeenth century, but even before that Calvin hinted at it:

> The carnal mind, when once it has perceived the power of God in the creation, stops there… In short, it imagines that all things are sufficiently sustained by the energy divinely infused into them at first. But faith must penetrate deeper. After learning that there is a Creator, it must forthwith infer that he is also a Governor and Preserver, and

that, not by producing a kind of general motion in the machine of the globe as well as in each of its parts, but by a special providence sustaining, cherishing, superintending, all the things which he has made, to the very minutest, even to a sparrow.
John Calvin, *Institutes of the Christian Religion* (1599)

How can a machine-like universe governed by the laws of nature (God's laws though they are), be compatible with the special providence of God? Part of the solution is to realize that the naturalism required by science need not be made into an absolute principle. Science requires methodological (or scientific) naturalism, but not ontological (also called metaphysical, or philosophical) naturalism.

Science is based on naturalism, the notion that all manifestations in the universe are explainable in terms of the known laws of physics and chemistry. This notion represents the cornerstone of the scientific enterprise. Unless we subscribe to it, we might as well close our laboratories. If we start from the assumption that what we are investigating is not explainable, we rule out scientific research. Contrary to the view expressed by some scientists, this logical necessity does not imply that naturalism is to be accepted as an a priori philosophical stand, a doctrine or belief. As used in science, it is a postulate, a working hypothesis often qualified as "methodological naturalism" by philosophers, which we should be ready to abandon if faced with facts or events that defy every attempt at a naturalistic explanation.
Nobel Laureate, Christian de Duve, "Mysteries of Life: Is There 'Something Else'?" (2002)

As an atheist de Duve certainly does not have a theological axe to grind; as a scientist, he affirms that we must do our very best to find a naturalistic explanation. But he avoids making naturalism into a philosophical dogma.

HUMAN ANCESTRY

All living creatures share a common ancestry, and humankind is no different in this (see p. 164). But all are agreed that humans are distinct in some way. Many criteria have been proposed as the significant feature of humanness – bipedalism, opposable thumbs, tool-making, learning ability, abstract thought, play, artistic sense – but all have fallen to our increasing knowledge of animal life and behaviour. The pioneer ethologist, William Thorpe, accepted that no single attribute can be unequivocally identified as unique to the human species, but he believed that there is such a tremendous chasm between us and our closest animal relatives that "there comes a point where 'more' creates a 'difference'". For Christians the absolute difference between animals and humankind is our creation "in God's image", we are *Homo sapiens* but we are also *Homo divinus* (p. 168).

MODERN HUMAN ORIGINS

We identify our species by shared anatomy and common ancestry, but above all, we identify fellow humans by shared mental function. This, of course, is hard to analyse in prehistoric populations. All we have to go on is preserved artefacts – which typically means items made of stone, bone, or shell. Symbolic thought is currently viewed as being most significant – as seen in artefacts such as pictures, ornaments, symbols, or very complex manufactured items. Obviously there is a lot of debate over the meaning of the remnants of cultures from such vast distances. However, one of the earliest such activities in general agreement is shell bead making. The earliest reports of this are from Qafzeh and Skhul caves 120,000 BC, followed by similar discoveries across North Africa (the Aterian Culture), and then after the collapse of the Saharan wet period (70,000 BC), in Blombas Cave, South Africa. In addition to the symbolic implications, all the sites at which these marine shells are found are located many kilometres from the sea, implying organized long distance trade networks.

Similar early South African indications of symbolic thought include scribed patterns in ochre blocks, soft-hammer flaking, skin working, burins (shaping tools), bone tips and awls, and complex composite tools (use of microliths and mastic).

The only reasonable conclusion supported by the physical data of bones, genes, and tools is that *Homo sapiens* arose in north-eastern Africa around 200,000 years ago, and did not leave Africa for another 140,000 years.

Are we "nothing but" apes? For a thorough-going reductionist the answer is easy, since the mind is the epiphenomenon of the brain, a mere symptom of the physical activity. The trouble is that this reductionist programme in the end subverts itself. Ultimately it is suicidal. If our mental life is nothing but the humming activity of an immensely complexly connected computer-like brain, who is to say whether the programme running on the machine is correct or not?

John Polkinghorne, *One World* (1986)

BRAIN AND MIND

Neuroscientists are virtually unanimous in claiming that the mind and consciousness arise from the brain, which is a mechanism made of cells. How a material mechanism can give rise to consciousness is a mystery, but this certainly happens, raising some serious questions for Christian believers. Must we abandon the notion of a soul and of life after death? Is there still scope for free will? Are our ethical (or unethical) and religious (or irreligious) tendencies pre-programmed in the brain? Most of these challenges stem from the mechanistic implications of modern neuroscience.

THE BRAIN: A MECHANISM MADE FROM BIOLOGICAL COMPONENTS

The brain works electrically, and the cells most involved in the electrical information processing of the brain are the neurons. The brain contains other cell types, most of which are termed *glial cells* (or *glia*). Some of these insulate the neuronal output wires, others regulate the nutrition of the neurons, others clear away rubbish, and so on. Like all cells, the neurons and glia work according to the laws of physics and chemistry, and the neurons communicate with each other by producing bursts of electricity that cause the release of chemicals called neurotransmitters that activate or inhibit other neurons.

In this age of sophisticated computers made of simple transistor elements, the idea that these connections are sufficient to produce the complex workings of the brain seems eminently plausible. Indeed, a wealth of evidence from electrophysiology, neuroanatomy, and cell biology strongly suggests that brain functions can be accounted for by the purely physico-chemical interactions between neurons.

THE BRAIN IS THE ORIGIN OF BEHAVIOUR, EMOTION, AND THOUGHT

The study of the human brain has been revolutionized in recent years by new techniques for localizing where activity is changing as a result of some task or stimulus. Techniques for recording such changes in brain activity with electrodes on the scalp have been available for more than half a century, but it is not easy to identify where the activity is coming from. This has changed as new imaging techniques have been developed, notably positron emission tomography, functional magnetic resonance imaging (fMRI), and magnetoencephalography. These methods can be used to pinpoint with great accuracy the changes in brain activity that accompany virtually any behaviour: performing a movement or even just imagining the movement, or performing mental arithmetic, or playing chess, or understanding language, or suffering pain.

The same is true for ethical decision-making and even religious experience. In an fMRI study on volunteers, ethical decision-making was shown to involve activity mainly in two particular

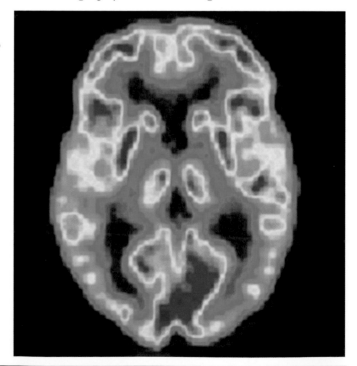

Scan of the brain by positron emission tomography (PET). The technique allows blood flow, oxygen, and glucose metabolism to be measured.

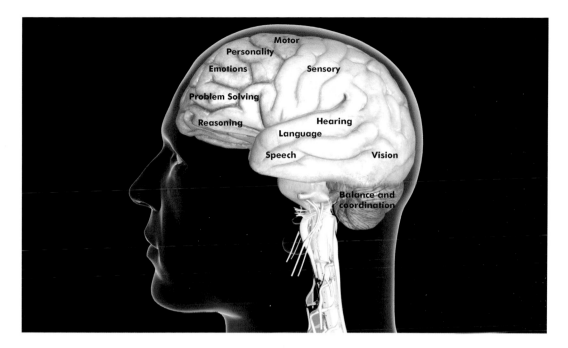

areas of the cerebral cortex, one in the temporal lobe and the other in the frontal lobe. In another study, Carmelite nuns underwent fMRI imaging while taking part in deep prayerful meditation, and possibly undergoing a mystical experience of union with God. This revealed the activation of many different brain regions including the lower part of the parietal lobe, the visual cortex, the caudate nucleus and part of the brain stem.

However, such studies can only tell us *where* in the brain the activity is changing. They do not address the causal relationships between mind and brain. They show that brain activity *correlates* with mental activity, but do not show that it actually *causes* it. Evidence for the latter comes from the fact that mental activity is affected by stimulating the brain, or damaging it, or modifying it with drugs.

BRAIN STIMULATION SHOWS A CAUSAL RELATIONSHIP BETWEEN BRAIN AND MIND

Fascinating results were obtained in the 1920s and early 1930s by the Swiss physiologist Walter Hess. He stimulated deep parts of the brains of cats with fine wire electrodes implanted previously under anaesthesia, and identified the hypothalamus, which lies close to the pituitary gland, as the site of the control centres for some of life's most basic functions. Stimulation of one small part of the hypothalamus made the animal aggressive. Its pupils would dilate, its hairs would bristle, it would start to spit, and when approached it would attack. In regions only a few millimetres away, stimulation would evoke complete, friendly submission. In still others it would evoke sleep, or feeding, or respiration changes, or bladder evacuation accompanied by the appropriate posture.

A remarkable extension of these results resulted from persuading the experimental animals to push the stimulation button themselves. In the 1950s James Olds implanted electrodes into the brains of rats and connected the electrodes to stimulators controlled by buttons in the cages. When the electrodes were in certain brain regions (which came to be called "pleasure centres"), the rats would press the buttons endlessly, as though they were receiving pleasure from the stimulation. In some experiments the rats would even cross electrified grids in order to be able to press the button. The "pleasure centres" were found in many regions of the brain, including a part of the basal forebrain called the nucleus accumbens (see p. 210).

But stimulation of the *human* brain provides the most direct evidence of the relation of brain activity to conscious states. Just as in rats, emotions can be elicited by the electrical stimulation of specific areas. Pleasure has been elicited from the septal region; fear from the amygdala and hippocampus, which lie deep in the temporal lobe; occasionally rage from the amygdala.

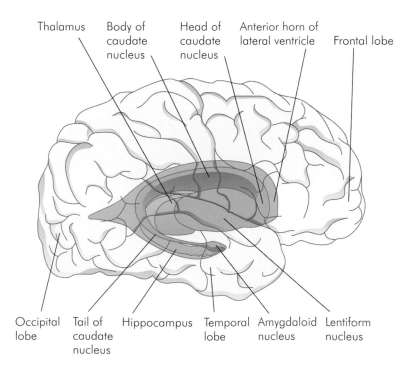

Thalamus · Body of caudate nucleus · Head of caudate nucleus · Anterior horn of lateral ventricle · Frontal lobe

Occipital lobe · Tail of caudate nucleus · Hippocampus · Temporal lobe · Amygdaloid nucleus · Lentiform nucleus

The Canadian neurosurgeon, Wilder Penfield, has shown that complex cognitive experiences can also be produced by stimulation of the temporal lobe. For example, upon stimulation of one point in a visually related part of her right temporal lobe, a

Regions of the brain

14-year-old epileptic girl suddenly cried, "Oh, I can see something come at me! Don't let them come at me!" Upon stimulation of an auditory part of the temporal lobe she said: "They are yelling at me for doing something wrong." Penfield deduced that he was stimulating an abnormal area that tended to produce epileptic discharges. He removed it and the epilepsy was cured.

In other patients, Penfield's electrodes evoked different complex hallucinations from the temporal lobe. "Music, a familiar air", in one patient. Another exclaimed, "I had the same very, very familiar memory in an office somewhere. I could see the desks. I was there and someone was calling to me, a man learning on a desk with a pencil in his hand." A woman under stimulation suddenly felt as if she was at home in her kitchen, and could hear from outside the voice of her young son against a familiar background of noises. Ten days after surgery, she denied that this was only an illusion and insisted that it was in fact a real memory.

BRAIN LESIONS AND CONSCIOUSNESS

Studying the effects of brain lesions on mental function has produced a wealth of data showing not only that the brain is necessary for consciousness and voluntary behaviour, but that different parts of the brain are necessary for different aspects of our mental life.

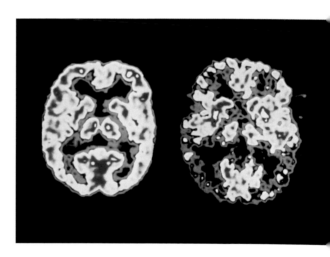

Take moral restraint. A real example is that of a previously respectable schoolteacher who began visiting child pornography websites and soliciting prostitutes. When he started making sexual advances to his preadolescent stepdaughter, his wife called the police. He was legally evicted from his house, found guilty of child molestation, and medicated for paedophilia. He himself felt that his new behaviour was unacceptable, but he said that his desire overrode his restraint. The judge ordered him to undergo a rehabilitation programme or face jail. He chose rehabilitation, but was expelled from the programme because he kept asking women for sex. Then the evening before his prison sentence, he went to a hospital complaining of headache and saying he was afraid he would rape his landlady. He was found to have an egg-sized tumour in the right frontal lobe. When

Alzheimer's disease leads to the death of nerve cells and loss of brain tissue, and the formation of plaques of fatty tissue.

this was removed, his salacious behaviour and paedophilia faded away. A year later the tumour started to grow back and the urges returned; but when the new tumour was removed they subsided again. It is not understood why the tumour had the effect it did, but there are other reports that damage to the frontal lobe can affect moral restraint, and it seems plausible that the tumour was releasing pre-existing urges by pressing on and inactivating a brain region necessary for their suppression.

Even our spirituality can be affected by brain lesions or neurodegeneration. Patients with Alzheimer's disease sometimes feel cut off from God. Disturbing though this is, it is not really surprising in view of the importance of memories and cognitive capacities in spiritual experience.

PHARMACOLOGICAL EFFECTS ON MIND AND MOOD

Drugs provide further evidence that changes in brain activity can affect all aspects of our consciousness. In the case of alcohol, this observation is so mundane as to be banal.

Another example is that of cocaine. Cocaine enhances the action of the neurotransmitter dopamine. One of the important sites of dopamine release is the nucleus accumbens. This is a "pleasure centre", and rats are enthusiastic to stimulate it if an electrode is implanted in their own nucleus accumbens. In a slightly different experiment, button-pushing by the rat caused dopamine or cocaine release from a tiny pipette into the nucleus accumbens; this too evoked powerful self-stimulation. This supports the view that pleasurable effects of cocaine are due to its enhancing the effects of dopamine in "pleasure centres" such as the nucleus accumbens. There is less direct evidence that the same is true in humans.

Another example of the power of drugs over mind and mood is the widely used anti-depressant "Prozac", which enhances the efficacy of serotonin by preventing the neurotransmitter serotonin being retaken by the nerve terminals that released it. At about the time Prozac was being introduced, further evidence for the mood-changing role of serotonin came from a new strain of mice genetically engineered to lack one of the 14 different kinds of serotonin receptor. These mice turned out to be particularly aggressive, attacking other mice much more than normal.

CONCLUSION

Thus, a considerable weight of evidence supports the view that our mental functions are not only paralleled by brain processes but are actually caused by them. Why this should be so may be a fundamental mystery, but it remains true that our mental life depends on brain processes.

THE SOUL AND THE QUESTION OF DUALISM

We will have nothing to do with the fantastic suggestion, that what the supersensitive "reactors" in the cortex react to, is the initiative of a virtually disembodied soul. To what, then, are we to say that they do react? What else, than to the motions of the embodied soul, that is to say, other motions in the same nervous system.
Austin Farrer, *The Freedom of the Will* (1957)

I believe in the ghost in the machine. That is to say, I think that the self in a sense plays on the brain, as a pianist plays on a piano or a driver plays on the controls of a car.
Karl Popper, in Popper and Eccles, *The Self and Its Brain* (1977)

TWO APPROACHES

When we speak of the soul we may be saying something about the fact that there is an essential "me" with conscious experience and the power to act and make choices. Or we may be expressing a belief about our existence continuing after death, that this same "me" will still have conscious experience, but in heaven. Modern neurobiology can only deal with the first question.

Christians tend to adopt one of two main approaches to the soul or *mind* – the two terms overlap, and usage varies.

i. *Interactive dualism.* **René Descartes** conceived of the soul/mind as an immaterial "me" separate from the brain and somehow interacting with it to produce willed behaviour. This is *substance dualism*, the position that we are made of two fundamentally different substances (in the philosophical sense). There are many different versions of substance dualism but the best known version is *interactive dualism* (or *Cartesian dualism*), the one proposed by Descartes himself.

ii. *Dual-aspect monism.* The alternative is *dual-aspect monism*, which views the soul as embodied in the functioning of the brain. On this view, the soul (or mind) does not act upon the brain; the soul/mind and brain are complementary aspects of the same entity, the human person. Our inner subjective experience (soul/mind), and the objective scientific view of the brain are two different views of the same entity, the human person.

Australian neurophysiologist and Nobel Prize winner John Eccles (1903–97), champion of dualism of body and soul.

GREEK AND CHRISTIAN NOTIONS OF THE SOUL

It is important to realize that the dualist notion of the soul widespread in our society is not really the biblical one. It comes from Socrates and Plato.

> *Does not death mean that the body comes to exist by itself, separated from the soul, and that the soul exists by herself, separated from the body?*
> **Socrates, in Plato's** *Phaedo*

The Greek notion of the immortal soul was developed by the philosophers who developed Plato's ideas (the Neoplatonists) and became deeply rooted in Western society. In the early centuries of the church, many Christian philosophers and theologians, including Origen and Augustine, combined it with their biblical understanding; theologians from Aquinas to Luther and Calvin likewise assumed it. But most modern scholars accept that the biblical notion of man is very different.

In the Old Testament, the word most often translated as "soul" is *nephesh*, whose primary meaning is simply *life* or *vitality*, with the underlying connotation also of *movement*. However, the word is used very frequently (754 times), and can take on many different meanings ranging from *personality* to *blood*. In Genesis 2, when God breathes into the nostrils of man the breath of life, the man becomes a "living being" (most modern versions) or "living soul" (King James Version) – a *nephesh*. The meaning is that he starts to live and move – just as the animals do, which is why they too can be called *nephesh*. The word translated "spirit" (*ruah*) in the Old Testament carries the basic idea of air in motion. In many cases it simply means and is translated "wind", but it can also refer to the "breath of life" that the whole animal creation shares with man (Genesis 6:17). When translated spirit, it usually expresses the vitality of the mind as expressive of the whole personality (Psalm 32:2; 78:8), or it may refer to human inclinations and desires (Hosea 4:12, for example).

Socrates (469–399 BC)

Neither *nephesh* nor *ruah* carries any hint of dualism. Admittedly, both are described occasionally as leaving man at death, but never as existing separately from the body. The Old Testament sees man as a unity. In the New Testament, it is more difficult to find out what is meant from the analysis of words, because the original manuscripts were written in Greek, and the available words were charged with the overtones of Greek philosophy, which included powerful dualistic influences. However, the New Testament writers do seem to emphasize the unity of the human person, and do not imply the idea of a disembodied soul. Thus, *psyche*, which is the New Testament equivalent of *nephesh*, carries meanings ranging from life and desire (in Paul's letters) to the whole personality.

Most strikingly, the New Testament doctrine of the resurrection of the body is very far from the Platonic concept of an eternal, immaterial soul able to exist in isolation from the body. This is particularly clear in 1 Corinthians 15 where Paul first affirms the physical resurrection of Jesus and that "those who belong to Christ" will likewise be raised. He then goes on to analyse the various uses of the word "body", showing that its meaning can vary, and he explains that after the dead are raised, their body will be a "spiritual body", very different from the previous "natural body" (or "physical body"), but a body nonetheless (pp.94–95). His notion of a "spiritual body" is radically different from the Platonic notion of an eternal, disembodied soul. Indeed, he states that the physical comes first, then the spiritual. Elsewhere Paul writes: "God,… who alone is immortal" (1 Timothy 6:16). Nowhere does the Bible countenance the notion of a disembodied soul or an intrinsically eternal soul.

ARGUMENTS IN FAVOUR OF DUALISM

Objections to monism

But if I do not have a separate soul, and if I am to have a new body in heaven, by what criterion will it still be "me"? This problem is not as great as it may at first seem. Even on earth, our personal identities persist without our being made of the same atoms and molecules throughout our lives. Most kinds of human cell have lives of only a few weeks or months, after which they die and are replaced by new cells. Neurons are admittedly an exception, in that they are not subject to such a turnover. But the molecules which constitute the neurons are continually turning over – sometimes every few minutes or hours. The most stable molecules are the chromosomes. These persist throughout life, but even they are subject to slow metabolic changes. The important point is that many of these changes in material content do not affect the basic information structure of the body and brain. If the metabolic changes in the DNA distort the encoded information, the resulting "errors" are corrected by special DNA-repair enzymes. Likewise, the basic stuff of neurons can be renewed without affecting the connectivity and functioning of the brain. Such changes are of course gradual ones within a continuously identifiable structure, and it is not suggested that they are perfectly analogous to the change between an earthly body and a heavenly body. The point is simply that the maintenance of personal identity does not depend on the matter we are made of but on the informationally relevant structure – just as a poem retains its essential qualities even if photocopied, or rewritten in a different script. Presumably, our resurrection bodies will preserve essential characteristics, even though they may be in other ways so different from our present bodies that we can scarcely conceive of them.

Attempts to defend dualism against the challenges of neuroscience

Interactive dualism is most commonly defended at the level of philosophy rather than neurobiology. Many modern philosophers are dualists, and some of these are interactive dualists. Philosophical defences usually emphasize the "hard problem of consciousness" and the problem of *qualia,* or the self-refuting nature of naturalism and determinism. These are important issues, but they are outside our present concern, which is the relationship between interactive dualism and neuroscience.

For Descartes, a separate soul was required to explain human intelligence. This no longer seems quite so necessary, although debate still takes place. Some of this is about whether standard algorithmic artificial intelligence can ever reproduce the performance of the human mind. Most specialists in computer intelligence seem to be optimistic that existing scepticism can be resolved by more subtle, non-algorithmic approaches, while most neurobiologists believe that current difficulties in artificial intelligence do not necessitate a separate soul acting on the brain, although they do not rule it out. Some of the uncertainty arises because a dualist could correctly argue that we do not have proof that all cerebral processes are entirely determined by the laws of physics and chemistry, and that brain processes central to our humanity such as intellectual creativity or ethical decision-making might still require a separate agent. The activation of particular brain regions during intellectual problem-solving or ethical decision-making could be due *partly* to the influence of a separate soul. Despite the total lack of supporting evidence, this is essentially the position that was taken by the late John Eccles, whose extensive and fundamental contributions to neuroscience were rewarded by a Nobel Prize in 1963, and who championed dualism throughout his long and productive career. Eccles's views are discussed below under the heading "Determinism and freedom".

Near-death experiences

Near-death experiences (NDEs) are reported remarkably commonly, usually (but not always) by people who have undergone profound cerebral **ischemia** (shortage of oxygen to the brain) and have in many cases been thought to have died. They may be triggered by stress or an emotional crisis, or more rarely occur spontaneously. NDEs vary somewhat between cultures, but many features are constant: the people concerned usually report an experience of being outside their own body and looking down on it; and then of rushing through dark space (often through a tunnel), seeing their lives pass before their eyes, and then entering a realm of light where they encounter deceased relatives or friends. There is a considerable literature on this phenomenon, but limited evidence on its neurobiological basis.

NDEs have long been cited by interactive dualists as evidence for a non-physical soul. The tradition extends as far back as Plato. Near the close of Plato's *Republic*,

Socrates tells of a Greek soldier, Er, who was believed killed in combat. But when the dead were collected for burial ten days after the battle, Er's body was undecayed, although he showed no signs of life. Before his comrades could bury him, Er came back to life and told them he had been in the afterworld. According to Er's account, when his soul left his body he found himself with other souls on a journey to a marvellous place where he saw many things including judges who determined the fate of the just and the unjust. The judges told Er that he was to observe and learn and then go back to earthly life and tell what he had seen. It seems likely that Er's NDE has contributed to the widespread belief in disembodied souls.

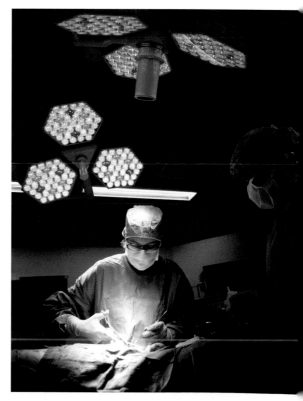

Some aspects of NDEs can be produced by brain stimulation. For example, during electrical stimulation of the temporal lobe, one of Wilder Penfield's patients exclaimed "Oh God, I am leaving my body". A more

recent case has been described in detail. Moderately weak electrical stimulation of the right angular gyrus (near the boundary between the parietal and temporal lobes of the brain) evoked the sensation of falling from a height. Slightly stronger stimulation evoked an out-of-body experience. The patient said "I see myself lying in bed, from above, but I only see my legs and lower trunk". In fact, the patient was lying in bed with her upper body supported at an angle of 45°, and so despite the illusory shift in the patient's vantage point, her description that she could only see her legs and lower trunk was correct. Subsequent stimulation led to illusions of lightness and floating close to the ceiling. When the patient was instructed to watch her legs, stimulation of the same site provoked the impression that her legs had become shorter or that they were moving towards her face. The region stimulated is known to be involved in the awareness of body position, and the authors interpreted the patient's sensations as resulting from a distortion of this awareness.

Out-of-body experiences such as these are only one aspect of an NDE, and a full NDE can apparently not be produced by stimulation of a single brain region. However, disruption of brain activity with drugs can produce more global NDEs, and this is particularly the case with ketamine, an anaesthetic that blocks a major class (NMDA-type) of receptors for the neurotransmitter glutamate; it is also used as a recreational drug. Ketamine can evoke the experiences of floating above the body, of travel through a tunnel, life review, and telepathic communication with a being of light.

How should we interpret such facts? There is a sizeable community of "believers" who maintain that NDEs provide irrefutable proof for a conscious soul that can leave the body, have experiences while in its disembodied state, and then return to the body. They point to numerous reports that people who "return to life" after an NDE describe things that they could apparently not have known by natural means. Such people often tell of friends or relatives they met in the other world who had died without their knowing, and that in this world, while floating near the ceiling, they saw things that they could not have seen by natural means. A typical example is a woman who underwent an operation under deep hypothermia (temperature below 16 °C) to remove an aneurysm from the basilar artery at the base of her brain. After the operation she reported having felt herself "pop" outside her body and hover above the operating table. She gave remarkably detailed descriptions of what happened during her surgery which were later verified to be very accurate. For example, she described a surgeon sawing into her skull with what looked to her like an electric toothbrush, and she reported accurately what the nurses in the operating room had said as well as many other details of the operation. There are many accounts of this kind.

On the other hand, such evidence does not convince everyone: some of the reports may be inaccurate, in others a patient who seemed unconscious may have had a marginal level of consciousness, and in still other cases the patients' descriptions may have had a semblance of accuracy by mere chance. Given that 5–15 per cent of the world's population claim to have had an NDE, it would not be surprising if some descriptions turned out to be accurate by mere chance.

Sceptics argue that the ability to produce NDEs by drugs or brain stimulation favours a naturalistic interpretation. The fact that many aspects of NDEs can be evoked by drugs certainly makes it at least conceivable that a disruptive event like cerebral ischemia could produce an NDE without any need for a disembodied soul. But the most important point in favour of the dualistic interpretation remains the apparent ability of people with an NDE to report facts that they could not have known by natural sensation. This is the critical issue, but the neurobiological data do not contribute to it.

Artificial intelligence and the soul

A related question is whether recent advances in artificial intelligence cast light on the question of monism versus dualism.

ARTIFICIAL INTELLIGENCE AND THE SOUL

Is it possible that technology will some day produce an artefact which is conscious – a machine that deserves to be called a person? Some who work in the field of Artificial Intelligence (AI) hold that this is the case, subscribing to a view known as "strong AI" or "Artificial General Intelligence".

The question is when, not if, we will build self-reproducing intelligent robots.
Rodney Brooks, the former director of the Computer Science and Artificial Intelligence Laboratory at MIT, in *Flesh and Machine* (2002)

Should Christians perceive strong AI as contradicting biblical teaching concerning the soul, or the teaching that humanity is created in the image of God? Do Christians have any necessary stake in the impossibility of creating a conscious artefact that deserves to be called a person? Would accomplishments in this field pose a challenge to the faith?

• •

Questions concerning the soul arise because consciousness or personhood is often attributed to "the soul". Body–soul dualists frequently understand Genesis 2:7 as teaching what amounts to a two-part creation of humanity: first God created a body and then (as a separate act) he breathed an immaterial soul into it. If human personhood stems from something separately created by God, then it seems a usurpation of his prerogatives to believe that humans could create an artefact that exhibits personhood.

However, Genesis 2:7 does not say that God created man's body, or that man acquired a soul; it says that God created man, and that man became a soul (or living being as modern translations tend to translate nephesh). Those who hold views like dual-aspect monism regard the mind (or personhood) and the body as two aspects of a single entity. In such views, human personhood can be understood as emerging from the activity of the neurons in the brain. Since emergence describes the origin of personhood rather than its nature, some dualists hold to it as well. If this is a correct understanding of the origin of personhood then, in principle, there is no reason to reject the possibility that personhood might emerge in a man-made artefact.

The human mind is produced by the human brain and is not a separate element "added to" the brain from outside.
William Hasker, The Emergent Self (1999)

What about the biblical teaching that humanity was created in the image of God? The precise meaning of the term has occasioned much discussion over the centuries. One understanding is that the *imago Dei* (image of God) is something unique in our constitution – something not part of any other creature – in which case perhaps the possibility of artificial persons poses a threat to this doctrine. But this understanding is far from universal among Christians. If the *imago Dei* is understood in terms of our value, purpose, and relationship to God, then it is not clear that the possibility of other entities having a similar purpose and relationship – or even a similar value – would necessarily challenge humanity's place in God's kingdom. Often an older sibling will ask the parents of a newborn child "Will you love me any less because you love my brother/sister?" The psalmist asked a similar question: "What is man, that you are mindful of him, the son of man that you care for him?" (Psalm 8:4), but never answers the question – perhaps because our relationship to God is rooted in *him*, not in something that is intrinsic to *us*.

All this is to say that the possible existence at some future time of an entity like Commander Data of *Star Trek: The Next Generation* poses no challenge to biblical teaching about human nature. At the same time, this is certainly not to claim that this will ever occur (although developments to date don't seem to suggest that this is likely in the near future, if ever.) But whether this will happen is ultimately a technological question, not a theological one.

CONCLUSION

Neuroscience provides no support for a separate, non-physical soul interacting with the brain, and the intriguing evidence from NDEs is no more than equivocal. There is overwhelming evidence that human behaviour, awareness, intentionality and even spirituality depend on brain activity. While the notion that certain key brain processes such as ethical decisions might be influenced by a non-physical soul cannot be strictly ruled out, it is not supported by any scientific evidence. Moreover, there is no known way in which a separate soul could influence the brain. There is no doubt that current neuroscientific data are more readily compatible with dual-aspect monism than with interactive dualism.

DETERMINISM AND FREEDOM

If the brain is a biological mechanism composed of cells whose components obey the laws of physics and chemistry, this implies that our behaviour and our decisions might be predetermined, which raises questions about free will. There are three main attitudes to this problem:

- *Compatibilism* ("soft determinism"): Determinism is compatible with free will and human responsibility (such as Spinoza, Hume, many modern philosophers including Daniel Dennett).

- *Libertarianism*: We do have free will, and this is incompatible with determinism (such as Thomas Reid, Kant, various modern philosophers including Robert Kane).

- *Hard determinism*: The past completely determines the future, including that of our own brains. Determinism is incompatible with free will and personal responsibility, which are therefore an illusion (such as Holbach, Nietzsche; most modern philosophers reject this label).

It would be beyond the scope of this book to consider in detail the arguments for these positions, but a few comments may be helpful. Hard determinism is unpopular, which is not surprising, because it undermines its own basis by implying that belief in hard determinism is not a free act. In contrast, compatibilism is favoured by a majority of modern philosophers. An important point made by compatibilists is that whereas determinism from the *outside* is compulsion, determinism from the inside is not. To say "my brain made me do it" is scarcely an excuse for an act, because if my brain did not "make me do it" then I would certainly not be responsible. The determinism inherent in a mechanistic understanding of the brain is not a problem for compatibilism.

Determinism is obviously a problem for libertarianism, so libertarians must propose a way for indeterminism to occur in the brain. By far the most popular modern approach is to invoke Heisenbergian uncertainty.

QUANTUM LIBERTARIANISM

Heisenberg's Uncertainty Principle states that there is an absolute limit to the precision of measurement when certain pairs of physical quantities are involved, such as the momentum and position of a particle. If h is Max Planck's constant, and

Werner Heisenberg (1901–76)

imprecision is expressed by Δ, then Δmomentum $\times$ Δposition $\geq h/4\varpi$. There is no limit to the precision with which the momentum alone of the electron, or its position alone, might be measured; but any gain in the precision of measurement of one member of the pair will inevitably be offset by decreased precision for the other member. Another such pair is: $\Delta E \times \Delta t \geq h/4\varpi$, where E is energy and t is time, and we shall use this below. Since h is very small indeed, Heisenbergian uncertainty is irrelevant to macroscopic objects such as golf balls; but it is very relevant to tiny entities such as electrons.

Heisenberg's principle was initially proposed as a practical limitation to measurement, but many physicists and philosophers have argued that it goes far deeper than mere practicalities, establishing a fundamental indeterminism in nature. Quantum libertarians argue that this provides for a fundamental indeterminacy of brain function, which can free us from the shackles of determinism and enable free will. The consequences of this interpretation for brain function have to be explored, but it should be recognized that it begins with the assumption that determinism is fundamental and not merely just a limit to measurement. It is contested by some physicists on these grounds.

A frequent criticism of quantum libertarianism is that the undirected randomness of Heisenbergian uncertainty would lead to disorder, rather than willed activity. This is to misunderstand what is being claimed: the quantum libertarians propose that, hidden by the fog of Heisenbergian uncertainty, the soul is actually exerting a tiny but *directed* influence on the activity of the brain.

However Heisenbergian uncertainty appears to be many orders of magnitude too small to allow significant impact of a non-physical soul on the brain. Quantum libertarians counter this by suggesting Heisenbergian uncertainty might allow a chemical bond to be modified in an ion channel in the synaptic membrane (the synapse is the site of communication between neurons). According to Heisenberg's principle, there is a limit to the precisions of energy (E) and time (t) given by $\Delta E.\Delta t \geq h/4\varpi$ where $h = 6.63 \times 10^{-34}$ Joules per second. In other words, an energy change ΔE can be "hidden" for a time Δt providing ΔE is of the order of $h/4\varpi\Delta t$. To have even a minimal effect on the synaptic function, Δt would need to be at least 10 microseconds, probably more. Substituting this value gives a ΔE of the order of 5.2×10^{-30} Joules. This is about 200,000 times too small to disrupt even a single Van der Waals interaction, the weakest of all the chemical bonds ($E = 1 \times 10^{-24}$ J). Even if, unrealistically, we took Δt as the time of a single ion to cross the channel (about 10 nanoseconds), ΔE is still 200 times too small. It is worth noting that recent supporters of quantum libertarianism do not address this problem, although Eccles's collaborator, the physicist Friedrich Beck calculated that their theory requires brain function to depend on events with a time-constant of 10^{-13}–10^{-14} seconds, which is about 10^9 times faster than any event known to be critically relevant to brain function. This is clearly problematic.

An alternative but unpopular possibility is that the soul itself might have energy, which would of course entail that it was a physical entity, not the non-physical sort of soul proposed by Descartes. Belief in a physical soul has occasionally been supported by people who attempted to estimate its mass by weighing the body before and after death, but there is no real evidence for a physical soul.

CONCLUSION

The question of determinism and free will is still a major topic of debate among philosophers. One thing seems certain: Heisenbergian uncertainty appears not to satisfy the requirement of libertarianism for functionally important indeterminism in the brain.

THE EVOLUTION OF RELIGION

One of the most vibrant debates in the scientific study of religion concerns how religion evolved. The debate has focused on two primary views: by-product and adaptationist. By-product theorists maintain that natural selection has not favoured religious beliefs and behaviours; rather, religion emerged as a by-product of cognitive mechanisms that evolved for other purposes. These scholars draw on a wealth of experimental research that demonstrates how supernatural agents activate the same cognitive mechanisms that humans employ when navigating ordinary social interactions, such as theory of mind. Supernatural agents are cognitively processed as humans, albeit humans with particular, and often extraordinary, physical and mental abilities. Supernatural agent concepts are formed by violating the basic expectations of universal ontological categories (person, animal, plant, and artefact). For example, ancestral spirits are cognitively processed as immaterial humans. By-product theorists have also explored ritual behaviour. For example, ritual performers and observers employ the same cognitive expectations and assumptions to perform ritual behaviour that we employ to understand all goal-directed action.

Most adaptationists do not dispute the by-product theorists' fundamental claim that the psychological mechanisms that produce religious beliefs and behaviours did not evolve to produce

A praying Buddhist

THE ORIGINS OF RELIGIOUS BELIEF

Virtually every culture is religious, regardless of its level of technology or education, or its political system. Religions vary greatly and do not always involve belief in a god (or gods), but the essential characteristics of a religion – beliefs concerning the origin, nature, and purpose of the universe; devotion to God or spirits or ancestors; symbolism, beliefs, and practices that give to life – are universal.

From at least the time of William James in the late nineteenth century, numerous attempts have been made to explain the universality of religion in evolutionary terms. These attempts have sometimes been used as propaganda by those who would explain away religion as nothing but an evolutionary relic, and therefore tend to be viewed with suspicion by believers. But to explain is not necessarily to explain away, and scientific study of the evolution of religion need not imply nothing-buttery.

religion per se. However, they argue that religion may best be understood as an adaptive complex of traits incorporating cognitive, affective, behavioural, and developmental elements. Religion consists of recurrent core features, including ritual, myth, taboo, emotionally charged symbols, music, altered states of consciousness, commitment to supernatural agents, and afterlife beliefs among others. These features receive varied emphasis across cultures; some cultures, for instance, place great emphasis on the afterlife (Christianity), others less so (Judaism). Moreover, the core features of religion clearly did not evolve together. Ritual, for example, has antecedents in many species and presumably has a much deeper evolutionary history in our lineage than other core features, such as myth. The evolution of religion consisted of uniting cognitive processes and behaviours that for the most part already existed.

A pilgrimage to Mecca is an obligation for all devout Muslims, demonstrating their solidarity with other Muslims and their submission to God.

Although the features of religions evolved separately, they coalesce in similar ways across all cultures and at some point in our evolutionary history they began to regularly coalesce into a functional system.

Adaptationists argue that we cannot evaluate whether or not the religious system is an adaptation or a by-product by examining its independent parts, such as supernatural agent beliefs or ritual behaviours, in isolation. We must consider the religious system more comprehensively, focusing on how the constituent parts contribute to the system and how the parts interact with each other to achieve functional goals. It is the religious system, not the constituent parts, that produces functional effects. Adaptationists have primarily focused on four types of fitness benefits produced by religious systems. Two types of benefits involve manipulation and thus may result in fitness gains only for those with power advantages: reproductive control and political control. And two types of benefits may be more widely distributed among communities: health and intra-group cooperation.

One potential resolution of the adaptationist–by-product debate is to view religion as an **exaptation**. An exaptation is a pre-existing trait that acquires a different role from that which it originally acquired through natural selection. If correct, the critical issue of the adaptationist–by-product debate is whether or not the cognitive and emotional mechanisms exapted by the religious system have been adaptively modified by the new socio-ecological niche created by religion. At the present time, we lack sufficient data to resolve this and other debates about the evolution of religion, but increasing research interest in this area suggests that a resolution might not be far off.

CONCLUSION

The scientific study of humanity and human life is an immense subject, drawing on numerous areas of science including evolutionary biology, palaeoanthropology, neuroscience, psychology, and artificial intelligence. This brief survey can only give a glimpse of current scholarly opinion. This may change in the light of new results, but it seems likely that much, though not all, will stand the tests of time and further investigation. For those who are both scientist and Christian, the light given by contemporary science tends to complement the picture provided by the Bible. The book of God's words (the Bible) and the book of God's works (nature) illuminate different dimensions of reality.

GENES FOR RELIGIOSITY

There have been suggestions about whether there are "God genes" that make some people more religious than others. It would be surprising if our genetic make-up were totally irrelevant to our spirituality, tendency to believe in God, and so on, but some accounts have exaggerated the issue out of all proportion.

One such suggestion was a book by Dean Hamer, *The God Gene: How Faith is Hardwired into our Genes*. *Time Magazine* for October 2004 asked: "Does our DNA compel us to seek a higher power? Believe it or not, some scientists say yes." Statements such as this were almost universally ridiculed by scientists. To understand why, it is necessary to understand the background

to Hamer's own research, the main theme of his book.

Previous research using twin studies found only a small genetic influence on parameters such as church-going or belief in God. If one twin goes to church (or believes in God), there is a good chance that his twin brother will do so too. However, the correlation is only slightly higher between monozygotic twins, who are genetically identical, than between dizygotic twins, whose genetic similarity is no greater than that of non-twin siblings. Hamer did not study faith or religiosity at all, but focused on responses to a psychological questionnaire designed to measure a combination of three factors: self-forgetfulness, the tendency to feel

connected to the universe, and an openness to believe things not literally provable, such as ESP. This combination has been called "self-transcendence", and earlier twin studies had shown a strong genetic influence on it. Hamer found a correlation (albeit weak) between a person's self-transcendence score and a particular variant of a gene called VMAT2 (vesicular monoamine transporter-2) which controls the levels of the neurotransmitters serotonin, dopamine, and noradrenaline in synapses.

Hamer's research (and his book) in fact provided no evidence that "Faith is Hardwired into our Genes" (to quote the book's title). A *Scientific American* reviewer objected: "The book… would be better titled: 'A Gene That Accounts for Less Than One Percent of the Variance Found in Scores on Psychological Questionnaires Designed to Measure a Factor Called Self-Transcendence, Which Can Signify Everything from Belonging to the Green Party to Believing in ESP, According to One Unpublished, Unreplicated Study'".

Despite sensationalist claims in the popular press, the weight of evidence (mainly from twin studies) indicates that genetic differences play only a minor role in determining who will be a religious believer.

Twin studies are a valuable method of separating genetic from environmental influences

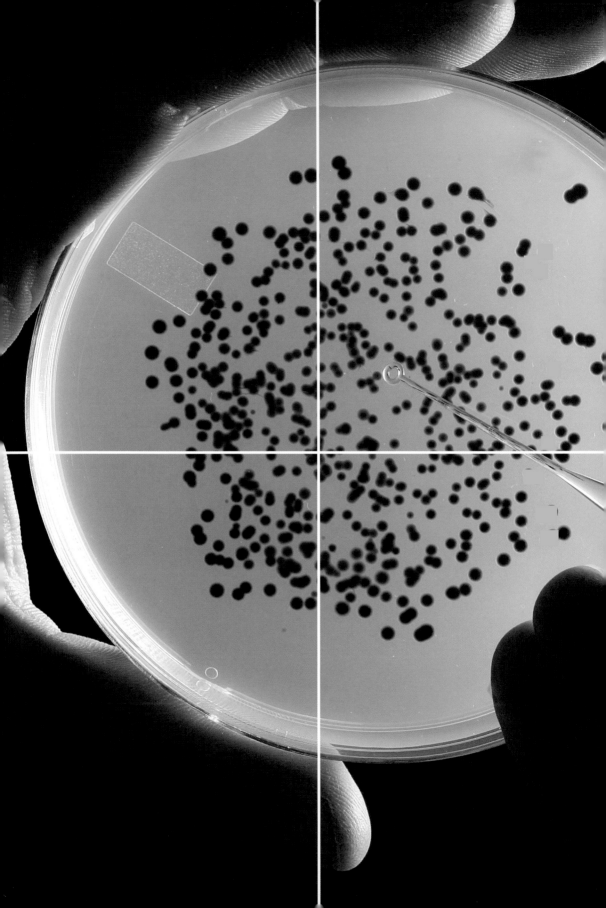

Science, Ethics, and Christianity

We need to understand the different positions that are taken on issues raised by modern science. This is a necessary preliminary for working out our own views, including whether there is a specifically Christian standpoint for any given issue. This understanding is the subject of ethics, broadly defined as a study of the principles involved in making moral decisions or, as the Oxford English Dictionary puts it, *"moral principles that govern a person's behaviour or the conducting of an activity... the branch of knowledge that deals with moral principles"*. Morals – the idea that some actions are right and some are wrong – are at the heart of ethics but the pressing questions that arise from this are "what are these moral principles, where do they come from and how do we find them?" There are four main approaches to these questions.

First, there is *natural law*, the idea that what is right is that which enables humans (and other entities) to reach their natural potential or to flourish. Aristotle is the best known proponent of this approach with his hierarchy of different elements within nature, going from totally inanimate objects such as stones, via plants, non-human animals, and humans to God. Each item within each level of the hierarchy had its own *telos*, its essential nature, and its reason for being; it was seen as morally wrong to prevent that *telos* from being expressed. Natural law reasoning features strongly in the writing of Thomas Aquinas. Natural law, in his view arises from the wisdom with which God rules the created order and which humans need to

Thomas Aquinas
(1225–74), proponent
of natural law

bring their thinking into line with this divine wisdom. Elements of natural law thinking, derived from Thomas Aquinas, are encountered today in the Roman Catholic prohibition of contraception.

Second, there are *deontological* systems (from the Greek *deon*, duty), systems based on rules and duties. Such systems lay down clear, "black and white" rules. To obey a rule is morally right; to disobey a rule is morally wrong. Deontological ethics is sometimes known as *Kantian* ethics because of the framing by Immanuel Kant of his imperatives, typified by the categorical "*Act in such a way that you treat humanity, whether in your own person or in the person of any other, never merely as a means to an end…*" or, in modern language, other human beings are not to be used as mere instruments for our wishes or desires. The Ten Commandments, with their straightforward rules, can be regarded as examples of **deontology**. In modern times, the UN Declaration of Human Rights, while clearly defining the *rights* of every human, also defines the *duties* of every human in not transgressing another's rights.

Third, there are *consequentialist* systems, moral systems in which the main consideration of whether an action is right or wrong is what happens as a result of that action being taken. Are the consequences "good" or "bad" (however an individual defines good and bad)? If the consequences are good, then the action is good. Consider the idea that lying is wrong. Under a deontological system one never lies. Under a consequentialist system, lying may be regarded as acceptable, or even right, if the outcome is good. For example, lying about someone's whereabouts in order to prevent their being found by people who would do them harm. Applied more widely, the version of consequentialism known as **utilitarianism** defines as good those actions that promote the most (or most widespread) happiness or satisfaction. Consequentialist thinking is very widespread, but it has its drawbacks. If only outcomes are considered, then we may ignore at our peril the means of reaching those outcomes. Further, in utilitarianism there is the danger of ignoring the minority through promoting the most widespread happiness or satisfaction.

In secular Western society, **consequentialism** in its various forms, tempered by deontology and occasionally nuanced by a smattering of natural law, is the main practice of most people in day-to-day moral decision-making (although most people do not analyse the means by which they reach such decisions).

However, there is still another way. We see it alongside natural law in the writing of both Aristotle and Aquinas. Aquinas emphasized that good ethical decision-making involves bringing our human wisdom into line with God's wisdom. In Aquinas's view, God's wisdom defines the natural law, but now we also have to accept that human character has to grow or to be changed to fulfil that law. In other words, character and virtue (including wisdom), contribute strongly to our decision-making in a system known as *virtue ethics*. That is not to say that virtue ethicists have thrown away the rule book or ignore the consequences of their actions. On the contrary, appropriate consideration of rules and consequences is part of a virtuous approach to moral decision-making (see below).

CHRISTIAN ETHICS

Christian ethicists and theologians are increasingly coming to regard Christian ethics as a virtue ethics system. Certainly there are some rules and outcomes of actions to be considered, but good moral decision-making comes from Christian character. Spiritual formation, openness to the transforming power of the Holy Spirit, growth of the fruit of the Spirit are all aspects of the development of Christian virtue. The philosopher Dallas Willard emphasizes the importance of this in stating that some Christians expend so much effort in getting people into heaven that they ignore "getting heaven into people". Jesus gave us a clear principle: "Love your neighbour as yourself" (Matthew 22:39). He also modelled Christian virtue in his own behaviour and told stories to show how Christian character should work out in practice.

What we do not find is Jesus held up or holding himself up, as an example of someone who "kept the rules", reinforcing or reinterpreting them. The way of life he was modelling was precisely not something that could be reduced to rules, or undertaken simply by the effort to conform to certain laid-down norms. Nor could it be arrived at… by the calculating and weighing the likely effects of certain behaviours, with those calculations leading to decisions and actions. Nor, certainly, was Jesus saying that people should "do what comes naturally": indeed, what comes "naturally" from the heart was precisely the problem as far as he was concerned. The only way we can get to the heart of understanding the moral challenge Jesus offered and offers still today, is by thinking in terms not of rules or of the calculation of effects or of romantic or existentialist "authenticity", but of virtue. A virtue that has been transformed by the kingdom and the cross.
Tom Wright, *Virtue Reborn* (2010)

Paul emphasized the primacy of love (1 Corinthians 13) and listed several aspects of Christian character as the fruit of the Spirit, "against such there is no law" (Galatians 5:22–23). Nevertheless, as has already been noted, rules play their part, albeit a subordinate part within the larger framework of virtue.

How then does this work out in the context of modern science with its range of previously untried choices? We cannot (and indeed should not) expect to find specific answers to such questions in the Bible; we are confronting situations and processes not even dreamt of in biblical times. Many writers warn against trying to fit verses or passages from the Bible into situations for which they were never intended, often in an attempt to justify a person's own preconceptions. It is very much a virtue-based approach that enables us to make wise decisions on such topics.

Moreover, along with communitarian theologians such as Richard Hays and Stanley Hauerwas, we need to emphasize that the development of Christian character ideally occurs in the context of a Christian community. This applies as much to discussion of bioethical issues as to other areas of life. It does not mean that all Christians will reach the same conclusions on all of these issues; we should be wary of those who purport to define *the* Christian view. There is often a range of opinions among Christians; it does not negate the communitarian aspect of Christian ethics. Such differences of opinion should be accepted with love within the Christian community, *maintaining the bond of peace in the unity of the Spirit*.

ETHICS AND THE PRACTICE OF SCIENCE

Ethical systems have evolved or been developed (or, for some, given to us) mainly for human society to function in the context of human actions and interactions. That is not to say that other living things (and perhaps the environment itself) do not have moral significance, merely that human activity and what we do with and to other humans has been the primary focus. Science has its own code of ethics, and scientific research has become a major activity of human society, at least within the developed nations. Obviously the practice of science does not preclude normal human interactions, and there is no reason to believe that scientists outside their laboratory are any more or any less "moral" than any other citizen. The practice of science involves the norms of social discourse and interactions between individuals and organizations just as much as any other sphere of activity. Whatever their occupation, Christians are expected to *love their neighbour as themselves* (Matthew 22:39).

However two issues are of especial importance to scientists. The first of these is fabrication and falsification of data. The progress of science depends on what has gone

Aftermath of Hurricane Katrina, New Orleans, 2005

before and if previously published data cannot be relied on, there can be no progress. The second is plagiarism, passing off of someone else's work as one's own. Both sadly occur: temptations arise whenever there is great pressure to succeed. If detected, they are dealt with very strictly by the scientific community, recognizing that the whole edifice of science and its credibility are threatened by such actions. In discussion of these issues we need scientists, whether or not they are Christians, to be open and honest about their work.

TECHNOLOGY, BIOTECHNOLOGY, AND ENVIRONMENT

Our ability to manipulate nature ("dominion") must be seen in the light of the principles of stewardship and creation care. The whole tenor of the Bible is that "the earth and everything in it is the Lord's" (Psalm 24:1) and that God cares about his creation. Further, it is usually the poor who suffer most from environmental damage. The principle of justice therefore enters into our environmental concern. How do we use these principles in given situations? A significant part of this must be to evaluate environmental risks and to use wisdom and discernment in weighing risks against benefits. We cannot know all the outcomes of our actions. Therefore to demand, or to claim, "100 per cent safety" would put humans in the place of God. Second, our growing perceptions of health and life expectancy perhaps make us more averse to the idea that something might go wrong, so that precaution may deny valid human judgments. Our recent ancestors risked travelling at an unprecedented 30 mph by train!

ETHICS AND RISK

Life is full of risks – crossing the road, climbing a ladder, living in an earthquake zone, investing one's savings, choosing a life partner. Some risks are just there, like a cliff edge; some happen, like lightning; and some we take voluntarily – abseiling or overtaking. Risk is not an aberration brought on by technology, nor simply blamed as a result of the fall. God created humans within biological limits. Hot deserts, icy cold lakes, and cliff edges all present natural dangers because we cannot exceed our body's thermostat, fly, or live under water. Part of being human is to learn how to live in the light of risk. Based on both our experience and others', we weigh the two main factors in a classical risk calculation – the size of harm that might occur from an action, and we judge how probable it is to happen.

Anyone developing a technology carries a responsibility to evaluate as far as possible the risk to individuals, to communities and social structures, and to God's creation. Scientists calculate risks of aircraft crashes or nuclear accidents based on engineering data and highly sophisticated modelling. But it is an ethical judgment whether the number which experts calculate is considered acceptable or not. This involves weighing risks against benefits, and often making difficult judgments. Is it irresponsible for scientists to piece together a pandemic virus from DNA fragments, when such research may be a vital way to reduce future outbreaks? Are nuclear power risks more acceptable than the risks of making climate change worse by continuing to burn fossil fuels?

We vary greatly in what we consider risky. Faced with uncertainty, some tend to be precautionary; others might grasp the challenge. Another element is the weighting we put on a certain risk. This is based on many unquantifiable factors – like our personal inclinations and experience, how much the risk lies in our control, our familiarity with it, what we compare it with if it is unfamiliar, and also our social context. Coal mining is a high risk occupation but if you were a man with family ties in a pit community, it was "what you did".

Some risks can be calculated on past data. In other cases, the precautionary principle mandates taking anticipatory action if we strongly suspect a risk, for example from climate change or from novel organisms created

by synthetic biology, even if we do not have sufficient information to be sure of the risk. However, there are limits to precaution; we can never be protected absolutely. Second, compared with past generations, high levels of health and life expectancy perhaps make us more averse to the idea that something might go wrong, so that precaution may neutralize other judgments. For example, most people accept the possible but uncertain risks of microwave radiation from a mobile phone. The benefits outweigh the uncertainty about damage. Similarly, we should not rule genetically modified organisms unacceptable simply because they might have some as yet unseen effect. An ethical judgment has to be made based on the best evidence available. Some applications with considerable benefits, and whose harmful effects were judged small, might be considered acceptable. In contrast, a

procedure especially risky to humans or the environment might be usable only in strictly contained conditions. Sometimes we may decide that we do not have the ability to handle a risk, either because it is too likely to happen or the consequences would be too great. We will discuss this further under nuclear power (see pp. 237–39).

A Christian view of risk would take all these aspects into account, but would especially seek to protect the vulnerable and those more at risk from a development, for risk is often unevenly spread. It also has to acknowledge our human tendency to play down the risks of our inventions through neglect, greed, or hubris. But ultimately it recognizes that our security does not lie in human risk protection, but in the grace and providence of God.

Risk-taking. A rock-climbing woman in the Verdon Gorge, Provence.

ENVIRONMENT AND ENERGY

The burning of fossil fuels (coal, oil, and natural gas) has led, to a dramatic increase in the atmospheric concentration of CO_2 since the Industrial Revolution with a concomitant rise in global temperature. Even the 0.6 °C rise that had occurred by 2010 has had detectable ecological effects. A rise of 2 °C (which seems likely to occur, if current usage rates are continued, by the end of the twenty-first century) is predicted to have very serious consequences. Climate scientists are concerned that the rise will eventually be even greater than this. There is thus an imperative to reduce very markedly the burning of fossil fuels. To this are added the pressures caused by the declining rate of discovery of oil. The probability is that recoverable stocks of oil will run out by the end of the present century, never mind the environmental hazards of oil production from difficult locations, exemplified in 2010 by the blow-out at the Deepwater Horizon oil-drilling rig in the Gulf of Mexico. There are therefore moves to replace fossil fuels with renewable and carbon-neutral energy sources. Thus, natural sources of energy such as wind, tide, water, waves, and solar energy are increasingly being used. (Wind and flowing water, have been widely used for centuries. The Rance barrage in northern France was the first modern tidal power station, built in the 1960s). However, widespread adoption of such technologies has its own problems. The quantity of fossil fuel used in construction must enter carbon-budget calculations. The principle of stewardship must lead us towards seeking a very clear benefit. Further, as typified by wind energy, there is a tension between different environmental priorities. In many parts of the world, the windiest places are often also scenically beautiful. Many are "wilderness" – wild, open, often montane places, the

Technological disaster. The oil rig Deepwater Horizon on fire in the Gulf of Mexico, 2010.

preservation of which has become an environmental priority. But dealing with climate change is also a priority. Which should take precedence?

Attention is now focused on two particular energy sources, nuclear fission, and biofuels. Both have been presented as partial solutions to current problems.

NUCLEAR POWER

The subject of nuclear power continues to evoke strong reactions. It brings together a complex set of ethical, environmental, and policy issues of great controversy, on which Christians sincerely differ.

A nuclear reactor harnesses the natural properties of the uranium nucleus, which emits neutrons, which in turn can split other uranium atoms into smaller atoms, with a great release of energy. The energy produced is far more than in any chemical reaction such as burning coal, oil, or gas. By bringing enough uranium close together, a controlled chain reaction can be set up, which can boil water to steam, generating electricity on a large scale. Nuclear fission chain reactions are a natural phenomenon in the universe, giving rise to all the chemical elements. On earth, aeons ago, chain reactions went on naturally for many thousands of

Technological development. A wind farm in Kansas.

years in uranium ore seams at Oklo in West Africa.

The first issue is whether finite and fallible humans can control this huge natural energy, with rigorous enough standards of design, construction, maintenance, and safety regulation, without subjecting people or God's creation to undue radiation risks, or catastrophic accidents? Nuclear power should only be used where there is a strong safety culture and firm infrastructure. Is this realistic? For some, the risk of severe health effects, loss of life, and environmental contamination, highlighted by the Chernobyl explosion of 1986, represent unacceptable consequences, no matter how unlikely such events may be. But Chernobyl resulted from extreme malpractice in a poor safety culture, and involved a design rejected in the West as unsafe. Despite severe damage to the Fukushima reactors following the catastrophic 2011 Japanese tsunami, health effects seem to have been small. Even such extraordinary events can be designed for. The Three Mile Island accident in the USA in 1979 arguably taught us more. A US reactor operating normally within safety regulations had a series of

faults leading to a partial melt down. Major harm was avoided, but were such failures under routine conditions to recur, one might fairly conclude that nuclear power was too risky an enterprise for humans to handle in practice.

The second major challenge is the acceptability of producing wastes that remain hazardous for unimaginable timescales, a legacy which every future generation must manage. For some, this rules out building any further nuclear power plants. Others argue that this not a unique problem. Humans have used copper, for example, in many different ways for thousands of years; yet copper salts remain poisonous for ever. Each generation bequeaths its technologies, assuming the next can handle their risks and benefits just as well. Deep repositories are now being built for long-lived radioactive wastes. In the very long term, small radioactive seepage may gradually occur but is not expected to have serious effects. A large accumulation of nuclear waste from weapons and civil power generation has to be stored, anyway. One more generation of nuclear power plants, to bridge the "energy gap" until renewable sources take over, would only make

Technological development. An "energy farm" of photovoltaic cells.

a small increase in the waste burden. Indefinite use of nuclear power would be a different matter. Nuclear fusion power, based on lithium and hydrogen, would almost eliminate long-lived wastes, and should be much safer from accidents, but it remains to be seen whether it will ever prove feasible and economic to engineer on the scale needed to be a major global energy supply.

Nuclear energy carries a large stigma because of "The Bomb". It is a classic example of human potential to put resources to both beneficial and malign uses. For some, the military origins and connections, which continue to pose threats in international relations, irredeemably render any peaceful uses of nuclear power unacceptable. But abandoning civil nuclear power would be no guarantee of removing military nuclear threats, because the knowledge, materials, and resources remain widely available.

One cannot evaluate nuclear power without considering its alternatives. There is no environmental "free lunch"; every energy source has its adverse side. An overwhelming proportion of world energy use is from fossil fuels. Their cumulative wastes are causing time-delayed, serious disruption of the planet's climate, with very dire consequences if we do not reduce our emissions urgently and very greatly. The UK Royal Commission on Environmental Pollution estimated that, unless we reduce our personal and national energy demand massively, even with extensive introduction of wind power on- and offshore, and other currently feasible renewable technologies, we would still fail to meet climate targets by 2050 without building many more nuclear power stations or fossil-fuel power stations with large scale capture of CO_2. It is a matter of ethical judgment which risk is more to be avoided. But if we wish both to eliminate nuclear power and to bring global warming to tolerable levels, the collective solution of major energy saving lies in our own homes and lives and choices.

Natural forces and technological disaster. The Fukushima nuclear power plant after tsunami damage, 2011.

Over the past century, agricultural production systems in developed countries have moved from self-sustainability to being highly dependent on cheap fossil fuel-derived energy inputs. Before fossil fuels were widely available, up to 25 per cent of land area used for farming was needed to provide on-farm energy in the form of food for working animals and wood for heat and power. It is now generally accepted that the use of fossil fuels to provide energy, not just for agriculture but right across the range of human activity, is playing a major role in current global climate change. Meanwhile, the human population of the world in 2010 was 6.8 billion and is expected to plateau at 9 billion in 2050. With the increasing population and changes in consumption patterns based on increasing dietary expectations (for example a "move to meat" in China), it is projected that current world food production will need to double by 2050. To grow enough food for everyone in a time of climate change is a huge challenge since global resources of arable land are more or less finite (and are under threat from the effects of climate change and the need to house the increasing population). Added

to this is the need to move away from fossil fuels in order to reduce emissions of the greenhouse gas, CO_2; this move includes the use of land for growth of biofuels. It has been described as a "perfect storm".

What decisions should be taken to ensure sufficient land for both food and fuel for everyone? A 2006 United Nations report *Livestock's Long Shadow* showed that about one-third of global crop production is used in the intensive rearing of animals for meat and dairy produce, omitting land used for the rearing of animals which is not suitable or only marginally suitable for food or biofuel crop growth. If the rich nations reduced their consumption of livestock-based foods significantly, much more land would become available both for growth of food crops and for valuable non-food uses such as biofuels. However, this is a moral decision involving other key issues such as creation care and global justice.

Turning more specifically to biofuels, trees (such as wood) have been used for fuel throughout human history. More recently, "ligno-cellulosic" energy crops (crops exploiting the cellular structure of plants) have become a

Deforestation in the Amazon Rain Forest

strong focus because they have the potential to produce higher yields. Over the past 20 years, increasing attention has been paid to a wild perennial grass species from eastern Asia – *Miscanthus giganteus* (elephant grass, Asian elephant grass, or giant silver grass). Trials have shown that once it is established, *Miscanthus* has a high productivity and requires very low inputs, resulting in high net energy yields per hectare. Admittedly, the best yields are obtained on good land which is mostly needed for food-crop production, but it will grow on lower-grade land. A challenge for breeders is to identify *Miscanthus* lines that, with suitable husbandry, will perform well on marginal land.

The pressure to move away from our dependence on fossil fuels is very clear. Equally clear is the tension between land use for fuel and land use for food. For these reasons, there is an increasing amount of research on biofuel sources that do not require agricultural land. These sources include micro-algae (tiny single-celled green plants) that may be grown in large tanks. However, taking all the different biofuel sources together and expecting that both plant breeding and biotechnology will lead to increased yields, it still remains very unlikely that these technical advances will be enough to meet the projected demands for food and energy.

There is therefore a moral imperative to reduce consumption. The lifestyles of developed countries, with their high demand for resources, have a largely negative impact on the populations of poorer countries. We are not loving our neighbours as ourselves (Matthew 22:39). Decisions need to be made to move away from over-consumption, from inefficient and environmentally costly products, and from waste. A truly virtuous approach is required, seeking God's gift of wisdom for guidance and for influencing decisions made at national and international levels. The words of Micah are very relevant: "And what does the Lord require of you, but to do justice, to love kindness, and to walk humbly with your God?" (Micah 6:8).

Left: Fixing the sun's energy in green algae
Right: One season's growth of Elephant Grass, *Miscanthus giganteus*

ENVIRONMENT AND AGRICULTURE: GENETICALLY MODIFIED (GM) CROPS

The basic techniques of genetic modification were developed in the early 1970s. The first successful plant GM experiment was carried out in 1983; by 1985 trials of GM plants were in progress. The first commercial product was Flav'Sav'™ tomatoes (and a paste made from the tomatoes) in which softening was delayed by "switching off" one of the plant's own genes; this appeared in 1995. Other GM crops quickly followed, in particular maize (corn), soybean, oil-seed rape (canola), and cotton. At the time of going to press, it is thought that GM rice will be marketed in 2011. The major genetic traits involved are resistance to herbicides (enabling farmers to better manage the control of weeds among their crops) and resistance to insect pests (reducing very markedly the use of insecticide, especially in cotton and maize crops).

GM CROPS

• • • • •

As the world's population increases (at the same time as the likelihood that the availability of agricultural land will decrease, through environmental degradation, global warming, and the living space requirements of the increasing population), it will not be even theoretically possible to feed everyone at current rates of agricultural production. In order to deal with this crisis we need higher yields coupled with the creation of crops able to grow in more marginal environments. This is the challenge facing plant breeders. One of the techniques available to them is genetic modification. This topic elicits strongly opposing reactions both within the Christian community and in wider society. So, is the employment of GM techniques in plant breeding programmes compatible with Christian ideals of creation care, global justice, and relief of suffering?

In respect of creation care, the first issue is whether moving genes between organisms is intrinsically wrong: is there a deontological or a natural law objection to this process? It is difficult to see why GM should be intrinsically wrong especially when we compare it with some of the other techniques used in plant breeding and when we note that gene transfer between species occurs widely in nature. Despite this, it is recognized that some peoples' objections to GM are based on the idea that it is of itself actually wrong.

Developing new rice cultivars at the International Rice Research Institute, showing the secure greenhouses for genetically modified studies.

By 2010, GM crops were being grown commercially on 134 million hectares in 25 countries, involving 14 million farmers. The USA has been the leading adopter of crop GM technology, followed by Brazil, Argentina, India, Canada, and China. In the European Union, commercial use of GM crops is, at the time of writing, confined to just six countries. Spain is the major European user of GM crops: 22 per cent of its maize crop (in 2010) was GM insect-tolerant, accounting for 80 per cent of the EU's growth of GM maize. In general, public opinion in the EU has opposed the use of GM crops (somewhat ironically, the first successful plant GM experiments were carried out in Belgium, the headquarters of the EU). The governments of EU countries apply the precautionary principle very rigorously and although the law in most EU countries does not prohibit the growth of GM crops, adoption is proceeding only slowly.

Second, there is the question of environmental safety. Plants may "escape" into non-agricultural environments (so-called "volunteers"), and there are some (actually very few) crop species that are able to hybridize (via cross-pollination) with very closely related wild species. However, these features are true whether a particular crop has been bred by GM or by "conventional" techniques. So evaluation of the possible environmental dangers of volunteer crops or of out-crossing needs to be based on the genetic traits that the crop possesses rather than the technique used to generate those traits. Nevertheless, it has to be acknowledged that GM techniques at present permit the introduction of a wider range of traits than conventional breeding. This will require adequate risk analysis on a case-by-case basis.

The third general environmental issue is that of biodiversity. One of the major traits initially introduced by GM techniques was herbicide-tolerance. Farm-scale trials showed that growth of herbicide-tolerant crops did indeed reduce biodiversity. However, this does not show that GM crops reduce biodiversity; it shows exactly what has been stated: growth of herbicide-tolerant crops reduces biodiversity. Plant breeders have produced herbicide-tolerant crop plants by conventional breeding which have not been subject to the same evaluation; under current regulations, these could be incorporated into commercial agriculture without such testing.

• •

Can GM crops be an aid in loving our neighbour (Matthew 22:39)? Leaving aside the non-softening tomato (which may be regarded as a rather novel application of the technology to "test the water"), the major traits in the first generation of commercial GM crops were of benefit to the farmer rather than the consumer. This is not in itself wrong: the growth of insect-tolerant crops reduces the need for insecticides, thereby decreasing environmental pollution. Further, growth of those crops by small farmers in less developed countries has led to increased yields at lower costs, and thus increased income. Second-generation GM crops include crops with benefits to the consumer, including Golden Rice™ which has the potential to relieve vitamin-A deficiency thus preventing thousands of cases of childhood blindness in parts of Asia (see Luke 4:18; 7:22).

However, the expense of developing GM technology (partly because of the cost of meeting regulatory requirements) has meant that ownership of crop GM technology was at the end of the twentieth century mainly concentrated in the hands of about six large agricultural biotechnology companies based in wealthy developed nations. Added to this is the highly contentious issue of the patenting of genes. Patent law in the USA and in the EU, until recently, forbade the patenting of discoveries; therefore parts of nature, including genes, were not regarded as patentable. From a Christian perspective, genes, as parts of nature are works of the Creator. However, biotechnology companies argued that in making copies of genes for use in GM techniques, they were inventing something, even if the copies had the same structure as the genes themselves. Patent agencies have accepted this argument and granted patents on a number of genes, thus placing yet more power in the hands of the already-powerful. There has been a widespread negative response to this from organizations and individuals (including scientists) who desire to see the earth's resources used more fairly. One reaction has been the publishing of gene sequences in public databases (thereby preventing their being patented). However, the patenting of plant genes, including those involved in drought- and temperature-tolerance (which are very relevant to the adaptation of plants to global warming) continues.

MORE THAN 1.02 BILLION HUNGRY PEOPLE

Distribution of chronically under-nourished people, 2010

Near East and North Africa **42**
Developed countries **15***
Latin America and the Caribbean **53**
Sub-Saharan Africa **265**
642 Asia and the Pacific

* Millions of people

Nevertheless, several less wealthy nations are now benefiting from GM technology. For example, 29 per cent of the 2009 cotton crop in Burkina Faso was GM insect-tolerant. More widely, 13 million of the 14 million farmers growing GM crops were "small" and resource-poor, from developing or less-developed countries. This has happened in several ways, including technology transfer via international agencies, some of which have deliberately ignored the patents on genes as unethical. Other agencies have bought the rights to exploit patented genes and in some instances, the patent holders have granted "freedom to operate". Further, there are increasing examples of "home-grown" GM initiatives, especially relevant to strains suitable for the countries in question. Among these is a blue rose developed in Japan, which, it might be said, is not an application relevant to feeding hungry people.

Is the use of GM crops compatible with Christian virtue-based approaches to the creation and to global justice? There are differences of opinion among Christians. Some proponents of GM crops, and especially certain commercial organizations, have exaggerated or even lied about possible benefits. Taking account of both this and practices such as gene patenting, it is no wonder that, at the very least, there are strong doubts about crop GM technology. However, it is equally true to say that some opponents of crop GM technology, while making valuable points about the concentration of commercial power, have also exaggerated or lied about possible risks. In actual debate, honest scientists with no vested interests have been accused of lying about their results while members of the public with genuine questions to ask have been called ignorant or stupid. None of this has helped individual or societal decision-making.

A blue rose created by inserting a gene from a petunia into a rose.

NANOTECHNOLOGY AND ENVIRONMENT

Nanotechnology is one of the newest branches of applied science, involving the use of devices constructed at the nanometre scale. It has been heralded as the key to the next industrial revolution, with applications in all aspects of human life. However, the

NANOTECHNOLOGY AND THE ENVIRONMENT

The term nanotechnology was first used in 1974 by the Japanese scientist, Norio Taniguchi. He used it to describe the methods and tools used to produce electronic circuits and devices with a precision in the range of one nanometre (nm), which is one thousand-millionth of a metre. Nanotechnology is currently used to describe scientific work carried out at the 1 to 100 nm range. It includes technology that can manipulate and manufacture items at this scale and many types of nanoparticles. Some of these are naturally occurring, including some of the particles produced during volcanic eruptions and forest fires, and of course, proteins and viruses.

New forms of carbon have been discovered which have nanoscale dimensions, including "buckyballs" and "carbon nanotubes". Buckyballs are hollow geodesic spheres made from carbon atoms which, in outline, look like a soccer ball. Carbon nanotubes have a similar arrangement of carbon atoms, but they form a sheet which rolls up to form a tube. These are a few nanometres in diameter, but can be up to millimetres long. Other engineered nanoparticles are being synthesized and investigated, including "quantum dots" (semiconductors containing only 10–50 atoms) and dendrimers (complex molecules in which a general spherical shape is achieved by branches radiating out from a central core). More visionary and futuristic possibilities are nanoscale machines, sometimes dubbed nanobots (nano-robots).

Nanotechnology is integral to developments in electronics, contributing to smaller devices with faster speeds and greater storage capacities. Nanoparticles are also of interest because

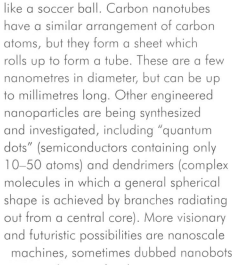

A bucky ball or fullerene

technology raises ethical issues both in relation to the environment, to the life of individual humans and to humankind in general.

of their novel chemical, physical, or biological properties. The same substance can have different properties as nanoparticles when compared to its bulk properties. For example, aluminium is relatively unreactive in bulk, but explosive as nanoparticles. Such different properties lead to interest in the potential value of these materials but also concerns about hazards.

Nanotechnology has been proposed as a source of new, inexpensive water-purification technologies. About 1.2 billion people do not have access to safe drinking water, and about 2.6 billion do not have adequate sanitation. Unsafe water leads to millions of deaths annually due to waterborne diseases. Water supplies are expected to deteriorate due to population growth, climate change, and other factors. Nanoparticles could be made which adsorb pollutants, while others could act as catalysts to degrade pollutants, and nanomembrane filtration systems could also be developed. Such systems would

be very welcome if the devices contribute to the provision of safe water and the reduction of disease. However, such nanotechnological developments raise some ethical concerns. Nanofiltration systems may remove pollutants or infectious agents, but what if they release nanoparticles into the environment that have adverse effects? Nanotechnology is plagued by a lack of information on the health and environmental hazards of nanoparticles. Such ignorance is exemplified by past mistakes. For example, chlorofluorocarbons were

Water is a basic human need; water, sanitation, and health are closely inter-related

developed as safer, more efficient refrigerants and firefighting chemicals. They were widely used for 50 years before their damage to the ozone layer was discovered. Fears have been raised that some nanoparticles could have detrimental effects on the environment.

There is an inevitable tension between the drive to bring new products to market and the importance of avoiding damage. When data exist on the known toxicities of compounds, risk-benefit analyses can be conducted. Nanoparticles are interesting because they have new, usually unpredictable, properties but little toxicological data exists for most of them. This makes it inherently difficult to know what the potential harms might be for the environment.

The precautionary principle is one way to address such uncertainties. This approach puts priority on the ethical principle of "do no harm", especially when the harm to the

environment could be serious or irreversible. However, it does not lead to straightforward solutions given that harm is already occurring because of the lack of (for example) adequate water filtration systems. Applying Christian wisdom and virtue is not straightforward. The precautionary principle at least leads to these ethical and environmental concerns being addressed before devices are released into the environment. Given the many other environmental applications of nanotechnology, including solar cell technology, enhanced batteries for electric cars, and greener manufacturing processes, the need for ethical evaluations of the potential risks and harms of nanotechnology is only going to increase.

GENETICS AND ETHICS

The extent of humankind's ability not only to interpret and understand the genetic basis of life but also to intervene and alter the DNA of organisms, including humans, stands as one of the most remarkable achievements of science during the past half-century. Such capabilities lie at the heart of many current and emerging bioethical controversies.

Misuse of genetic information

It has been argued that genetic data need to be treated with greater sensitivity than other information about a person. This view (sometimes termed "genetic exceptionalism") is partly prompted by concern that a third party (for example an employer or an insurer) might discriminate again someone on the basis of their heredity make-up. Moreover, knowledge of the genetic constitution of an individual may reveal the probability (or even the certainty) that one or more family members share a given condition. This raises issues regarding violation of the relatives' autonomy and rights to privacy.

Stewardship

Christians have a mandate in Genesis to act as stewards of God's creation. On the one hand this involves a need to be proactive and not shirk our responsibilities to take part in management of the planet, but on the other to recognize times when we need restraint. A number of potential genetic interventions move beyond mere analysis into actions that may lead to the long-term modification of a species or directly on to decisions of life and death. The accusation is sometimes made that the scientists or doctors involved in such procedures have violated a boundary of appropriate responsibility and are therefore "playing God".

Justice and fairness

Justice is an important biblical principle (see Amos 5:14–15; Matthew 23:23). Although the costs of certain genetic procedures are falling, it remains true that many interventions are relatively expensive. This raises the spectre that genetic medicine will only be available to those who can afford it, reinforcing divisions in society between the "haves" and the "have-nots".

Consent

It is sometimes argued that those affected directly by a decision (for example relating to genetic screening) or future generations influenced indirectly by a decision made now have not been in a position to grant consent.

Therapy and enhancement

Deciding whether a given intervention is ethical becomes further complicated by the fact that an apparently identical procedure might be conducted either to counter an existing illness (such as therapy) or to select positively for or add additional characteristics beyond the "normal" situation (such as enhancement). For example, gene therapy may be used to deliver a gene that will provide a cure to a disease that is caused by absence of a functional copy or to introduce a gene that might contribute to better athletic performance.

Genetic engineering

Genetic engineering is a term used rarely by scientists but widely employed by the general press and in school curricula. Prior to the 1970s, and even before the genetic basis of inheritance had been truly understood, attempts to influence the inheritance of physical characteristics had been conducted in a relatively crude manner. Farmers, racehorse owners, and dog breeders have always selected for particular traits by

PRE-IMPLANTATION GENETIC DIAGNOSIS

News stories often refer to "Designer babies" (a term rarely used by scientists) when discussing the ability to modify the genetic make-up of an embryo. The possibility of looking at the DNA of an embryo before it is transferred into the uterus of the mother is a technique developed from in vitro fertilization (IVF); it is more accurately referred to as pre-implantation genetic diagnosis (PGD). PGD exploits the fact that a cell may be removed from an embryo when it consists of only eight cells without apparent damage to the remaining cells. The extracted cell can then be tested either to ensure it has the correct number of chromosomes, to determine the sex and/or to see if it has a specific version of the gene(s) of interest.

PGD was initially used to detect whether the new embryo was carrying a faulty gene that would result in a serious illness, such as cystic fibrosis. Its applications have been broadened to include screening to ensure that the new embryo does not have other diseases and sometimes even to discover if it might provide a suitable tissue match to an older brother or sister suffering from the condition, particularly if it is a blood disorder. In such a case, stem cells from the umbilical cord can be grown in culture and used in transplants to replace the bone marrow of an older child. Some opponents have argued that this might have adverse psychological effects on the younger sibling, particularly if the therapy does not produce the desired

A saviour sibling: blood cells from the umbilical cord of baby Adam Nash were cultivated and then injected into his sister who was suffering from Fanconi anaemia.

orchestrating the mating of their animals or by crossing particular species of plants. Much more controversially, *eugenic* movements in Europe and America during the first half of the twentieth century sought to encourage reproduction by "worthy" members of society and to resist the transmission of less desirable characteristics, even going as far as forcibly sterilizing "less worthy" individuals.

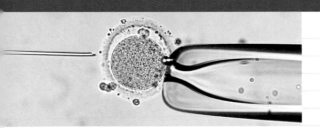

improvement in the older child, never mind the possible need for additional interventions such as bone marrow or organ donation. This kind of "saviour sibling" procedure was first used in the USA in 2000 when Adam Nash was conceived in order to be a donor for his older sister Molly who was suffering from Fanconi anaemia. The ethical issues involved were given prominence in Jodi Picoult's novel *My Sister's Keeper* and a subsequent film of the same name.

PGD has also been employed to select a new child to be a donor in circumstances under which they were not themselves at risk of the condition suffered by their older relative. Although this sounds very similar to the previous examples, it differs since the embryo may receive potential harm but has no corresponding benefit for them as an individual. This has led to "fertility tourism", where people refused treatment in one jurisdiction (usually their home country) travel to another place where the rules are less stringent. It is also used when parents have sought to specify the sex of their next child for non-medical reasons, such as "family balancing", the desire to have a girl after a string of male children (or vice versa).

In vitro fertilization: injecting a sperm into an ovum outside the body

THE ETHICS OF PRE-IMPLANTATION GENETIC DIAGNOSIS

Christians may object to PGD on the ground that life begins at conception (fertilization). They are concerned about the fate of embryos that are found not to have the desired combination of genes. These embryos are likely to be allowed to die or be donated for use in medical research. Alternatively (or additionally), Christians may be unhappy with the notion that interfering with the genetic make-up of an individual is "playing God". They may be uncomfortable that the notion of choosing certain characteristics marks a fundamental shift to a "consumerist" approach to child-rearing rather than gratitude to God for a child whatever gender and whatever health issues it may have.

Other Christians are less opposed to PGD. They argue that a high proportion (probably around two-thirds) of embryos of eight cells (and more) fail to implant naturally. Rejection of inappropriate embryos using PGD represents only a very small percentage of the total number of conceptions that do not go on to develop into babies. They might also counter the "playing God" argument by pointing out that failure to use technology at our disposal to, for example, remove the gene for an inherited illness (and from subsequent children) perpetuates suffering that we can easily alleviate.

Slippery slope? Even if the merits of using PGD to counter life-threatening or other serious conditions per se is acknowledged, opponents condemn the technology because of their belief that once the door is opened there will be an inevitable drift towards using it to influence characteristics such as musical talent, sporting ability, intelligence, and/ or physical appearance. Such arguments get increasingly complicated. There have already been cases, for example, where deaf parents have applied to use PGD to ensure that their child would be deaf, on the basis that a child can only be truly immersed in their parents' world if they share their perception of that world. For others, this represents a wilful act to ensure that a child receives a handicap and is akin to (say) inflicting deliberate harm on a child to improve the likelihood of greater donations while begging.

The advent of modern genetic techniques has facilitated much more accurate characterization and purposeful manipulation of the genetic make-up of organisms. Scientists are able with significant accuracy to control whether a particular gene is switched on or off, to move genes between species, and to gather vast amounts of information about a person merely by examining their DNA.

Genetic testing

Testing the DNA of an individual can take place at a variety of stages in life and for a variety of reasons. Screening for certain genes (usually where a single gene is responsible for a particular disease) can be conducted on adults, on newborn infants, on babies *in utero* (pre-natal), and, in the case of IVF-based technologies, before an embryo is implanted into the mother (pre-implantation).

Genetic knowledge can be a double-edged sword. On the one hand, the routine testing of newborns for such debilitating inborn errors of metabolism as phenylketonuria and medium-chain acyl dehydrogenase deficiency can forewarn parents of the need for careful dietary interventions to maintain the well-being of the child. Testing of an adult for inheritable diseases might alert them to the risk that they will pass on a serious condition to their children. At the same time there are dangers that receipt of bad news about genes may cause significant distress or make them ineligible for insurance or open to discrimination.

There are particular concerns about the promotion of genetic testing in which an interested individual can order a battery of tests on their own DNA (or that of someone else). In some cases our knowledge of how closely the gene variants included in such

Frozen sperm, available for artificial semination

screens correlate with a disease is actually fairly speculative. Even if it is well established, it may be necessary for several genes to work together and often in combination with environmental factors for illness to occur. There is thus some quite complex uncertainty in determining the risk. Without the intermediary role of a qualified doctor to provide advice, the customer may be misled or not adequately prepared to receive potentially bad news.

There are also technical questions about the accuracy of some tests. Without appropriate care, DNA sequences may be misread, giving false results. There has been at least one case where a muddle with a batch of results by one of the major providers of

DNA SEQUENCING AND THE HUMAN GENOME PROJECT

Stories describing the outcome and the impact of DNA sequencing have become regular features of news bulletins. However, the ability to determine the complete order of the four-letter alphabet for an organism is a relatively new phenomenon. When Robert Holley published the sequence of a small RNA molecule in 1966 it was the fruit of seven years of work. The molecule was only 80 **nucleotides** (building blocks or "letters') in length. Sequencing of DNA only really became an established laboratory technique in 1977 when two rival methods were launched. The favoured method, known as dideoxy sequencing (or Sanger sequencing, after its inventor Fred Sanger) allowed scientists to unambiguously describe about 300 nucleotides in one experiment, but it remained labour-intensive and involved the use of radioactively labelled

materials. The human genome consists of about 3 billion (3×10^9) nucleotides and although the fundamental principles of Sanger sequencing remained central to the approach used in the original Human Genome Project (HGP), a number of scientific and technological developments (such as fluorescent-labelling of nucleotides, liquid-handling robots, increased computing power) were required to allow automation of much of the process. It was these technical advances that led to President Clinton, Prime Minister Blair, and the scientists heading up the research being able to gather on 26 June 2000 and declare the completion of a draft version of the entire genetic "blueprint" of humankind.

For much of the following decade, the anticipated avalanche of genetically inspired medicines has failed to

```
90        100            110
TAGCTGTTTCCTGTGTGAAATTG
TAGCTGTTTCCTGTGTGAAATTG
60        170            180
GTAAAGCCTGGGGTGCCTAATGA
GTAAAGCCTGGGGTGCCTAATGA
30        240            250
GTCGGGAAA C TGTCGTGCCAGC
GTCGGGAAA C TGTCGTGCCAGC
00        310            320
GGCGCCAGGGTGGTTTTTCTTT
```

genetic tests led to reports being delivered to the wrong clients.

In addition to testing for specific genes, there is a very real possibility that it will soon be possible to conduct a complete audit of the DNA of a patient for less than $1,000 and that knowledge of the entire genome of an individual could be stored routinely with their medical records. This emphasizes the need for secure handling of the material in order to maintain confidentiality.

materialize. During this time, however, the methods used to sequence DNA have entirely changed; amazingly it is now possible to read the bases of DNA some 50,000 times faster than in 2000 and at a small fraction of the cost. These additional developments seem at last to be delivering real benefits.

In particular, it has become feasible to look for differences and similarities in a series of different genomes (a process known as comparative genomics). This may involve comparison of the DNA of different species, for example to investigate evolutionary relatedness or to see why a particular strain of bacteria has developed antibiotic resistance where a similar strain has not. It is also possible to compare the DNA of large numbers of people suffering from a particular genetic condition and contrast these with a similar number of other individuals that do not have that illness, and hence identify the genes involved in either causing or modulating the severity of symptoms. These kinds of genome-wide association studies as they are termed, are starting to bear fruit and are expected to do so more and more in the future. Armed with better knowledge about the genetic basis of a disease it should be possible to develop medicines tailored to the specific need of the patient.

A further application of genome technology now makes it possible to compare the DNA in different cells of the same individual and identify cells that have become cancerous and where the cancer has then spread around the body. This has relevance for both diagnosis and prognosis of the disease, and may serve to direct doctors towards appropriate treatments.

Printout of a small part of the human genome

THE ETHICS OF SEQUENCING PROJECTS

As these examples illustrate, the potential benefits of large-scale sequencing projects are vast. However they raise a number of ethical concerns. One issue is the expense of such investigations. Worries have also been expressed that the whole rationale of sequencing work overstates the role of genes in our humanity, at the expense of both environmental factors and the influence of society (emphasizing nature over nurture). The HGP has shown how surprisingly few are our protein-coding genes and how little we know about the regulation of gene action. On the positive side, the growing evidence that a variety of non-DNA or *epigenetic* factors affect which genes are turned on or off has served to dampen fears over *genetic determinism*.

Some conditions are almost confined to particular groups (for example sickle cell disease in black Africans or Tay Sachs disease in Ashkenazi Jews). There is some trepidation that further revelations about inherited diseases segregating along ethnic lines may be exploited by individuals or groups with a vested interest in promoting racial tension.

PATENTING HUMAN GENE SEQUENCES

Some human gene sequences have been patented. This places power in the hands of the already-powerful and potentially affects the availability and costs of treating specific inherited diseases.

The *forensic use of DNA* is increasingly important in crime detection. Following the initial invention of *genetic fingerprinting* during the 1980s, the use of *DNA profiles* has become a mainstay of police work in many parts of the world. The United Kingdom has been at the forefront of this trend, with the establishment of a National DNA Database. Although an effective tool for solving crime, the database has been criticized by civil libertarians, particularly regarding the retention of information belonging to people arrested but subsequently found not guilty or released without charge.

Pharmacogenetics

When a patient is given a medicine, the drug has to be processed by the body, either to convert it to an active form or to clear it from the system once it has done its job. Much of this role is played by a collection of metabolic enzymes. Different genetic versions (alleles) of a particular enzyme may process the drug in a different way. This explains why a drug that is effective in one patient may have no effect in another or, worse, may lead to a life-threatening adverse drug reaction (ADR). By knowing which version(s) of the key enzymes the patient possesses it ought to be possible to tailor their medication to maximize the beneficial effects and reduce the occurrence of ADRs. Pharmacogenetics of this kind is one example of the growth of individual or *personalized medicine*, which is currently emerging and is expected to become far more common in the near future.

Gene therapy

Illnesses arising from faults within the DNA often mean a patient needs intrusive treatment throughout their lives (which may also be shortened as a consequence). If it were possible to do so, it would be much more satisfactory not only to act to alleviate the symptoms, but to intervene at the root cause and thus remove the illness completely. This is the rationale of gene therapy. In its simplest form, an individual whose illness was the consequence of having two non-functional copies of a gene would be cured by delivery into their cells of a working copy of the gene. This strategy has seen some success, notably in the treatment of blood disorders where some of the patient's bone marrow can be extracted and altered outside the body (*ex vivo*) before being reintroduced.

Such application of the technology per se is one of the less controversial applications of genetic knowledge; it does not, for example, involve research on embryos. There have also been some issues relating to patient safety either as the result of immune response raised against the virus used to deliver the new gene into cells, or as a consequence of disruption to the expression of their other genes caused by arrival of the new DNA (so-called *insertional mutagenesis*).

Ethical questions about gene therapy, however, develop from the fact that the same mechanism might allow two further uses. First, DNA might be transferred into germline cells (eggs or sperm) rather than standard body (somatic) cells. This means that the change to the genetic make-up is likely to be passed on to the next generation. Second, there is the issue of therapy versus enhancement. The World Anti-Doping Agency is concerned about the potential for "*gene doping*" and the rise of genetically enhanced athletes. At the time of writing there are no known examples of this use, but many observers feel it is an issue of "when" not "if" such an approach is made.

Genetically modified organisms (GMOs)

The ability to move genes between species (or altering ones that are there) has now become an established scientific procedure. Effective first with microbes, it has subsequently proven possible to introduce genes into plants (see box on GM crops) and animals (sometimes termed transgenic animals). GM mice carrying human "disease genes" are widely used in medical research, and there have also been more direct applications, such as the creation of GM sheep producing pharmaceutical proteins in their milk. Basing their arguments essentially on natural law, some Christians have argued that transferring human genes into other animals offends against the *telos* of those animals. *Cloning* of animals has also become possible with some species, with Dolly the sheep being the most famous example to date. This is an area where accusations of "playing God" have been particularly common.

Embryonic stem cells

Of all recent developments in biomedical science, those that have caused probably the most disquiet in the Christian community are those involving embryonic stem (ES) cells. ES cells are cells in the *blastocyst* stage of the early (pre-implantation) embryo that will give rise to all the different types of cell that contribute to the makeup of the fully formed individual. ES cells are described as *pluripotent*. They were first isolated from mouse embryos in 1981, and scientists learned how to maintain them in culture. This set the scene for work on human ES cells, first isolated and cultured in 1998. The motive for this is that ES cells may have a role in regenerative medicine – the repair of tissues and organs damaged by trauma, disease (or even ageing). It is argued that the pluripotent nature of ES cells enables them to repair a wide range of tissues, provided that they can be "persuaded" to differentiate into appropriate types of cell. The potential of this technique led to the modification of law in the UK to allow the extraction of stem cells from the blastocyst stage of human embryos that had been created by *in vitro* fertilization. The modification to the Act also saw provision for the creation of human embryos by cloning, for the purpose of extracting ES cells. This is known as "therapeutic cloning" in contrast to reproductive cloning (as with Dolly the sheep); reproductive cloning of humans remains illegal. There was extensive public debate about the ethics of these developments although, because the modification to the Act in reality confirmed the legality of procedures that were already taking place, that debate was a case of trying "to close the stable door after the horse has bolted". Indeed, at the time of writing the first small-scale trial of the use of ES cells in repair of the spinal cord is taking place in the USA.

Some of the aspects of the ethical debate are presented on p. 260. However, it is probably true to say that some of the focus of stem cell research is shifting from ES cells to adult stem cells, such as those in bone marrow (which have been shown to have the potential to repair certain body tissues) and to ES-like cells, generated from the adult stem cells that occur in skin (and which in that tissue, participate in the turnover of skin cells and in wound healing). Future developments are thus awaited with interest.

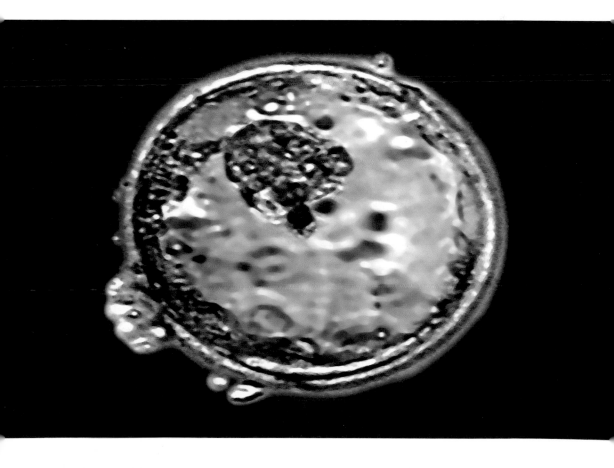

A human blastocyst – an embryo after approximately five days of development.

THE "MORAL STATUS" OF THE EARLY (PRE-IMPLANTATION) HUMAN EMBRYO

Aristotle regarded the earliest stages of the embryo as plant-like, needing and drawing nutrition like any plant; the embryo then becomes an animal creature, sensitive and responsive like other animals; and only thereafter does it become a creature with fully human characteristics. This understanding saw the form of the embryo as the projection of inward animating principles (Greek *psyche*, Latin *anima*, English soul): animating the plant was a vegetative soul, animating the animal was a sensitive soul, and animating the human form was a rational soul. The early Christian fathers accepted this interpretation. It seemed to accord with Exodus 21:22–23, which is the only reference in the Bible to abortion. These verses clearly affirm a worth for foetal life, but its application is not straightforward. The Septuagint translation says that life is to be given for life if the embryo is "formed". Both Jerome and Augustine explained that an act producing a miscarriage was not homicide if the foetus was "unformed", "since there cannot yet be said to be a live soul in a body which lacks sensation when it is not formed in flesh and so not yet endowed with sense" (Augustine

on Exodus 21:22). While Jerome and Augustine were agnostic regarding (in traditional language) the point at which the soul entered the body, they were not prepared to affirm that this had taken place while the embryo was "unformed". There are many references in the Bible to "life" before birth, but none which identify the point at which this "life" began. The Psalms often refer to God's care and protection in the womb (notably Psalm 139:13–16). Both Isaiah and Jeremiah were called before birth (Isaiah 49:1; Jeremiah 1:5); indeed Jeremiah's call came *before* he was "formed in the womb". Our being chosen as Christians was much earlier, "Before the creation of the world" (Ephesians 1:4). Prior to a papal bull of 1869, both canon and common (secular) law accepted that full protection of the embryo only occurred at "ensoulment" and this took place some time after fertilization. In practice this was taken as the time of "quickening", when a pregnant woman begins to feel her foetus moving.

New impetus was given to this debate by the possibility of *in vitro* fertilization (IVF), a procedure that has been available since 1978. How should we

Louise Brown, the first test-tube baby, born 1978 from an egg and sperm provided by her parents.

261

of the cells in the blastocyst form the placenta. Only the ES cells (which form the Inner Cell Mass) go on to form the foetus. Any genetic or developmental continuity from fertilized egg to foetus therefore only involves a sub-population of cells in the blastocyst. The success rate for implantation is low, achieved by about 30 per cent of human blastocysts. Implantation is a specific "bottle-neck" in development, particularly emphasized in those mammals (bears, badgers, kangaroos) in which implantation is delayed, often for several months. In humans, completion of implantation more or less marks the end of the embryo's potential for twinning, a process which has sparked theological debate: if "life" begins at conception, do twins only have half a soul?

A government appointed body in the UK (the Warnock Committee) proposed ethical and practical governance for IVF. They declared "the embryo of the human species [should] be afforded some protection in law". There was however a minority of the Committee that ascribed full human personhood to the early embryo.

view the very early human embryo: does it have moral significance in the way that a human person has moral significance at birth? Indeed, is the early human embryo a person? If not, at what stage of development does human personhood become apparent? This question is sometimes phrased as "when does human life begin?", which does not convey fully the ethical problem, since the one-cell embryo (never mind the egg and sperm from which it is formed) is clearly "human life".

In order to inform the discussion, some have turned to science. Human pre-natal development is not a steady uninterrupted process. For several days after fertilization the embryo undergoes cell divisions and then reorganizes to form the blastocyst, the stage at which ES cells are obtained. A pregnancy is only established if the blastocyst implants into the wall of the uterus. A large proportion

Looking to the future

One of the features of modern science is the speed at which it develops. There is often little time for ethical reflection and ethical concerns are often expressed after lines of research or of application are well established.

Synthetic life forms

In 2010, the media announced that an American scientist, Craig Venter, and his team had created life. Venter himself was happy to go along with this description of his work. In fact, he had done no such thing. His team had synthesized in the laboratory a complete DNA molecule, consisting of about one million nucleotides (building blocks/ letters) of a *Mycobacterium*, a micro-organism, adding some small extra sequences to "watermark" the molecule. This was an amazing achievement: it was by far the longest DNA molecule ever assembled in the laboratory. The team then transferred the synthetic DNA molecules to cells of another *Mycobacterium* species from which the DNA had been removed. Those cells functioned, grew, and divided as if they were the species represented by the synthetic chromosome. Venter gave the name *Synthia* to this new life form, adding to the impression that somehow synthetic life had been created. However, creation of life requires much more than making a DNA molecule, and as biological commentators were quick to point out, the experiment required there to be pre-existing cells into which to transfer the DNA. Despite this, the print and broadcast media buzzed with "creation of life" stories with widespread use of that overused and misused phrase, "playing God".

Although some have suggested that this work is simply a rather gross example of human *hubris* it does have a wider and more laudable aim, namely to produce microbes with a minimal set of genes necessary to sustain life, into which additional "cassettes" of genes could be added to equip them to fulfil a defined purpose, such as the biodegradation of spilt oil. "Synthetic" life forms of this kind may thus ultimately prove invaluable; however, there are cautionary voices warning that we may not fully understand and may not be able to control the organisms we are producing, or that groups with more malevolent goals might utilize the technology for bioterrorism.

Nanotechnology

Nanotechnology – technology on a nanometre scale – is now being used commercially. Some of the current uses involve medical, pharmaceutical, cosmetic, and personal products. The range of applications in these areas is still small but is predicted to expand rapidly over the next ten years.

NANOTECHNOLOGY AND HEALTH

The application of nanotechnology to healthcare is an area of intense interest. New diagnostic devices use nanotechnology to give faster turnaround times with smaller samples. Nanoparticles may detect cancer at earlier stages, and then home in specifically to destroy cancer cells. Conventional drugs are being reformulated as nanoparticles with better solubility, allowing lower doses with fewer side-effects.

The small size of nanoparticles allows them to penetrate deep inside tissues and cells. Some cross the blood–brain barrier, raising the possibility of treating parts of the brain which standard drugs cannot reach. But these same properties raise questions about unknown harms. The blood–brain barrier exists to protect the brain from harmful chemicals, so great care is required to ensure these treatments do not have serious adverse effects. In addition, some nanoparticles enter cells via the active transport systems used by proteins and other biochemical molecules. This system is not easily reversed, making it more challenging to remove excess nanoparticles or prevent their over-accumulation.

All these factors create uncertainty. Participants being recruited for clinical trials must be informed of the potential risks and benefits of experimental interventions. Making informed decisions will therefore be challenging, especially with interventions that work by novel mechanisms. In spite of these unknowns, some health-related products containing nanoparticles have already reached consumers. Sunscreens were one of the first, incorporating nanoparticles which leave no white residue on the

Ultraviolet radiation from the sun can cause cancer

• •

skin compared to products with larger particles. These nanoparticles were also said to block damaging UV rays better. Several dietary supplements are marketed in the US as containing nanoparticles.

Such products have generated ethical questions similar to those on nanotechnology and the environment. There are questions as to whether nanoparticles can be absorbed into the body through the skin and whether there might be long-term adverse effects. Also, the fate and effects of these nanoparticles once they are washed off the skin remain uncertain. For example, research with socks containing nano-silver (added to prevent odours and athlete's foot) has demonstrated that some brands lose almost all their nano-silver after two to four washings. Consumer-advocacy groups want manufacturers to label their products to make it clear whether they contain nanoparticles or not. Norwegian observers have noticed that sunscreen advertising originally highlighted when products contained nanoparticles but that more recent advertisements rarely comment on whether products contain nanoparticles or not.

Broader ethical issues can be raised about nanomedicine. For example, quick and simple diagnostic devices could be used to select embryos for various traits, but this raises concerns about eugenics – driven by individuals' desire for perfect children (as in relation to pre-implantation genetic diagnosis). Constant monitoring of health status may help guide doctors and patients, but might lead to privacy violations. New drug devices that deliver important treatments could easily be used to deliver performance-enhancing drugs. Such issues are not unique to nanotechnology, but point to the importance of examining the worldviews motivating developments in nanotechnology.

Nanotechnology has the potential to do great good if the underlying motivations are to relieve illness and provide people's basic needs. Otherwise, high-tech enhancement and cures for the "worried well" will only contribute to a widening gulf between the rich and poor. Christians should be concerned that the poor and the afflicted receive justice (Psalm 82:3–4).

Transhumanism and human enhancement

The idea that we can use science, not only to improve the health of humans but to actually enhance the human species or at least individuals, may seem like science fiction. But it is not pure fiction. The Transhumanist Movement (slogan *Better than well*) is devoted to the use of biotechnology, neuroscience, genetics, computing, and nanotechnology to enhance human function. In the therapeutic arena, there are now some very sophisticated artificial limbs that can be interfaced with the amputee's nervous system giving a much higher level of control and even feeling than is possible with more conventional prostheses. Rather more trivially, several transhumanist enthusiasts have had IT devices implanted within them and are exploring other ways of directly linking with computer systems. So, while some of scenarios that are presented about human enhancement are very fanciful, it is not a topic that should be ignored.

HUMAN ENHANCEMENT

Human enhancement refers to the aim to make changes in our minds or bodies to enhance our capacities. This could be still within normal human abilities, but allow me to do something better than I could naturally do. But some speak of radical changes beyond what *anyone* can do. Much of this is speculative and often very exaggerated. But developments across a range of Nano-Bio-Information-Cognitive sciences make at least some modification of the human body plausible enough to need serious societal debate about the body, human nature, society, and human destiny.

Possible enhancements could take many forms, including chemicals to enhance physical or cognitive performance or mood; functional implants within the body; computer chips linked to parts of the brain; changes to body cells; maybe extending lifespan. Genetic enhancement is less likely since most characteristics of interest are not easily alterable by manipulating a few genes. Cosmetic surgery, drugs in sport, and recreational drugs are examples of enhancement used in limited situations, but the idea is improvements available all, not for medical or health reasons, but for personal preference.

Some strong promoters of enhancement belong to a movement called transhumanism which believes that humans are destined to go beyond our current biological limitations through

● ●

radical technological change to our bodies and minds. Advocates promote this agenda as both desirable and inevitable. Christians have challenged this as a quasi-religious vision for the technological transformation of humanity as a misleading, naturalistic illusion. Perhaps "playing God" has real meaning here. But enhancement is not an inevitable course; society needs to decide what course to take, what to explore or what not to pursue.

Laying superhuman dreams aside, what might God expect us to do with God-given creativity, inventiveness, and aspirations to better ourselves, if we have the technology? Can we improve on God's "design" of ourselves? Can finite and fallen humans understand the complexity of body and mind well enough to be sure that an "enhancement" would be for the better, seen as a whole? A risky medical intervention may be offset by the hope of treating a serious condition; an enhancement unrelated to any medical condition has no comparable ethical "good" to balance its risks. There are also risks of proceeding faster than we understand, impelled by hubris, or by commercial, political, or military pressures.

Many supposed enhancements are ambiguous. If retinal implants enabled us to see in infrared, would we use enhanced sight to drive more safely at night, or just to drive faster but not more safely? Again, suppose some students take a concentration-aiding drug for competitive advantage in exams. Perhaps against their values, all the class now feel they have to use it for fear of falling behind. This means that no one has a competitive value, but no one dares not use it and fall below the new norm. No one gained, but everyone became dependent. Was that an enhancement?

A major ethical criticism is that enhancement is self-centred. If benefits were as radical as claimed but available mainly to the rich, it would inevitably increase injustice in an already deeply inequitable world. Am I a truly "enhanced" human if I take enhancement for myself, not caring about those worse off? The Christian view of the human person stresses solidarity with the have-nots. Could enhancement be devised primarily for the poor?

It might be nice to think more quickly or not to get tired so easily, but would we be more satisfied? If we achieved

The Earth — the only one we have

a goal, or beat our rival in an exam or sports competition, only with the aid of an enhancement, did *we* really achieve it? Some suggest the best satisfactions in making a finer work of art or craft, or to help someone else, are less to do with enhancing myself and more with loving my neighbour or loving God.

Finally, would it actually make us better humans? What view of humanity is emphasized by the idea of enhancement? In Christ, our humanity is not defined by how well our bodies function, but is a far richer account, of body, mind, spirit, morality, spirituality, and so on, in relationship to God and each other. A stress on human functional performance would miss the point about what most needs changing about our humanity, which is less in physical limitations than in our moral, relational or spiritual failings. These would remain no matter how much we were to enhance ourselves, because they call for solutions beyond technical fixes.

Technical enhancement carries a logical contradiction, because it is a treadmill that can never reach its goal. There would always be that *next* enhancement. Christian theology teaches us that we are created by God for relationship with God, and can never ultimately be satisfied with merely created things, however good they may be. They still leave us wanting what only God can meet.

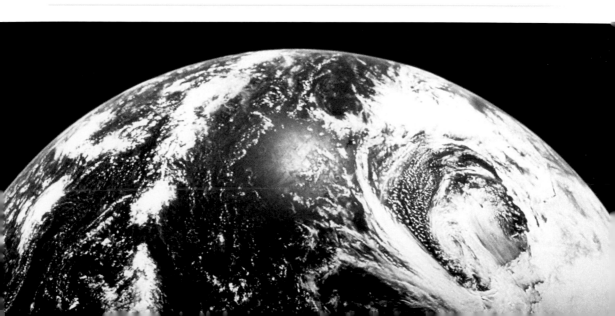

Glossary

Aetiology: the study of causation; enquiry into the origin or causes of anything, especially the cause of a disease.

Anthropic: relating to humankind; commonly used for the argument that the physical universe is fitted (or possibly even "designed") for human existence.

Anthropocentric: the assumption that humans are the central and most significant entities in the universe.

Aristogenesis: evolution in one direction over a long period of time, commonly taken to imply directing by an internal factor.

Atemporalism: the idea that God is outside time and hence unaffected by events within time. This may mean that he has an entirely non-temporal existence or that all times are simultaneously present to him.

Consequentialism: that the consequences of an action are the basis for judging the rightness of that action (as distinct from deontology, which judges the rightness of a behaviour on the nature of the behaviour itself).

Cosmogony: concerning the origin or coming into being of the universe.

Cosmology: the branch of astronomy that deals with the structure and space-time relationships of the universe.

Deduction: arguing from a generalization to specific instances, as opposed to induction, where the conclusion is assumed to emerge from empirical data.

Deontology: "duty" or "obligation" ethics where the morality of an action is based on fulfilment of duty or adherence to rules (contrast consequentialism). Deontological theories differ on what are the grounds of duty: for some it may be God, for others, rationality; for others, duties are merely brute and groundless facts.

Dysteleology: the assumption that existence has no final purpose. The term was invented by Ernst Haeckel; the belief is now associated with the type of atheism proclaimed by Richard Dawkins and Christopher Hitchens.

Eisegesis: using one's own ideas to interpret a text, as distinct from exegesis where the meaning of the text is critically examined.

Entelechy: actuality; a vital principle assumed to give life to an entity, directing its processes to the realization of an end.

Entropy: a measure of randomness, involving a loss of organization or information over time.

Epistemology: the nature or scope of knowledge, belief, or experience, asking what we know and how we know it.

Exaptation: change in function or a trait during evolution, often used of a trait which is pre-adapted to a function which subsequently becomes useful to the organism.

Exegesis: the critical explanation or interpretation of a text (contrast eisegesis).

Hermeneutics: the study of the theory and practice of interpretation, usually of a written text but also of any act of communication.

Immanence: divine activity from within; contrast transcendence, where the divine acts from outside.

Induction: arguing from data or particular cases to general conclusions (contrast deduction).

Instrumentalism: the view that a process or scientific theory may produce new predictions or techniques, irrespective of its truth or falsity.

Interactionism: the belief that matter and mind are independent but exert causal effects on each other; it involves the assumption of dualism – the coexistence of body and mind.

Isch[a]emia: restriction of blood supply to an organ, leading to tissue damage because of a lack of oxygen or nutrients.

Kenosis: literally means "emptiness"; commonly used of the self-emptying of oneself (or Jesus) in subjection to God, more controversially refers to the status of the divine in the incarnate Christ.

Metacognition: knowing about knowing, including how to use particular strategies for learning or problem solving.

Monism: the assumption that all reality is ultimately one; the belief that nothing exists outside a particular category, often used in distinction to dualism.

Noogenesis: the emergence of mind or of intelligent forms of life.

Nucleotides: subunits of nucleic acid molecules, comprising phosphoric acid, a purine or pyrimidine base, and a sugar. There are only four such bases in DNA: adenine, thymine, guanine, and cytosine; they are linked in chains, with their sequence forming the genetic code.

Ontology: the study of the nature of being, a branch of metaphysics.

Orthogenesis: the idea that life that has an innate tendency to develop in a linear way, due to some intrinsic driving force (see also aristogenesis).

Panentheism: the view that the universe is God, although God is more than the universe; God is the animating force behind the universe. Distinguish from pantheism where God and the universe are identical, and God penetrates everything.

Panspermia: the idea that life exists throughout the universe, that life on Earth originates from space.

Phenotype: an organism's appearance or characteristics; distinguished from genotype, which is the set of genetic instructions of the organism.

Reductionism: an assumption that a whole is nothing more than the sum of its parts, so that a complex entity can be explained wholly by its simplest components.

Teleology: the belief that there is a purpose or final end to natural processes.

Utilitarianism: a form of consequentialism, holding that the proper course of any action is one that maximizes the overall "good" of society, that is, it produces the greatest happiness for the greatest number of people.

Xenotransplantation: transplanting of cells or tissues from one species to another.

Significant People and Events

GREEK AND ROMAN INFLUENCES

The early Christian church took on contemporary views of the nature of world, derived from Hebrew thinkers but also from Greek and Roman sources. It inherited a notion of the primacy of reason over observation or experiment, together with an assumption of the impossibility of change from Plato and of naturalism from Lucretius. The early Christians sought to interpret these ideas in the light of the Bible, but their interpretations often had to be modified in the light of later discoveries.

MEDIEVAL TIMES

Robert Grosseteste, Bishop of Lincoln (1175–1253) wrote on optics, astronomy, and geometry. He affirmed that experiments should be used to verify a theory and test its consequences.

Albertus Magnus (1193–1280) expounded Aristotle (384–322 BC), but also emphasized the importance of observation and experiment. He wrote: "Natural science does not consist in ratifying what others have said, but in seeking the causes of phenomena."

Roger Bacon (1214–94), English philosopher who emphasized empiricism, regarded as one of the earliest advocates of the modern scientific method. He joined the Franciscan Order around 1240, where he was influenced by Grosseteste; was influential in propagating the concept of "laws of nature".

Thomas Aquinas (1225–74) combined the biblical idea of God as lawgiver with the Platonic and Aristotelian views of "natural laws" immanent in the universe; pupil of Albertus Magnus.

Jean Buridan (1300–58) was unafraid to criticize other scholars, including his own teacher, the nominalist William of Ockham. He developed the theory of impetus, which was an important step toward the modern concept of inertia and understanding determinism.

Nicolaus Copernicus (1473–1543), Polish author of *De Revolutionibus Orbium*, argued that a solar system with the Sun at its centre rather than the Earth was a possible interpretation. In 1616, in connection with the Galileo affair, this work was forbidden by the church "until corrected". Only in 1835 was the original uncensored version dropped from the *Index of Prohibited Books*.

William Turner (1508–68), the "father of English botany", author of *A New Herbal*, the first original plant book in English; exiled several times for preaching in favour of the Reformation.

Andreas Vesalius (1514–64), Flemish anatomist who insisted on dissection and accurate description rather than reliance on authority; published *De Humani Corporis Fabrica* in 1543. This year is often regarded as the time when modern science began, marked by the publication of Copernicus's demonstration of the need to challenge received beliefs and Vesalius's demonstration of the importance of observation and experiment.

Tycho Brahe (1546–1601) discovered a new star in 1573, supporting the Copernican model (which he only partly accepted) and in flat contradiction to the alleged immutable celestial spheres postulated by Aristotle and Ptolemy.

SEVENTEENTH CENTURY

Francis Bacon (1561–1626), Lord Chancellor of England, popularized inductive methodologies for scientific enquiry (often known as the "Baconian method"); expressed clearly the idea of God's "Two Books".

Johannes Kepler (1571–1630), Brahe's pupil, developed a model of the cosmos explicitly driven by religious ideas; his later and most famous scientific contribution, his Laws of Planetary Motion and the elliptical path of the planets was based on empirical data that he obtained from Tycho Brahe's meticulous astronomical observations.

Galileo Galilei (1564–1642) had many problems with the Inquisition for defending heliocentrism in the convoluted period brought about by the Reformation and Counter-Reformation. In regard to the Bible, he took Augustine's position: not to take every passage too literally, particularly when the biblical book in question is a book of poetry and songs, not a book of instructions or history. Galileo's *Dialogue of the Two Chief World Systems* (1632) led to his trial on a charge of heresy, a banning of the book for over a century, and a persisting assumption that the church was anti-science.

William Harvey (1578–1657) wrote *De Motu Cordis* (1628) establishing the circulation of the blood driven by the heart as a pump; emphasized the body as mechanism.

Pierre Gassendi (1592–1655), Catholic priest who tried to reconcile Atomism with Christianity. He published the first work on the Transit of Mercury and corrected the geographical coordinates of the Mediterranean Sea.

René Descartes (1596–1650), one of the key thinkers of the Scientific Revolution in the Western World. His *Meditations on First Philosophy* partially concerns theology and he was devoted to reconciling his ideas with the dogmas of the Catholic faith to which he was loyal. He saw the universe in strictly mechanical terms. The human body was controlled by a discrete soul.

Blaise Pascal (1623–62), known for Pascal's law (physics), Pascal's theorem (mathematics), and Pascal's Wager (theology).

Robert Boyle (1627–91), pioneering chemist who argued that the study of science could glorify of God; saw the universe as a vast interlocking mechanism.

Nicolas Steno (1638–86) was a pioneer in both anatomy and geology and one of the first to argue that fossils are the remains of living organisms; largely abandoned science after his religious conversion, when he became a significant advocate of the Counter-Reformation.

EIGHTEENTH CENTURY

John Ray (1627–1705), "Father of Natural History" and author of *The Wisdom of God manifested in the Works of the Creation* (1691). Applied the rigorous approach to the Bible used by the Protestant Reformers to purge science of mythology.

Thomas Burnet (1635–1715), his *Sacred Theory of the Earth* (1681) impressed Newton and influenced cosmogony throughout the eighteenth century.

Isaac Newton (1643–1727) produced *Philosophiae Naturalis Principia Mathematica*, (1687), strengthening the concept of a mechanical universe. Newton wrote more on biblical hermeneutics and occult studies than on science and mathematics.

Gottfried Leibniz (1646–1716), Newton's rival. A polymath who worked on determinants and a calculating machine; he was a Lutheran who worked with convert to Catholicism John Frederick, Duke of Brunswick-Lüneburg in the hope of a reunification between Catholicism and Lutheranism. He also wrote *Vindication of the Justice of God*.

The Enlightenment = supremacy of rationalism and the "de-deification" of the natural world.

Stephen Hales (1677–1761), pioneer physiologist and inventor who designed a type of ventilation system, a means to distil sea-water, ways to preserve meat, and so on. In religion he was an Anglican curate who worked with the Society for the Promotion of Christian Knowledge and for a group working to convert black slaves in the West Indies.

Thomas Bayes (1701–61), Presbyterian minister who wrote *Divine Benevolence, or an Attempt to Prove That the Principal End of the Divine Providence and Government is the Happiness of His Creatures*, better known for Bayes' theorem.

Carl Linnaeus (1707–83), Swedish taxonomist; natural theology and the Bible were important to his *Systema Naturae* and *Systema Vegetabilium*.

Leonhard Euler (1707–83), founder of much modern mathematics who also wrote *Defence of the Divine Revelation against the Objections of the Freethinkers*.

David Hume (1711–76), Scottish philosopher who argued strongly for the pre-eminence of reason; challenged the so-called argument from design (*Dialogues Concerning Natural Religion*, 1779), and the plausibility of miracles.

Rise of deism.

NINETEENTH CENTURY

Erasmus Darwin (1731–1802), medical practitioner, inventor, pantheist, member of the Lunar Society, and propounder of evolutionary ideas in *Zoonomia* (1794–96) half a century before his grandson, Charles.

Joseph Priestley (1733–1804), Unitarian minister and pioneering chemist; member of the free-thinking "Lunar Society", which included a number of early industrialists (Josiah Wedgwood, Robert Watt, Matthew Bolton) and others, such as Erasmus Darwin.

Rise of geology; debates about "flood geology" (diluvialism or Neptunism) and Vulcanism;

catastrophism or uniformitarianism; recognition of "deep time" – a long period of Earth's history.

Awareness of "deep space" from the observations of William Herschel (1735–1822) indicating that the Solar System was moving through space, leading to the recognition of an expanding universe, and the likelihood of a "Big Bang".

Worship of nature, influenced by William Wordsworth (1770–1850) and (especially) Samuel Taylor Coleridge (1772–1834).

William Buckland (1784–1856), first Professor of Geology at Oxford University, later Dean of Westminster Abbey. Wrote *Vindiciæ Geologiæ; or the Connexion of Geology with Religion Explained* (1820), justifying the new science of geology and reconciling geological evidence with the biblical accounts of creation and Noah's flood. Author of one of the "Bridgewater Treatises" in 1836, by which time he acknowledged that the biblical account of Noah's flood could not be confirmed using geological evidence.

Adam Sedgwick (1785–1873), Cambridge University geologist, teacher of Charles Darwin, and strong opponent of evolution.

Michael Faraday (1791–1867), a devoted Sandemannian (a sect seeking to practise "primitive Christianity"); discoverer of benzene and electromagnetic induction.

Baden Powell (1796–1860), High church mathematician at Oxford; initially conservative but moved theologically to become the only scientific contributor to *Essay and Reviews* (1860), which challenged biblical authority.

Charles Robert Darwin (1809–82). Naturalist and workaholic. Never formally renounced his Christian faith and refused to criticize believers, but certainly moved from a fairly orthodox Anglicanism to deism.

Philip Henry Gosse (1810–88), marine biologist and regular preacher; author of *Omphalos* (1857).

Asa Gray (1810–88): Harvard botanist and foremost advocate of Darwinism in North

America; found no conflict between evolution and his orthodox Christianity.

James Clerk Maxwell (1831–79), demonstrator of electric and magnetic fields; caused Psalm 111:2 ("Great are the works of the Lord, studied by all who delight in them") to be carved on the gate of the Cavendish Laboratory in Cambridge, which he headed.

Publication of **The Origin of Species**, *1859.*

Debate at the British Association for the Advancement of Science in Oxford between Samuel Wilberforce, Bishop of Oxford, and Thomas Henry Huxley, 1860.

Darwin's **The Descent of Man** *published 1871.*

Bishop Frederick Temple's 1884 Bampton Lectures regarded as formal acceptance of Darwinian evolution by the Christian establishment.

George Jackson Mivart (1827–1900), zealous convert to Roman Catholicism; zoologist who originally supported Darwin but later heavily criticized him.

Herbert Spencer (1820–1903), self-taught philosopher and sociologist; begetter of "social Darwinism".

Henry Baker Tristram (1822–1906), pioneering ornithologist, originally persuaded by Darwin's ideas, but later opposed them; author of *The Natural History of the Bible* (1867).

William Thomson (Lord Kelvin) (1824–1907) – formulated the laws of thermodynamics; convinced Christian, but calculated the age of the Earth to be too short for evolution to have taken place, although he later revised his estimate up by a factor of ten.

TWENTIETH CENTURY

Independent rediscoveries of Gregor Mendel's work (originally published 1865) in 1900 by Hugo de Vries, Carl Correns, and Erich von Tschermak, and establishment of the science of genetics. Apparent conflict between the variation studied by the geneticists and that assumed by the Darwinians. This produced an eclipse of Darwinism and a proliferation of teleological hypotheses into the subsequent void, leading to widespread confusion and an assumption that new ideas had to be found to replace Darwinian evolution.

Max Planck (1858–1947), founder of quantum mechanics and a Lutheran church elder.

Albert Einstein (1879–1955), discoverer of relativity; called himself an agnostic, disbelieving in any idea of a personal God.

George Lemaître (1894–1966), Roman Catholic priest and proposer of Big Bang theory.

Michael Polanyi (1891–1976), chemist who developed the concept of "different levels" of thought and investigation.

In 1925, the "Monkey Trial" took place in Dayton, Tennessee where a young school teacher, John Scopes, was prosecuted for teaching evolution,

contrary to a State law. Although Scopes was found guilty, the anti-evolutionists who brought the case were so ridiculed that they retreated, surfacing again in the creation science movement of the 1960s.

Publication of **Evolution: the Modern Synthesis** *by Julian Huxley (1942), reintegrating Darwinian ideas into mainstream biology.*

Francis Crick (1916–2004) and Jim Watson (1928–) unravel the structure of DNA, 1953.

Theodosius Dobzhansky (1900–75), geneticist and Russian orthodox believer; known for his essay "Nothing in biology makes sense except in the light of evolution", a challenge to an Arabian scholar who wanted to ban the teaching of evolution.

David Lack (1910–73), Oxford ornithologist and author of *Evolutionary Theory and Christian Belief* (1957).

Charles Coulson (1910–74), mathematician and Methodist; *Science and Christian Belief* (1955) clarified the futility of belief in a God of the gaps.

William Pollard (1911–89), Anglican priest and Executive Director of the US Oak Ridge Institute of Nuclear Studies (1960–74); author of *Physicist and Christian: a dialogue between communities* (1961).

Henry Morris (1918–2006), hydraulic engineer and fervent advocate of "scientific (young earth) creationism"; founder of the Institute for Creation Research. Authored *The Genesis Flood* (1961) with Old Testament scholar John Whitcomb.

Donald MacKay (1922–87), physicist and communications scientist; key thinker on science–faith issues, particularly in extending ideas of complementarity into a dynamic mode.

Robert Boyd (1922–2004), Director of the UK Space Programme in its early days and early member of the Research Scientists' Christian Fellowship.

Arthur Peacocke (1924–2006), biochemist and Anglican priest, influentially advocated process theology and argued for panentheism.

The Genesis Flood *by John Whitcomb and Henry Morris(published in 1961), reinvigorated "young earth creationism". An attempt in Arkansas to interpret "creation science" as a scientific subject was disallowed in the US Supreme Court in 1968 on the grounds that creation science was religion.*

Influential lecture (1966) by Lynn White on "The historical roots of our ecologic crisis" blamed environmental degradation on Christian arrogance towards the natural world.

Anthropic Principle (first proposed 1974) seen by many to be a strong evidence of providence (or even design) in the construction of the universe.

The Selfish Gene, *the first book by Richard Dawkins (1941–) published in 1976, argued a naturalistic reductionism for evolutionary processes. It has been followed by other books by Dawkins (notably* **The Blind Watchmaker,** *1986;* **The God Delusion,** *2006), and stimulated other works in a similar vein by so-called "neo-atheists" (for example* **Darwin's Dangerous Idea,** *by Dan Dennett, 1995;* **God is Not Great,** *by Christopher Hitchens, 2007).*

First outline of human genome with 20,500 genes published in 2000.

"Intelligent design" ruled in a US Court (Kitzmiller v Dover Area School District, December 2005) to be religion and not science, and thus not a proper subject for science teaching.

Further Reading

The following is intended solely as a guide and introduction to a very large literature. Neither is it a list of "recommended reading". A number of the works listed are critical of Christianity or unhelpful for the science–faith dialogue.

ENCYCLOPAEDIAS AND HANDBOOKS

Clayton, P. (ed.), *The Oxford Handbook of Religion and Science,* Oxford: Oxford University Press, 2006.

Ferngren, G. (ed.) *History of Science and Religion in the Western Tradition*, New York: Garland, 2000.

Harrison, P. (ed.), *The Cambridge Companion to Science and Religion,* Cambridge: Cambridge University Press, 2010.

Richardson, W. M. & Wildman, W. J. (eds.), *Religion and Science,* New York: Routledge, 1996.

Southgate, C. (ed.), *God, Humanity and the Cosmos,* London: T&T Clark, revised edition, 2005.

Van Huyssteen, W. (ed.), *Encyclopedia of Science and Religion*, New York: Macmillan, 2003.

HISTORICALLY SIGNIFICANT OR IMPORTANT

BEFORE 1900

Bacon, F., *The Proficience and Advancement of Learning*, London, 1605.

Boyle, R., *Some Physico-Theological Considerations about the Possibility of the Resurrection*, London, 1675.

Burnett, T., *The Sacred Theory of the Earth*. London, 1690 (original published in Latin, 1681).

Chambers, R., *Vestiges of the Natural History of Creation*, London: John Churchill, 1844.

Darwin, C. R., *The Origin of Species*, London: John Murray, 1859.

Darwin, C. R., *The Descent of Man*, London: John Murray, 1871.

Derham, W., *Physico Theology*, London, 1713

Draper, J. W., *History of the Conflict Between Religion and Science*, New York: Appleton, 1874.

Galton, F., *Hereditary Genius*, London: Macmillan, 1869.

Gore, C. (ed.), *Lux Mundi*, London: John Murray, 1889.

Gosse, P. H., *Omphalos*, London: Van Voorst, 1857.

Gray, A., *Darwinia*, New York: Appleton, 1876.

Hale, M., *The Primitive Origination of Mankind*, London, 1677.

Hodge, C., *What is Darwinism?*, New York: Scribner, Armstrong, 1874.

Hume, D., *An Inquiry Concerning Human Understanding*,London, 1748.

Huxley, T. H., *Evidence as to Man's Place in Nature*, London: Williams and Norgate, 1863.

Lamarck, J. B., *Philosophie Zoologique*, Paris, 1809.

Lyell, C., *Antiquity of Man*, London: John Murray, 1863.

Moore, A., *Science and Faith*, London: Kegan, Paul, Trench, 1889.

Newton, I., *Philosophiæ Naturalis Principia Mathematica*, London, 1687.

Paley, W., *Natural Theology*, London, 1802.

Ray, J., *The Wisdom of God as Manifested in the Works of Creation*, London, 1691.

Temple, F., *The Relations Between Religion and Science (Bampton Lectures of 1884)*, London: Macmillan, 1885.

Ussher, J., *The Annals of the Old and New Testament*, London, 1658.

White, A. D., *A History of the Warfare of Science with Theology*, New York: Appleton, 1886.

1900–70

Barbour, I. G., *Issues in Science and Religion*. London: SCM Press, 1966.

Bergson, H., *L' Evolution Créatrice*, Paris: Les Presses Universitaires de France, 1907 (English translation, *Creative Evolution*, 1911).

Butterfield, H., *The Origins of Modern Science*. London: Bell, 1949.

Coulson, C. A., *Science and Christian Belief*, Oxford: Oxford University Press, 1955.

Farrer, A., *A Science of God?*, London: Geoffrey Bles, 1966.

Gillispie, C. C., *Genesis and Geology*, Cambridge, MA: Harvard University Press, 1951.

Glacken, C. J., *Traces on the Rhodian Shore*, Berkeley, CA: University of California Press, 1967.

Huxley, J. S., *Religion without Revelation*, London: Chatto & Windus, 1957.

Huxley, J. S. (ed.), *The Humanist Frame*, London: Allen & Unwin, 1961.

James, W. *Varieties of Religious Experience*, London: Longmans, Green, 1902.

Kellogg, V., *Darwinism Today*, London: Bell, 1907.

Lack, D., *Evolutionary Theory and Christian Belief*, London: Methuen, 1957.

Lewis, C. S., *Miracles*, London: Geoffrey Bles, 1947.

Lovejoy, A., *The Great Chain of Being*, Cambridge, MA: Harvard University Press, 1936.

Polanyi, M., *Personal Knowledge*, Chicago: University of Chicago Press, 1958.

Pollard, W. G., *Chance and Providence*, New York: Scribner, 1958.

Price, G. McC, *The New Geology*, Mountain View, CA: Pacific Press, 1923.

Ramm, B., *The Christian View of Science and Scripture*, Grand Rapids: Eerdmans, 1954.

Raven, C. E., *Natural Religion and Christian Theology*, Cambridge: Cambridge University Press, 1953.

Schaeffer, F. A., *The God Who Is There*, London: Hodder & Stoughton, 1968.

Schrödinger, E., *What Is Life?*, Cambridge: Cambridge University Press, 1944.

Short, A. R., *Modern Discovery and the Bible*, London: IVF, 1942.

Teilhard de Chardin, P., *Le Phénomène Humain*. Paris: Éditions du Seuil, 1955 (English translation, *The Phenomenon of Man*, London: Collins, 1959.)

Whitcomb, J. C. & Morris, H. M., *The Genesis Flood*, Nutley, NJ: Presbyterian and Reformed Publishing, 1961.

Whitehead, A. N., *Process and Reality*, Cambridge: Cambridge University Press, 1929.

1970–90

Berry, R. J., *God and the Biologist*, Leicester: Apollos, 1996.

Black, J. N., *The Dominion of Man*, Edinburgh: Edinburgh University Press, 1970.

Dawkins, R., *The Selfish Gene*, Oxford: Oxford University Press, 1976.

Hardy, A. C., *The Biology of God*, London: Collins, 1975.

Henry, C. F. H. (ed.), *Horizons of Science*, San Francisco: Harper & Row, 1978.

Hookyaas, R., *Religion and the Rise of Science*, Edinburgh: Scottish Academic Press, 1971.

Kevles, D. J., *In the Name of Eugenics*, New York: Knopf, 1985.

Livingstone, D. N., *Darwin's Forgotten Defenders: the Encounter between Evangelical Theology and Evolutionary Thought*, Grand Rapids, MI: Eerdmans, 1987.

Lovelock, J. E., *Gaia. A New Look at Life on Earth*, Oxford: Oxford University Press, 1979.

MacKay, D. M., *The Clockwork Image*, Leicester: IVP, 1974.

Mayr, E., *The Growth of Biological Thought*, Cambridge, MA: Harvard University Press, 1982.

Mayr, E. & Provine, W. B. (eds.), *The Evolutionary Synthesis*, Cambridge, MA: Harvard University Press, 1980.

Medawar, P., *The Limits of Science*, New York: Harper & Row, 1984.

Monod, J., *Le Hasard et la Nécessité*, Paris: Éditions du Seuil, 1970 (English translation, *Chance and Necessity*, London: Collins, 1972).

Moore, J. R., *The Post-Darwinian Controversies*, New York: Cambridge University Press, 1979.

Peacocke, A. R., *Creation and the World of Science*, Oxford: Oxford University Press, 1979.

Russell, C. A., *Cross-Currents: Interactions Between Science and Faith*, Leicester: IVP, 1985.

Ward, B. & Dubos, R., *Only One Earth*, London: André Deutsch, 1972.

Wilson, E. O., *Sociobiology*, Cambridge, MA: Harvard University Press, 1975.

SINCE 1990

Alexander, D. R., *Rebuilding the Matrix*, Oxford: Lion, 2001.

Bookless, D., *Planetwise*, Nottingham: IVP, 2008.

Bowler, P. J., *Monkey Trials and Gorilla Sermons*, Chicago: Chicago University Press, 2007.

Brooke, J. H., *Science and Religion*, Cambridge: Cambridge University Press, 1991.

Brown, W. S., Murphy, N. & Malony, H. N. (eds), *Whatever Happened to the Soul?*, Minneapolis, MN: Fortress, 1998.

Bruce, D. & Bruce, A. (eds), *Engineering Genesis*, London: Earthscan, 1998.

Bruce, D. & Horrocks, D. (eds), *Modifying Creation?*, Carlisle: Paternoster, 2001.

Collins, F. S., *The Language of God*, New York: Free Press, 2006.

Conway Morris, S., *Life's Solution: Inevitable Humans in a Lonely Universe*, Cambridge: Cambridge University Press, 2003.

Gould, S. J. *Rocks of Ages*, New York: Ballantine, 1999.

Harrison, P., *The Bible, Protestantism, and the Rise of Natural Science*, Cambridge: Cambridge University Press, 1998.

Hawking, S., *A Brief History of Time*, London: Bantam, 1988.

Houghton, J., *Global Warming*, Oxford: Lion, 1994.

Jeeves, M. A., *Mind Fields*, Grand Rapids, MI: Baker, 1994.

Jeeves, M. A. & Berry, R. J., *Science, Life and Christian Belief*, Leicester: Apollos, 1998.

Johnson, P. E., *Defeating Darwinism*, Downer's Grove, IL: IVP, 1995.

Jones, D. G., *Designers of the Future*, Oxford: Monarch, 2005.

McGrath, A. E., *Dawkins' God: Genes, Memes, and the Meaning of Life*, Oxford: Blackwell, 2004.

McGrath, A. E., *Science & Religion*, 2nd edition, Oxord: Wiley-Blackwell, 2011.

MacKay, D. M., *Behind the Eye*, Oxford: Blackwell, 1991.

Midgley, M., *Science as Salvation*, London: Routledge, 1992.

Miller, K. R., *Finding Darwin's God*, New York: HarperCollins, 1999.

Numbers, R. L., *The Creationists*, New York: Knopf, 1992 (3rd edition, 2006).

Pennock, R. T., *Tower of Babel: The Evidence Against the New Creationism*, Cambridge, MA: MIT Press, 2000.

Polkinghorne, J. C., *Science and Christian Belief*, London: SPCK, 1994.

Porter, R., *Enlightenment*, London: Allen Lane, 2000.

Rees, M., *Just Six Numbers*, London: Weidenfeld & Nicolson, 1999.

Ruse, M., *Can a Darwinian Be a Christian?*, Cambridge, MA: Harvard University Press, 2001.

Russell, R. J., Stoeger, W. R. & Ayala, F. J. (eds), *Evolutionary and Molecular Biology: Scientific Perspectives on Divine Action*, Vatican City: Vatican Observatory Publications, 1998.

Ward, J. F. K., *God, Chance and Necessity*, Oxford: One World, 1996.

Ward, J. F. K., *The Big Questions in Science and Religion*, Conshohocken, PA: Templeton Press, 2008.

There are also a number of testimonies written by (or about) scientists who are Christians or who have contributed to the science–faith debate. These give an indication of how the debate is worked out in practice:

Berry, R. J. (ed.), *Real Science, Real Faith*, Crowborough: Monarch, 1991.

Berry, R. J. (ed.), *Real Scientists, Real Faith*, Oxford: Monarch, 2009.

Frankenberry, N. K. (ed.), *The Faith of Scientists*, Princeton, NJ: Princeton University Press, 2008.

Hermann, R. L. (ed.), *God, Science and Humility*, Radnor, PA: Templeton Press, 2000.

Rupke, N. A. (ed.), *Eminent Lives in Twentieth-Century Science and Religion*, revised edition, Frankfurt: Lang, 2009.

Stannard, R., *Science and Wonders*, London: Faber & Faber, 1996.

In addition to the books listed, there are several periodicals in the science–faith area. The most venerable is the series of Boyle Lectures, endowed by Robert Boyle (1627–91) "for proving the Christian Religion against notorious Infidels, viz. Atheists, Deists, Pagans, Jews and Mohometans" and delivered annually from 1692 to 1732, many of them published. They have recently been revived.

In 1829, the Earl of Bridgewater charged the executors of his will to pay eight scientists £1,000 each to examine "the Power, Wisdom, and Goodness of God as manifested in the Creation". The "Bridgewater Treatises" were bestsellers in the mid nineteenth century. In a similar vein, Alexander Gifford, a Scottish judge, left money for lectures on "Promoting, Advancing, Teaching, and Diffusing the Study of Natural Theology". The Gifford Lectures have been given regularly at the Universities of St Andrews, Edinburgh, Glasgow, and Aberdeen ever since (see

Witham, L., *The Measure of God*, New York: HarperCollins, 2005).

The Victoria Institute was founded in London in 1865 "to investigate fully and impartially the most important questions of Philosophy and Science, but most especially those that bear upon the great truths of Holy Scripture, with the view of defending these truths against the oppositions of Science, falsely so called". Its annual *Transactions* were influential for more than half a century, but their impact declined in the twentieth century. Since 1989, the Institute has joined with Christians in Science (formerly the Research Scientists' Christian Fellowship, founded 1950, "to develop and promote biblical Christian views on the nature, scope and limitations of science, and on the changing interactions between science and faith; and to bring biblical Christian thought on scientific issues into the public arena") to sponsor a biannual journal *Science & Christian Belief*.

Perspectives in Science and Christian Faith is published quarterly by the American Scientific Association (founded 1941 and "committed to providing an open forum where controversies can be discussed without fear of unjust discrimination"). It first appeared in 1949.

Zygon is a quarterly journal, founded in 1966, providing "an international forum for exploring ways to unite what in modern times has been disconnected: values from knowledge, goodness from truth, religion from science".

Theology and Science has been published three times a year since 2003 by the Center for Theology and the Natural Sciences (founded 1981) in Berkeley, California, with the aim of "building bridges between theology and science".

The European Society for the Study of Science and Theology publish the proceedings of their biennial conferences in book form.

The Faraday Institute for Science and Religion (http://www.faraday-institute. org) at Cambridge University produces a number of "Faraday Papers" which can be downloaded without cost. The Institute has also collaborated in a series of DVDs with associated resource material on science and religion topics (http://www. testoffaith.com).

There are also more specialized journals and newsletters for Christian doctors, environmentalists, and so on.

A handbook of this nature is not the place to include a full list of references to the issues dealt with. For readers wanting to follow up particular topics described in this handbook, this section gives references to help those wanting to pursue such enquiries. It should not be taken as an exhaustive guide to all the topics in the handbook.

Alexander, D. R., *The Language of Genetics*, Philadelphia: Templeton Foundation Press, 2011.

Atran, S., *In Gods We Trust: The Evolutionary Landscape of Religion*, Oxford: Oxford University Press, 2002.

Ayala, F. J. & Dobzhansky, T. (eds), *Studies in the Philosophy of Biology*, London: Macmillan, 1974.

Barrow, J. D. & Tipler, F. J., *The Anthropic Cosmological Principle*, Oxford: Oxford University Press, 1986.

Berry, R. J., "Adam or Adamah?", *Science & Christian Belief*, 2011, **23**, pp. 23–48.

Berry, R. J., "What to believe about miracles", *Nature*, 1986, **322**, pp. 321–22.

Boyer, P., *Religion Explained: The Evolutionary Origins of Religious Thought*, New York: Basic Books, 2001.

Bratton, M. (ed.), *God, Ethics and the Human Genome*, London: Church House Publishing, 2009.

Brooke, J. H., "The Wilberforce–Huxley debate: why did it happen?", *Science & Christian Belief*, 2001, **13**, pp. 127–41.

Bruce, D. & Bruce, A. (eds), *Engineering Genesis: the Ethics of Genetic Engineering in Non-Human Species*, London: Earthscan, 1998.

Bryant J., Baggott la Velle, L., & Searle, J. (2005) *Introduction to Bioethics*. Chichester: Wiley.

Burke, D., "Assessing risk: science or art?", *Science & Christian Belief*, 2004, **16**, pp. 27–44.

Bussey, P. J., "Beyond materialism: from the medieval scholars to quantum physics", *Science & Christian Belief*, 2004, **16**, pp. 157–78.

Carroll, S. B., "Genetics and the making of *Homo sapiens*", *Nature*, 2003, **422**, pp. 849–57.

Cairns-Smith, A. G., *Seven Clues to the Origin of Life*, Cambridge: Cambridge University Press, 1990.

Clayton, P. & Peacocke, A. R. (eds), *In Whom We Live and Have Our Being: Panentheistic Reflections on God's Presence in a Scientific World*, Grand Rapids, MI: Eerdmans, 2004.

Collins, F., "The Human Genome Project: tool of atheistic reductionism or embodiment of the Christian mandate to heal?", *Science & Christian Belief*, 1999, **11**, pp. 99–111.

Dawkins, R., *The God Delusion*, London: Transworld, 2006.

Day, A. J., "Adam, anthropology and the Genesis record", *Science & Christian Belief*, 1998, **10**, pp. 115–43.

Do, K. Q., Cabungcal, J. H., Frank, A., Steullet P., & Cuenod, M., "Redox dysregulation, neurodevelopment, and schizophrenia", *Current Opinion in Neurobiology*, 2009, **19**, pp. 220–30.

Doye, J. *et al.*, "Contemporary perspectives on chance, providence and free will", *Science & Christian Belief*, 1995, **7**, pp. 117–39.

Dunstan, G., "The moral status of the human embryo: a tradition recalled", *Journal of Medical Ethics*, 1984, **10**, pp. 38–44.

Finlay, G., "Evolution as created history", *Science & Christian Belief*, 2008, **20**, 67–89.

Finlayson, C., "Biogeography and evolution of the genus *Homo*", *Trends in Ecology and Evolution*, 2005, **20**, pp. 457–63.

Finocchiaro, M., *The Galileo Affair: a Documentary History*, Berkeley, CA: University of California Press, 1989.

Foster, M. B., "The Christian doctrine of Creation and the rise of modern science", *Mind*, 1934, **43**, pp. 443–68.

Fukuyama, F., *Our Posthuman Future*, London: Profile Books, 2002.

Gleick, J., *Chaos: Making of a New Science*, London: Cardinal, 1998.

Green, J.B., Eschatology and the nature of humans: a reconsideration of pertinent biblical evidence. *Science & Christian Belief*, 2002, **14**, pp. 33–50.

Hahn, Robert A., *Sickness and Healing: an Anthropological Perspective* New Haven, CT: Yale University Press, 1995.

Harrison, P., "Religion and the early Royal Society", *Science & Christian Belief*, 2010, **22**, pp. 3–22.

Hasker, W., *The Emergent Self*, Ithaca, NY: Cornell University Press, 1999.

Houghton, J. T., *Global Warming: The Complete Briefing*, 3rd edition, Cambridge, Cambridge University Press, 2004.

Jeeves, M. A., "How free is free? Reflections on the neuropsychology of thought and action", *Science & Christian Belief*, 2005, **16**, pp. 101–22.

Jeeves, M. A. (ed.), *Rethinking Human Nature*. Grand Rapids, MI: Eerdmans, 2011.

Jones, D. G., "Human cloning: a watershed for science and ethics?", *Science & Christian Belief*, 2002, **14**, pp. 159–80.

Judge, S., "How not to think about miracles", *Science & Christian Belief*, 1991, **3**, 97–102.

Larson, E. J. & Witham, L., "Scientists are still keeping the faith", *Nature*, 1997, **386**, pp. 435–36.

Lewis, C. L. E. & Knell, S. J. (eds), *The Age of the Earth: from 4004 BC to AD 2002*, London: Geological Society Special Publication No. 190, 2001.

Loewe, L. & Scherer, S., "Mitochondrial Eve: the plot thickens", *Trends in Ecology and Evolution*, 1997, **12**, pp. 422–23.

McGrath, A. E., *Darwinism and the Divine*, Chichester: Wiley-Blackwell, 2011.

May, G., *Creatio Ex Nihilo*, Edinburgh: T&T Clark, 1994.

Merton, R. K., "Science, technology and society in seventeenth-century England", *Osiris*, 1938, **4**, pp. 360–632.

Middleton, J. R., *The Liberating Image: The imago Dei in Genesis 1*, Grand Rapids, MI: Brazos Press, 2005.

Nagel, T., "What is it like to be a bat?", *Philosophical Reviews*, 1974, **83**, pp. 435–50.

O'Mathúna, D. P., *Nanoethics: Big Ethical Issues with Small Technology*, London: Continuum, 2009.

Polkinghorne, J. C., *From Physicist to Priest: an Autobiography*, London: SPCK, 2007

Poole, M. W., "Explaining or explaining away? The concept of explanation in the science-theology debate", *Science & Christian Belief*, 2002, **14**, pp. 123–42.

Nuclear Power and the Environment, Sixth Report of the Royal Commission on Environmental Pollution. London: HMSO, Cmnd, 6820, 1976.

Torrance, T. F., *Theological Science*, Oxford: Oxford University Press, 1969.

Turl, J., "Theodesy and geodesy: who is to blame?", *Science & Christian Belief*, 2011, **23**, pp. 49–66.

Van Till, H. J., "Are bacterial flagella intelligently designed?", *Science & Christian Belief*, 2003, **15**, pp. 117–40.

White, L., "The historical roots of the ecologic crisis", *Science*, 1967, **155**, pp. 1203–07.

Wigner, E., "The unreasonable effectiveness of mathematics in the natural sciences", *Communications in Pure and Applied Mathematics*, 1960, **13**, pp. 1–14.

Index

PICTURE ACKNOWLEDGMENTS

PHOTOGRAPHS

3D4Medical.com: p. 207

Alamy: pp. 12br, 38bl Mary Evans Picture Library; p. 15 Lebrecht Music and Arts Photo Library; pp. 34–35 PhotoAlto; p. 49bl Michael Ventura; p. 50 Bildarchiv Monheim GmbH; p. 55 Interfoto; p. 85 The Art Gallery Collection; pp. 89, 259 Phototake Inc.; p. 111 Jeff Morgan 11; p. 121 Art Directors & TRIP; p. 130t All Canada Photos; p. 137 Classic Image; p. 146 Mark Hodson Photography; p. 158 The Print Collector; p. 182 The Art Archive; p. 189 Pictorial Press Ltd; p. 191 Jim West; p. 199 David Chapman

Art Archive: p. 102; p. 12tr Jean-Leon Huens/NGS Image Collection; pp. 18, 162, 230 Musée du Louvre Paris/Gianni Dagli Orti; p. 29 Victoria and Albert Museum London/Sally Chappell; p. 31 Isabella Stewart Gardner Museum Boston/Superstock; p. 63 Private Collection/Eileen Tweedy; p. 74 Museo della Civilta Romana Rome/Collection Dagli Orti; p. 80 Galleria Borghese Rome/Collection Dagli Orti; p. 97 Reproduced with the permission of the Trustees of Wesley's Chapel, City Road, London/John Wesley's House/Eileen Tweedy; p. 101 Jean-Leon Huens/NGS Image Collection; p. 133 Global Book Publishing; p. 170 Sistine Chapel Vatican/Superstock

Bridgeman: p. 42; p. 65 Ken Welsh; p. 128 Private Collection; p. 143 Leeds Museums and Galleries (City Art Gallery) U.K.

British Museum: p. 204

Corbis: pp. 59, 267; p. 1 Bernard Radvaner; pp. 2, 119 Roger Ressmeyer; pp. 6, 22, 245 Ocean; pp. 8–9 Danny Lehman; pp. 10, 66 Chris Andrews; Chris Andrews Publications; p. 16 William Taufic; p. 19 Stapleton Collection; pp. 32, 109, 145, 167, 188 Bettmann; p. 36 Pete Saloutos; p. 37t Ron Watts; p. 41t Richard Bryant/Arcaid; p. 41cr Eric Nathan/Loop Images; pp. 46–47 Chris Hill/National Geographic Society; p. 52 William Radcliffe/Science Faction; p. 70 Philadelphia Museum of Art; p. 73 Uwe Zucchi/dpa; p. 76 Andy Rouse; p. 79 Ian Trower/JAI; p. 82 Dave G. Houser; p. 87 Sandro Vannini; p. 91 Francis G. Mayer; pp. 112–13, 132, 157 Frans Lanting; p. 122 Warren Toda/epa; p. 129 Sanford/Agliolo; p. 139tr Martial Trezzini/epa; p. 144 Micro Discovery; p. 151 Andy Rain/epa; p. 165 George Steinmetz; p. 172 Michael Nicholson; pp. 186, 206 Visuals Unlimited; p. 192 Adrianna Williams; p. 195(molecule) David Arky; p. 195(human cell) DK Limited; p. 197 Tetra Images; p. 200 NASA/JPL-Caltech; p. 201 Dr. Richard Kessel & Dr. Gene Shih/Visuals Unlimited; p. 205 Fiona Rogers; p. 212 Angelo Cavalli; p. 215 Owen Franken; p. 223 Sam Diephuis; p. 227 Randy Faris; pp. 228, 241tl Michael Macor/San Francisco Chronicle; p. 233 Smiley N. Pool/Dallas Morning News; p. 235 Keith Ladzinski/Aurora Photos; p. 237 Jim Richardson; p. 253 Ted Horowitz; p. 261 Adrian Arbib

Dr Gordon Chancellor/Flickr: p. 156

Getty: pp. 33, 37br, 123, 125, 175, 185, 251tr; p. 20 Time & Life Pictures; p. 98 NASA/ESA/STSCI/M.Robberto, HST Orion Treasury Team/SPL; p. 99bl SSPL; p. 159 Planet Observer; p. 236 MCT; p. 238 Felipe Rodriguez Fernandez; p. 239 DigitalGlobe

International Rice Research Institute: pp. 242–43

iStock: p. 40 Evgeny Kuklev; p. 49t mohamed sadath; p. 56 Alexander Shirokov; p. 195(cluster of cells) Henrik Jonsson; p. 195(3d atom) Andrey Prokhorov; p. 195(human heart) Max Delson Martins Santos; p. 195 (female body muscles) red_frog; p. 263 jan kranendonk; (telescope icon) O'Luk

John Bryant: p. 241tr

Lebrecht: p. 173; pp. 23, 211 Horst Tappe; p. 75 culture-images; p. 220 Interfoto

Photolibrary: p. 64 Ken Welsh; p. 118 NASA; p. 225 Das Fotoarchiv; p. 240 Juan Pablo Moreiras/FFI; p. 246 Oxford Scientific; p. 247 Lineair; p. 251cl Imagebroker

Royal Society: p. 25

Science Photo Library: pp. 106–07 Jacopin; p. 130br Christian Darkin; p. 139b Vincent Moncorge/Look at Sciences; p. 209 Dr Robert Friedland; p. 210 Peter Gardiner; p. 255 Philippe Plailly

Topfoto: pp. 176–77 Scanpix Sweden

ILLUSTRATIONS

Lion: pp. 108, 131, 166, 245

Q2A Media: pp. 135, 147, 163, 164, 165b